Humanitarian Intervention

THIRD EDITION

War and Conflict in the Modern World Series

Humanitarian Intervention

Ideas in Action

THIRD EDITION

Thomas G. Weiss

polity

First edition published in 2007 by Polity Press
This edition published in 2016 by Polity Press
Reprinted 2017, 2018

Polity Press
65 Bridge Street
Cambridge CB2 1UR, UK

Polity Press
350 Main Street
Malden, MA 02148, USA

ISBN-13: 978-1-5095-0731-3
ISBN-13: 978-1-5095-0732-0 (pb)

A catalogue record for this book is available from the British Library.

Library of Congress Cataloging-in-Publication Data

Weiss, Thomas G. (Thomas George), 1946-
  Humanitarian intervention / Thomas G. Weiss. -- Third edition.
      pages cm
  Includes bibliographical references and index.
  ISBN 978-1-5095-0731-3 (hardback) -- ISBN 978-1-5095-0732-0 (paperback) 1.
Humanitarian intervention. I. Title.
  JZ6369.W448 2016
  341.5'84--dc23
                                                          2015031612

Typeset in 10.25 on 13pt Scala by
Servis Filmsetting Ltd, Stockport, Cheshire
Printed and bound in the United States by LSC Communications

For further information on Polity, visit our website: www.politybooks.com

Contents

About the Author

Thomas G. Weiss is Presidential Professor of Political Science at The Graduate Center of The City University of New York (CUNY) and director emeritus of the Ralph Bunche Institute for International Studies. Past President of the International Studies Association and recipient of its Distinguished IO Scholar Award 2016, he was also editor of *Global Governance* and research director of the International Commission on Intervention and State Sovereignty as well as Chair of the Academic Council on the UN System. He has written extensively about international organization, peace and security, humanitarian action, and sustainable development. Recently authored books include *What's Wrong with the United Nations and How to Fix It*, 3rd edn (2016); *The United Nations and Changing World Politics*, 8th edn (with David P. Forsythe, Roger A. Coate, and Kelly-Kate Pease, 2016); *Governing the World? Addressing "Problems without Passports"* (2014); *Global Governance: Why? What? Whither?* (2013); *Humanitarian Business* (2013); *Humanitarianism Contested: Where Angels Fear to Tread* (with Michael Barnett, 2011); *Thinking about Global Governance: Why People and Ideas Matter* (2011); *Global Governance and the UN: An Unfinished Journey* (with Ramesh Thakur, 2010); and *UN Ideas That Changed the World* (with Richard Jolly and Louis Emmerij, 2009). Recently edited volumes include *Emerging Powers and the UN: What Kind of Development Partnership?* (with Adriana Erthal Abdenur, 2015); *Wartime Origins and the Future United*

Nations (with Dan Plesch, 2015); *International Organization and Global Governance* (with Rorden Wilkinson, 2014); *Post-2015 UN Development: Making Change Happen?* (with Stephen Browne, 2014); *The International Politics of Human Rights: Rallying to the R2P Cause?* (with Mónica Serrano, 2014); and *The Responsibility to Protect: Cultural Perspectives in the Global South* (with Rama Mani, 2011).

Foreword to the Third Edition

Mass murder and ethnic cleansing – of the kind the world witnessed in Rwanda and the Balkans in the 1990s, and has seen again in this new century in Darfur, Sri Lanka, Libya, and Syria – shock the conscience like nothing else. The shock is compounded when we think about how much the international community has known since the Holocaust and Cambodia as to how these catastrophes begin and gather momentum, and how readily so many of them could have been averted. But every few years we found ourselves, humbled and shamefaced, acknowledging once again that such a catastrophe has occurred and pledging not to allow anything like it ever to be repeated.

Professor Thomas G. Weiss, in his writings over many years, is one of those who have made it impossible for the international community to claim that these situations are unforeseeable or irremediable. Many academics and journalists and think-tanks have analyzed their dynamics, making clear what needs to be done, who needs to do it, and the many constraints that stand in the way of effective action. But few have been as well versed in the issues and as articulate as the author of this book. Few have brought to the task such knowledge of the relevant global history, and such a clear understanding of the normative principles involved and how they can be made to work in international institutional practice.

Humanitarian Intervention – now updated and expanded in this timely third edition – is pitched not only for students of international affairs, but for attentive citizens who want a clear and readable guide to how this great moral and political challenge of our time has repeatedly been fumbled by the world's leaders, how those leaders can and should do better, and how in recent years they have been showing at last some signs of doing just that. But above all, it is written for, and should be read by, those very policymakers who have so often sat on the sidelines wringing their hands and making excuses as genocide, ethnic cleansing, and other major crimes against humanity have been screened in slow motion before them.

The good news, for more than a decade now, is that policymakers are no longer operating, as they did for so long, in an almost principle-free and consensus-free vacuum, in which no one could agree what, if any, limits there were on a sovereign state's freedom of action when it came to internal matters not immediately threatening a neighbor's or the wider world's security, and where there was particularly acute disagreement about when and where it was ever right to use coercive military force. In 2005, the more than 150 national leaders attending the World Summit to commemorate the sixtieth anniversary of the United Nations unanimously agreed that there is a principle which explains and justifies engagement and concern, and in extreme cases forcible intervention.

This principle, "the responsibility to protect," had its origins in the precedent-setting report of that title by the International Commission on Intervention and State Sovereignty, a distinguished international group, which I had the honor to co-chair with Mohamed Sahnoun, and which had the pleasure and benefit of having its research directed by Tom Weiss. The core idea of the responsibility to protect – or "R2P," as it has become familiarly known – is that the perspective that matters is that of suffering human beings. States have the primary responsibility for protecting their own citizens from

human-made catastrophe, but when a state abdicates that
responsibility – through either incapacity or ill-will – it shifts
to the wider international community, to regional and global
organizations (such as the African Union or United Nations),
and to the governments and citizens of other countries.

It is not a matter of any state having the "right of humanitarian intervention." The commission argued strongly for the
abandonment once and for all, in any policymaking context, of
that very divisive terminology. The issue is not the right of any
state to throw its weight around, but rather the *responsibility* of
every state to play its appropriate role, with the objective not
being intervention as such, but the *protection* of men, women,
and children threatened by the horror of mass violence.
Coercive military action, authorized under the UN Charter, still
has its place in extreme situations when civilians can be protected in no other way. But it is just one element within a larger
and more nuanced policy framework, in which prevention is
given as least as much weight as response, and nonmilitary
measures are always to be preferred if they can do the job.

No idea has moved faster in the international normative
arena than "the responsibility to protect," defined this way.
Ideas in Action is Weiss's subtitle, and this book details the
steady journey of this idea from a gleam in a small group's
eyes to acceptance as a norm of international behavior by the
leaders of the whole global community – the idea that when it
comes to the fundamental issues of human security involved
in genocide, ethnic cleansing, and other major crimes against
humanity, the rights of individual humans trump the sovereignty of the thuggish states in which they live.

Initial efforts by some countries – most visibly Cuba,
Nicaragua, Sudan, and Venezuela – to wind back the 2005
consensus and reassert a more absolutist view of sovereignty have manifestly failed. Successive debates in the UN
General Assembly every year since 2009, and the continued

willingness of the Security Council to use R2P language in its resolutions – more than 30 of them since 2011, notwithstanding the scars left by disagreement over that year's Libya intervention – have made it abundantly clear that the basic principles of the responsibility to protect command huge majority support and that the norm is here to stay.

The high-water mark in the military application of the responsibility to protect was undoubtedly the Security Council's decision in March 2011 to authorize the intervention led by the North Atlantic Treaty Organization in Libya to protect civilians at risk of massacre by the Qaddafi regime. Had it acted equally decisively and robustly in the 1990s, the 8,000 men and boys murdered in Srebrenica and the 800,000 men, women, and children slaughtered in Rwanda might still be alive today. But with high tides come high risks. The atmosphere in the council quickly soured as it became clear that the United States, United Kingdom, and France interpreted their civilian protection mandate as requiring nothing less than regime change, and they would listen to no argument to the contrary from the likes of Russia, China, Brazil, India, or South Africa. And with this breach was lost any prospect of consensus on an effective response to the explosive new situation in Syria, a paralysis which continues to this day.

The Libya and Syria cases make it clear that, at the sharpest end of the R2P response spectrum, there will always be difficulty in reaching, and sustaining, consensus as to how to act. The prospect of coercive military intervention, even for the noblest of humanitarian motives, invariably arouses visceral responses. And the current environment of wider geopolitical tensions – not least between the United States and Russia – make it unlikely that consensus over the hardest cases will be restored any time soon.

That said, the seeds for future constructive discussion have been sown with the proposal, first floated by Brazil in 2011, and the subject of much backroom debate since, that R2P be supplemented, not replaced, with a complementary set of "responsibility *while* protecting" principles and procedures. The core "RwP" ideas are twofold: that agreed prudential criteria should be much more fully debated by the Security Council before mandating any use of military force, and that there should be an enhanced monitoring and review process during the implementation phase to ensure that, so far as possible, consensus is maintained throughout the course of such operations. The United States, United Kingdom, and France have been reluctant so far to accept such disciplines, but are beginning to recognize that unvetoed majority support for any robust responses – not just military ones – to politically sensitive atrocity crime cases in the future may prove very elusive unless they do.

Given these developments, and the strong normative support for basic responsibility to protect principles that continues to be so evident in UN and other international forums, there are plenty of grounds for optimism that R2P's future is not behind it. But there is still a long way to go, as Tom Weiss makes evident, to translate agreed principle into universally delivered practice: to consolidate the intellectual consensus, build the institutional capacity, and generate the political will that are all necessary ingredients if R2P is to be effectively operational every time a case for its application arises. How to finish this unfinished business is in many ways the central theme of this important book. But finish it we must if we are to avoid the shame of uttering ever again that *cri de coeur* of "never again."

Gareth Evans
President Emeritus, International Crisis Group
Co-Chair, International Advisory Board, Global
Centre for the Responsibility to Protect
Canberra, July 2015

Preface and Acknowledgments

No topic is more pertinent for the series "War and Conflict in the Modern World" than *Humanitarian Intervention: Ideas in Action.* It is a perfect platform to tease out not only the political but also the ethical, legal, strategic, operational, and economic tensions underlying one of the most controversial, yet for me personally satisfying, developments of the post-Cold War era: the use of military force for human protection purposes.

When Louise Knight contacted me, I was at first uneasy, because I had been working in this vineyard for a long time – perhaps too long, I thought, to write something creative. But she explained that the challenge would be to re-examine as succinctly as possible various pieces of a puzzle that I have been struggling to assemble for almost two decades. She also reminded me that Polity expected me to call into question shibboleths. She was uncommonly kind in her evaluation – and flattery does work. So I decided to synthesize the most essential elements of international efforts to rescue human beings trapped in the throes of war. For me, the norms to aid and protect such populations are of the essence. I am thankful that she twisted my arm ever so slightly; and I trust that she is still glad that she did so. And this third edition is very much in order to update developments, political and operational, as well as substantial new scholarship and policy analysis since late 2011 when I finished the second edition.

In my career, I have worked closely with a number of individuals from whom I have learned about humanitarian action.

I have no talent as a natural scientist, but I may have been one in a former life, because I prefer their normal collaborative style to the more solitary routine of social scientists. And over the years, I have written jointly with colleagues a number of books and articles. As such, pride of authorship always gave way to getting the analysis right and pushing out the envelope on important issues. In the pages that follow, I have pulled together my current thinking, which necessarily reflects my intellectual debt to a number of people whose work and mine were melded over the years. They certainly find traces of themselves in this extended essay even if they receive no royalties.

First is Larry Minear. When he proposed that we build on our book on Operation Lifeline Sudan,[1] I was delighted to help launch and direct the Humanitarianism & War Project, which was an essential early contribution to applied research in the turbulent 1990s. There must be a better way to assist and protect people, we thought. That conviction helped us keep the faith in spite of empirical evidence to the contrary provided by the alphabet soup of agencies that we habitually encountered in subsequent crises. Lessons learned versus lessons spurned became the theme song of almost a decade together codirecting the project from 1990 to 1998 at Brown University, before I joined the CUNY Graduate Center faculty and Larry moved the research to Tufts University. I cherish the memories of that productive and congenial time. Larry's capacity for work borders on the heroic. It did not hurt that each of us was vying for the Type-A personality of the year award. With reference to this book, Larry and I had our intellectual differences over the desirability and impact of outside military forces in war zones. I nearly always lost our arguments, but I benefited from the clashes, and those subtleties have undoubtedly found their way into this volume.

Don Hubert worked as part of my team at the Research Directorate for the International Commission on Intervention and State Sovereignty (ICISS).[2] The commission's report, *The Responsibility to Protect*, has been widely circulated and is the focus of chapter 4. Don and I were the principal authors of an accompanying research volume, which contains the intellectual underpinnings for the ICISS report and informs the first two chapters of this book. Don first joined me as a post-doc at Brown University, and has subsequently chosen to make his contribution as a government official working on human security in the government of Canada, prior to a short stint as an academic at the University of Ottawa and his return to the more practical world of international development. It is delightful to count him among my younger intellectual comrades-in-arms.

Similarly, I would like to acknowledge another younger sidekick, who now teaches at the New School. Peter Hoffman completed his insightful dissertation on private military companies (PMCs) and will contribute substantially to international relations scholarship. It has been fun to mentor him over the past decade and a half – he suffered through one of my seminars and still came back for more in the ICISS Research Directorate (2000–1) and as the coordinator of the Inter-University Consortium for Security and Humanitarian Action (2002–6). We collaborated on a book about confronting new wars and humanitarian crises,[3] and its contents crop up, especially in chapters 3 and 5.

I got to know David Korn through our book that charts the itinerary of international efforts to assist and protect internally displaced persons.[4] This predecessor of the responsibility to protect is key to chapter 4's analysis. And the protagonists of that story, Roberta Cohen and Francis M. Deng, are a source of inspiration to analysts who hope to make a difference.

Michael Barnett and I have worked together over the past decade. We began with an edited book that asked some "unusual suspects" to take a fresh look at the ongoing crisis in humanitarian action and then we continued with our own volume on the topic.[5] A professional field is emerging that reflects the acute crises of the post-Cold War era that have continually challenged aid personnel and forced the best of them to rethink their standard operating procedures and principles. Michael's own scholarship is as inspiring as his sense of humor is contagious; and our work helps inform parts of the first and last chapters of this book.

I would also like to mention my collaboration with Richard Jolly and Louis Emmerij in the United Nations Intellectual History Project between 1999 and 2010. This long-overdue effort to document the world organization's intellectual contribution to economic and social development has opened up new vistas. While that project stresses economic and social rather than humanitarian issues, the general approach and our collaboration have contributed to my own thinking.[6] The subtitle of the current book, *Ideas in Action*, reflects some of what I have learned from them. On a parallel track under the project's auspices, another younger collaborator, Sam Daws, and I had edited an authoritative handbook covering crucial aspects of 60 years of the United Nations.[7] Our cooperation has taught me much, and the 40 chapters for that volume provide guidance to me and hence, indirectly, to readers.

I wish clearly to acknowledge the intellectual and editorial inputs of Danielle Zach, another very promising former PhD student in political science at The CUNY Graduate Center, who is now a post-doc continuing her work on diasporas and armed conflict, and transnational radicalism more broadly. All editions of this book would not have been as readable and sharp without her careful attention. She applied the remarkable editorial skills that she has honed steadily over the past several years in working on a number of book projects at the Ralph Bunche Institute. She also made good use of her own teaching experience and pointed out how to bring to life many generalizations, as did Nina Connelly's research assistance and critical commentary for this third edition. Both Danielle and Nina have improved the texts immeasurably, and I am deeply grateful.

I am also extremely grateful that Gareth Evans, now chancellor of the Australian National University and president emeritus of the International Crisis Group, agreed once again to grace these pages with a new foreword. I learned a great deal during the 15 months that he spearheaded the forced-march pace by ICISS. His work ethic and vision were exemplary; he was always in the trenches during the various battles to get the report drafted and agreed. It would simply not have happened without him. No person has worked harder to get R2P on the international radar screen and keep it there. I am honored to have him as a colleague in this business, aptly summarized by the subtitle of his own book *The Responsibility to Protect: Ending Mass Atrocity Crimes Once and for All.*[8]

Finally, this book is dedicated once again to the memories of Fred Cuny and Sergio Vieira de Mello, who were murdered while trying to alleviate suffering in Chechnya (in April 1995) and in Iraq (in August 2003). Over the years, they shared with me generously their time and insights in various settings around the world; and hopefully some of their dedication and passion for life have found their way into these pages as well.

Notwithstanding this truth in packaging and the help of many individuals, I alone am responsible for remaining errors of fact or interpretation.

T.G.W., New York City, October 2015

Abbreviations

ALNAP	Active Learning Network for Accountability and Performance in Humanitarian Action
AU	African Union
CAR	Central African Republic
CDC	Centers for Disease Control (US)
CHR	Commission on Human Rights
DAC	Development Assistance Committee (OECD)
DRC	Democratic Republic of the Congo
ECOMOG	Military Observer Group of the Economic Community of West African States
ECOWAS	Economic Community of West African States
EU	European Union
HRC	Human Rights Council
HRW	Human Rights Watch
IASC	Inter-Agency Standing Committee (UN)
ICC	International Criminal Court
ICISS	International Commission on Intervention and State Sovereignty
ICJ	International Court of Justice
ICRC	International Committee of the Red Cross
ICTR	International Criminal Tribunal for Rwanda
ICTY	International Criminal Tribunal for the former Yugoslavia
IDP	internally displaced person
IFOR	Implementation Force (in the former Yugoslavia)

IGO	intergovernmental organization
ISIS	Islamic State of Iraq and Syria
LRA	Lord's Resistance Army
MISAB	Inter-African Force to Monitor the Implementation of the Bangui Agreements
MNF	Multinational Force (in Haiti)
MONUC	UN Mission in the Democratic Republic of the Congo
MONUSCO	UN Organization Stabilization Mission in the Democratic Republic of the Congo
MSF	Médecins Sans Frontières (Doctors without Borders)
NAM	Non-Aligned Movement
NATO	North Atlantic Treaty Organization
NGO	nongovernmental organization
NSA	nonstate actor
OAU	Organization of African Unity
OCHA	Office for the Coordination of Humanitarian Affairs (UN)
ODA	official development assistance
OECD	Organisation for Economic Co-operation and Development
OHCHR	Office of the High Commissioner for Human Rights
PID	Project on Internal Displacement
PMC	private military company
PSD	Presidential Study Directive
RSG	representative of the secretary-general
R2P	responsibility to protect
SADC	South African Development Community
SFOR	Stabilization Force (in the former Yugoslavia)
UNAMET	UN Assistance Mission in East Timor
UNAMID	UN–AU Mission in Darfur
UNAMIR	UN Assistance Mission in Rwanda

UNAMSIL	UN Mission for Sierra Leone
UNDP	UN Development Programme
UNHCR	UN High Commissioner for Refugees
UNITA	National Union for the Total Independence of Angola
UNITAF	United Task Force (in Somalia)
UNMISS	UN Mission in the Republic of South Sudan
UNOCI	UN Operation in Côte d'Ivoire
UNOSOM	UN Operation in Somalia
UNPROFOR	UN Protection Force (in the former Yugoslavia)
UPR	universal periodic review
USAID	US Agency for International Development
USSR	Union of Soviet Socialist Republics
WHO	World Health Organization
WMD	weapons of mass destruction

Introduction

A remarkable development of the post-Cold War era has been
the routine use of military force to protect human beings
trapped in the throes of wars. With the possible exception of
the 1948 Convention on Genocide, no idea has moved faster
in the international normative arena than "the responsibility
to protect," the title of the 2001 report of the International
Commission on Intervention and State Sovereignty (ICISS).
At the same time, international dithering in Darfur, northern Uganda, Zimbabwe, Sri Lanka, and the Democratic
Republic of the Congo (DRC) indicates the dramatic discon-
nect between political reality and pious rhetoric, as do the
world powers' inconsistent responses to civilian vulnerability
in Libya, Côte d'Ivoire, and most especially Syria, as well as
the host of other ad hoc reactions to a motley assortment of
nonstate actors ranging from Al Qaeda to the Islamic State of
Iraq and Syria (ISIS) to Boko Haram.

The two are rarely in synch. Sometimes norm entrepreneurs scramble to keep up with political reality, and
sometimes they are ahead of the curve. In this case, depicting
instances of crises that may have warranted the responsibility
to protect – or "R2P," as it has come to be known in international circles – on a graph would reflect a steady growth since
the early 1990s, whereas the curve depicting the operational
capacity and political will to engage in humanitarian intervention would resemble the path of a roller coaster. Hence,
the US-led and UN-approved intervention in northern Iraq

in 1991 took place largely without any formal discussion of moral justifications. In spite of continual fireworks in debates about international responses to conscience-shocking events from Central Africa to the Balkans, the September 2005 World Summit represented the zenith of international normative consensus about R2P, which has endured since 2009 in a series of annual General Assembly interactive dialogues on the responsibility to protect. With only a handful of states – Cuba, Nicaragua, Sudan, and Venezuela – expressing outright opposition to the R2P doctrine and seeking to roll back normative progress, these discussions continued to crystallize the R2P's normative status and also led to the establishment of a new UN bureaucratic unit in the shape of the joint office at UN headquarters.[1] At the same time, the blowback from 9/11 and the war on terrorism and in Iraq during the first decade of the twenty-first century resulted in a nadir in the actual practice of humanitarian intervention. Security Council action to forestall atrocities in Libya in March 2011 represented a new upswing in the implementation of R2P. Council resolution 1973 authorized prompt, robust, and effective international action to protect Libya's people from the kind of murderous harm that Muammar al-Qaddafi inflicted on unarmed civilian protestors and the opposition, whom he called "cockroaches" – eerily echoing terminology wielded by Rwanda's genocidal regime in 1994. At the same time, the international paralysis in Syria resulted in record-breaking bloodshed and displacement, and the lack of peacebuilding in Libya created chaos and suffering that made some long for the days of the deposed despot.

This book is about the need to override state sovereignty and rescue suffering civilians who live in a state that is unable or unwilling to protect and succor them. Have we entered the beginning of a new normative era? Are we witnessing a new dawn or dusk for the practice of humanitarian intervention?

This short volume seeks to answer these questions in five chapters.

Chapter 1, "Conceptual Building Blocks," places before the reader notions to be kept in mind throughout the book. It begins by parsing the contested notion of humanitarian intervention itself. It continues with the two main principles of the Westphalian order: state sovereignty as encapsulated in UN Charter Article 2(7) and the basic "hands-off" of non-intervention in domestic affairs. At the same time, they are complemented by a fundamental tension in the Charter's Preamble and Articles 55 and 56 and elsewhere: namely, a respect for fundamental rights. Another building block is a discussion of the nature of continuity and change in world politics, or the extent to which nothing is new or much has changed – a discussion, like most of international relations, that revolves around the anarchical nature of the international system.

Chapter 2, "'Humanitarian' Interventions: Thumbnail Sketches," provides a historical overview of numerous cases of humanitarian intervention in order to provide empirical background to understand the controversy surrounding this notion in the contemporary world order. There are brief discussions of the examples of colonial "humanitarian" interventions, as well as those between 1945 and 1990 when the UN Charter regime was circumscribed by the East–West conflict. The explosion of interventions with largely humanitarian justifications in the post-Cold War era follows; and because of their continuing salience for the contemporary debate, the trends of the turbulent 1990s are discussed in depth. The chapter then highlights four crises – in the DRC, Uganda, Zimbabwe, and Darfur – where there has been little evidence of any new imperative to save strangers in spite of substantially new discourse about the responsibility to do so. The section concludes with the council's inconsistent responses to civilian vulnerability and mass atrocities in Libya, Syria, and Côte d'Ivoire. These cases show a shift away from the hostility to R2P's implementation encountered during the George W. Bush administration, especially in the wake of the US-led invasion of Iraq in 2003. They also reveal that, although normative consensus is robust, practical action still lags behind and is unevenly implemented. And the story is further complicated with the new medievalism in the scourge of attacks by fundamentalist terrorist groups that manipulate religion for political purposes.

Chapter 3, "New Wars and New Humanitarianisms," discusses the contemporary reality of armed conflicts and of outside efforts to come to the rescue. Much of the ugly reality consists of the challenges on the ground from what are dubbed "new wars," which by now is a somewhat dusty label. Another part is the variety of humanitarian experiments and reactions in the post-Cold War era, called "new humanitarianisms," also a shop-worn label but one that accurately depicts a range of challenges for those who try to help war victims. Determining precisely what is "new" is an important part of the conceptual and actual battle. A final section in this chapter discusses some of the difficulties in trying to measure the impact of outside military forces.

Chapter 4, "New Thinking: The Responsibility to Protect," provides the details of the contemporary norm that grew from the Security Council's inaction in both Rwanda and Kosovo. In the former, it authorized action too little too late, and in the latter it was paralyzed and left the North Atlantic Treaty Organization (NATO) to engage in "humanitarian bombing" – an oxymoron, and far too much too early for some observers. A way to square the circle of state sovereignty and human rights emerged from ICISS and its 2001 report, *The Responsibility to Protect*. No idea is without antecedents, and I dwell on two in detail. The first is the conceptual framework

that seeks international access to, and protection of, the growing number of war victims who do not cross an international
boundary: internally displaced persons (IDPs). The seismic
idea that there was an international responsibility to enforce
human rights standards inside the boundaries of states grows
from the work of Francis M. Deng and Roberta Cohen. The
controversial use of the bully pulpit by the UN's seventh
secretary-general, Kofi Annan, also contributes to the story, as
does the acknowledgment of R2P by the 2005 World Summit
and the subsequent General Assembly debates on this essentially new middle ground in international relations.

Chapter 5, "So What? Moving from Rhetoric to Reality,"
concludes by examining what difference changing norms
make to victims on the ground. In looking toward the next
decade, further normative progress is of secondary importance. It is far more crucial to understand and address the
political shortcomings standing in the way of making R2P
an operational reality – of turning "here we go again" into a
genuine "never again." Many developing countries still fear
humanitarian intervention as a subterfuge for big-power
meddling. However, General Assembly debates over the last
decade have revealed that there is indeed consensus, with
only a few states, indeed the usual suspects, totally remaining
outside the R2P fold. The international community of states
appears to be recovering from the US and UK ex post facto
morphing of the justification for the war in Iraq into some
vague humanitarian benefits. The overwhelming military
strength of the United States, however, continues to raise
questions as to what happens when any US administration
is ideologically opposed to military deployment for human
protection purposes – can other actors go it alone? Can they
rally sufficient force to effectively address the stated goals?
Moreover, even when the administration at the helm is sympathetic to R2P, American involvement in Afghanistan and Iraq

– not to mention insecurity in Pakistan and enduring threats from Iran and North Korea – limits resources and impinges on political will in support of humanitarian intervention. This was clearly demonstrated in the Obama administration's commitment to "days not weeks" of US military intervention in Libya, which also ruled out any possibility of boots on the ground. Meanwhile, Europeans complain but invest too little in more military capacity. The privatization of international relations and security – and thus also of the aid and protection "business" – poses additional challenges for a humanitarian sector already deeply in crisis.

CHAPTER ONE

Conceptual Building Blocks

This chapter outlines the main concepts that reappear subsequently. It begins with humanitarian intervention itself, including the crucial distinction between coercion for human protection purposes and classic UN peacekeeping. A discussion follows of the principles underpinning the international system – state sovereignty along with nonintervention, that is, a "hands-off" approach concerning matters that supposedly are in the domestic jurisdiction of states. These principles, however, confront a fundamental tension in the UN Charter and elsewhere: namely, the widespread call to respect fundamental human rights. The final section discusses change and continuity in the international system, focusing on the issues of self-determination, borders, and state capacity.

Humanitarian intervention: a contested concept

Military interventions beginning in the 1990s – against the wishes of a government, or without meaningful consent, and with humanitarian justifications – are the focus of this book. Cases where these criteria are met amount to "humanitarian intervention," which in Adam Roberts's succinct definition is "coercive action by one or more states involving the use of armed force in another state *without the consent* of its authorities, and with the purpose of preventing widespread suffering or death among the inhabitants."[1]

Some commentators argue that the definition of intervention should cover the deployment of both "solicited" and "unsolicited" military force. The emphasis here is on the unsolicited variety. The absence of consent is clearest when there is explicit opposition from a recognized government (in Iraq, the Federal Republic of Yugoslavia, Rwanda, and Libya). Because "the existence of *de facto* control is generally the most important criterion in dealing with a regime as representing the state,"[2] consent was controversial and of little practical meaning in other cases (Liberia, Haiti, and Sierra Leone) and irrelevant in one case (Somalia). In East Timor, consent was ambiguous – it emanated from an illegal occupying power (Indonesia) after significant international pressure that verged on coercion.

The second criterion is the prominence of a genuine humanitarian justification for action by intervening states. The International Commission on Intervention and State Sovereignty set the bar very high – the threat or actual occurrence of large-scale loss of life (especially genocide) and massive forced migration. The commission did not, for example, include the overthrow of a democratically elected government or an environmental disaster, or even widespread abuses of human rights – unless one of the results was large-scale loss of life. The intergovernmental resolution by the UN General Assembly at the September 2005 World Summit was more specific still: "genocide, war crimes, ethnic cleansing and crimes against humanity."

The motives behind a government's decision to commit military muscle to help war victims vary. They may be ethical – because it is the right thing to do to halt a humanitarian catastrophe – or legal – because states are parties to the Genocide Convention, for example. They may also involve legitimate calculations of national interests – either because acting can mitigate the direct and negative impact of a particular humanitarian disaster on national security or on the economy, or because doing so builds international society and norms. Motives may also be disingenuous – self-interested pursuit of gain disguised as "humanitarian."

Purists would hope that only the ethical or legal would be in play for humanitarian intervention, and many would also judge as legitimate decisions involving a calculation to strengthen international society. Others would readily admit that self-interested motives can be an important element in a decision, as is what often is closely correlated, namely political will and available military capacity. Almost no one would try to justify as "humanitarian" a so-called humanitarian intervention that really reflected ugly strategic or economic interests – which should be viewed as hijacking humanitarian intervention.

Motives behind humanitarian interventions are almost invariably mixed. Looking for parsimony in motives does not really advance the discussion. If significant national interests disqualified potential humanitarian intervention, there would rarely be sufficient motivation to get involved in the first place or to stay the course – the feeble international military involvement in Darfur since 2003 and the US withdrawal from Somalia after losing 18 Rangers in October 1993 are apt illustrations. Indeed, whether one is a proponent of the "Realist" (capital "R") perspective in international relations theory or merely a realist, one of the keys to decision-making about humanitarian intervention involves persuading states that it is in their interests to act and see actions through despite hardships or unexpected danger. As with decisions from time immemorial about just wars, those about humanitarian intervention involve thorny subjective judgments.[3]

While the ethical humanitarian rationale need not be exclusive or even foremost, it should be explicit and prominent. This rationale must be one of the conspicuous hooks on which humanitarian intervention hangs. In some cases, mainly nonhumanitarian justifications have predominated and prevailed – for instance, the regional security concerns of Nigeria in Liberia or of the United States about the nature of the regime in Haiti. However, responding to the needs of populations at risk remained not only in evidence but was also specifically cited as a visible component of the domestic and international sales pitch for coming to the rescue.

The evolution of peace operations

Humanitarian intervention, and other types of military enforcement action, are distinct from traditional peacekeeping, which the United Nations pioneered.[4] Traditional peacekeeping operations since Dag Hammarskjöld and Lester Pearson's time have been called "Chapter VI-and-a-half" for its metaphorical location between UN Charter Articles VI and VII. The mathematics can be misleading, especially when applied to what a quarter-century ago I first called "military humanitarianism."[5] "Chapter VI.25" would be a more accurate label for UN operations because even the most vigorous reflect consent and should be rounded down to "the pacific settlement of disputes." Meanwhile, halting mass atrocities by invoking the responsibility to protect requires overriding the expressed wishes of political authorities and should be at least "Chapter VI.9" and rounded up to Chapter VII coercion.

Public and media perceptions are misleading if blue-helmet UN peace operations are equated with humanitarian interventions. There have been UN operations that were both, the most infamous being Somalia. The Security Council authorized the first Chapter VII operation under UN command-and-control with a resolution that mentioned "humanitarian" 18 times. When the second UN Operation in Somalia turned into humanitarian enforcement, crucial distinctions evaporated for the US-led coalition. The unceremonious display of dead US Rangers in the streets of Mogadishu resulted in the "Somalia syndrome," which made problematic future commitments of troops with humanitarian justifications if more than zero casualties were in the offing.[6]

It is difficult to recall the unrealistic expectations surrounding the so-called UN Renaissance at the Cold War's end after the reversal of Saddam Hussein's aggression against Kuwait. The UN-authorized and US-led Operation Desert Storm in January 1991 was followed closely by the first use of what ICISS would later label "military force for human protection purposes."[7] In April, Operation Provide Comfort's no-fly zone successfully protected Kurds who had fled their homes. Enforcement in Iraq followed a series of more complex yet successful traditional peacekeeping operations in the late 1980s, dubbed "second generation" – in Cambodia, Angola, Namibia, Iran-Iraq, and Central America. For a brief moment, there was seemingly nothing that the UN could not do.

Euphoria was evident in January 1992 when the Security Council requested newly elected UN secretary-general Boutros Boutros-Ghali to draft a forward-looking overview. Six months later, *An Agenda for Peace*[8] conveyed an over-the-top enthusiasm for all manner of UN operations – peacekeeping, peacemaking, peacebuilding, and peace enforcement – which was short-lived after the fiasco in Somalia and troubles in Bosnia-Herzegovina. The quick success in northern Iraq spawned deployments with minimal military muscle. For example, humanitarian "safe areas" had insufficient firepower and boots-on-the-ground and were the least safe places in the Balkans. July 2015 marked the twentieth anniversary, for instance, of the massacre of some 8,000 men and boys in Srebrenica, one of those areas that was observed by the UN's Dutch battalion.

Eventually, the North Atlantic Treaty Organization (NATO)

bombed Serbian positions in Bosnia-Herzegovina with UN authorization, and the Dayton Accords in November 1995 halted the humanitarian and political disaster. The previous year set the record for hapless humanitarian nonintervention in Rwanda's genocide. Despite heroic acts, including by UN force commander General Roméo Dallaire, the inadequate 2,500-member UN Assistance Mission for Rwanda (UNAMIR) was cut to 270 and witnessed the slaughter of some 800,000 people between April and June 1994.

In 1995 Boutros-Ghali recanted his earlier bullishness in *Supplement to "An Agenda for Peace."*[9] After three bitter and painful years, the UN retreated from humanitarian interventions or military enforcement of any type. The 2000 report by the Panel on United Nations Peace Operations – the "Brahimi Report" named after its chair – repeated the message: the UN should not be in the enforcement business.[10]

Additional confusion arises because UN-authorized, but occasionally regionally led or hybrid, peace operations sometimes follow humanitarian interventions from coalitions of the willing or regional organizations. Examples range from the minor presence of some 500 members of the UN Guards Contingent that took over after Operation Provide Comfort in Iraq to the 50,000 NATO-led Kosovo Force that followed the alliance's air attacks against the Federal Republic of Yugoslavia.

Another variation of the blurring was the UN Operation in Côte d'Ivoire (UNOCI), a traditional peacekeeping force first deployed in 2004 at the request of President Laurent Gbagbo. The UN later turned down his request to withdraw amidst violence against peaceful protestors and the flight of tens of thousands who resisted the incumbent's refusal to recognize the election of Alassane Ouatarra. For three months the Security Council dragged its collective feet. A predictable humanitarian disaster – refugees, massacres, full-scale civil war, and a ruined economy – pushed the council in March 2011 to authorize UNOCI to "use all necessary means" to protect civilians and in self-defense. The resolution-rattling ended early in April, when Paris unleashed its 1,650-strong Licorne contingent to rout Gbagbo's forces.

Military humanitarian intervention ranges across a variety of tasks from compelling compliance and coercive protection to war-fighting. It involves tactics aimed to alleviate suffering. But such efforts are distinct from consensual operations in which there is "peace to keep," the agreed comparative advantage of the United Nations, even if US ambassador Samantha Power notes that "we are asking peacekeepers to do more, in more places, and in more complex conflicts than at any time in history."[11] Consent clearly is implausible from those abusing their populations or manifestly unwilling or unable to protect them, which brings us to the responsibility to protect.

In short, traditional peacekeeping is based on the principles of consent, neutrality, and the nonuse of force except in self-defense. This unusual form of military deployment is designed to create and maintain conditions in which political negotiations can proceed – in effect, to monitor compliance with an agreement that belligerents have committed themselves to implement. It involves patrolling buffer zones between hostile parties, monitoring cease-fires, and helping defuse local conflicts. Ongoing examples of traditional peacekeeping include unarmed military observers in the Western Sahara and armed infantry-based forces in Cyprus. Soldiers are not the only people who can carry out such functions, but they are more easily deployed in such large numbers in dangerous situations to act as international constables. UN peacekeepers won the 1988 Nobel Prize for having used this creative conflict-management method for more than 40 years since the first unarmed military observers were posted.[12]

At the other end of the spectrum of international military

action lies a well-understood concept, war fighting. Here the objective is to defeat a clearly defined adversary, and it is undertaken by fully combat-capable troops. NATO's 1999 air campaign in Kosovo and 2011 bombing in Libya fall into this category, as does Tanzania's 1979 overthrow of the thuggish regime of Idi Amin Dada in Uganda, discussed in further detail later.

However, activities falling between the two extremes have become a more common form of international military operation, with pertinence for humanitarian crises. Here it is useful to distinguish between two related but distinct sets of objectives: compelling compliance and providing protection. The former, commonly referred to as "peace enforcement," involves the search for comprehensive political settlements leading to sustainable peace. It includes traditional peacekeeping tasks such as monitoring cease-fires, but it also encompasses more complex ones whose ultimate success requires a willingness and a capacity to use deadly force. These include the "cantonment and demobilization of soldiers; the destruction of weapons; the formation and training of new armed forces; [and] monitoring existing police forces and forming new ones."[13]

Examples of this form of military operation include the Implementation Force (IFOR) and the Stabilization Force (SFOR) organized by NATO in Bosnia, the US-led Multinational Force (MNF) in Haiti, and the UN Mission for Sierra Leone (UNAMSIL). A variant of this approach is the use of force to compel parties to the negotiating table. Examples here include NATO air strikes preceding the signing of the Dayton Accords on Bosnia, or the early phase of intervention in Liberia, where the Economic Community of West African States (ECOWAS) deployed a Monitoring Group (ECOMOG) that fought Charles Taylor's rebels in order to secure a cease-fire and a secure environment for the establishment of an interim government.

The other form of enforcement consists of protecting civilians. "Coercive protection" can take a variety of forms, but the most common are the maintenance of humanitarian corridors, the protection of aid convoys, and the creation of safe havens or protected areas. Prominent examples include the no-fly zone in northern Iraq after the First Gulf War and the so-called safe areas of Bosnia. A particularly important dimension of this kind of operation is the force posture of intervening troops. Coercive protection is distinct from the other categories of operations, which have military forces oriented in relation to other military forces: war fighting involves combat against designated opponents, peacekeeping is the monitoring of military cease-fires or the interposition of forces between armed parties to the conflict, and compelling compliance involves the use of force against conflicting parties or spoilers. In contrast, coercive protection requires the interposition of forces between well-armed potential attackers (armies, militias, and gangs) and civilians.

Finally, humanitarian intervention entails many tasks about which militaries around the world are uncomfortable, in part because they are dangerous but have restrictive rules of engagement and in part because career advancement does not typically result from so-called peace operations.[14] Buried in this gray area is thus a host of challenges: the forcible disarmament of belligerents (especially in refugee camps like those in eastern Zaire); the meaningful protection of safe areas (in stark contrast to Srebrenica, where 8,000 Muslim men and boys were slaughtered in the presence of UN forces); and the protection of humanitarians (as Fred Cuny, Sergio Vieira de Mello, and many others would testify if they were still alive). Thus, humanitarian intervention ranges across peace enforcement and coercive protection, and sometimes amounts to war fighting; however it is parsed, it is distinct from peacekeeping, a situation in which there is "peace to keep."

The terminology surrounding humanitarian intervention and the tasks associated with such operations are the
subject of heated controversy among a variety of actors, ranging from UN member states to humanitarian practitioners,
from nongovernmental organizations (NGOs) to academics.
Commentators of all stripes often prefer to eliminate the
modifier "humanitarian." Many civilian aid staff dislike the
association with the use of military force, viewing "humanitarian intervention" itself – let alone "humanitarian bombing" in
Kosovo – as a contradiction in terms. Former colonies recall
the disingenuous application of the term for purposes that
were anything but humanitarian. And many observers do not
want the high ground automatically occupied by those who
claim a humanitarian justification for going to war without a
serious scrutiny of the specific merits of a case. "Of course,
military intervention may be undertaken for humanitarian
motives," cautions former UN secretary-general Kofi Annan,
but "let's get right away from using the term 'humanitarian'
to describe military operations."[15]

Such preoccupations are understandable and may serve
some diplomatic or analytical purposes. However, "humanitarian intervention" constitutes the title of this book because
the term is widely employed in academic and policy literatures. Semantics aside, truth in packaging requires an
accurate shorthand description for outside military coercion
to protect civilians caught in war zones to prevent or halt
mass atrocities. It made no sense to insert either "so-called"
throughout this text or to use scare quotes. Human suffering
and the need to provide humanitarian relief to affected populations are prominent considerations of publics and politicians
who back the use of military force for such objectives – and
they almost always employ the term "humanitarian intervention." In fact, David Rieff argues that we should call a spade
a spade – referring to "humanitarian war" would make clear

the bloody costs as well as the benefits.[16] And Taylor Seybolt prefers "humanitarian military intervention," which he points out "is not humanitarian in character but it can be humanitarian in outcome."[17] While "the responsibility to protect" is more acceptable normative diplomatic terminology, an additional argument for occasionally using the old lexicon would be the overt treatment of the essential but often downplayed military elements of R2P.

The politics of normative change

As for too many issues, UN secretary-general Ban Ki-moon's operating style is to avoid controversy. His January 2009 report laid out three pillars for R2P – state responsibility, capacity building, and international responses.[18] Part of his purpose was to gloss over the third one, which includes using or threatening to use military force to stop mass atrocities. This focus became clear in his 2011 report when the secretary-general noted, in the wake of the Libyan intervention, that the more progress is achieved on the first two pillars "the less recourse will there be to the third pillar."[19]

This evasiveness was evident a year earlier in his July 2010 report on early warning,[20] as if better information and the establishment of a joint office were the real challenges or the real solution to making "never again" more than a slogan. The need for greater prevention is indisputable, but it is hard to fathom why UN officials and Alex Bellamy find it "reasonable" to view R2P "as a policy agenda in need of implementation rather than as a 'red flag' to galvanize the world into action."[21] Moreover, it is curious that "discussions of prevention continually return to the need for an early-warning system," writes William Zartman, "when the real need is for an authoritative list of proximate triplines and for a determination to act."[22] Indeed.

My position is close to this skepticism about political cor-
rectness because we have witnessed not too much but, rather,
too little armed force to protect human beings. After Kosovo
in 1999 – other than a small British deployment in Sierra
Leone in 2000 and a smaller essentially French one in eastern
Congo in 2003 – there was no substantial multinational effort
until Security Council resolution 1973 authorized "all necessary measures" against Libya to enforce a no-fly zone and
to protect civilians. Except for the bullish but as yet unused
article 4(h) of the African Union's Constitutive Act – which
stipulates "the right of the Union to intervene in a Member
State pursuant to a decision of the Assembly in respect of
grave circumstances, namely: war crimes, genocide and
crimes against humanity"[23] – the hard edge of the R2P stick
has thus been largely ignored in order to make the norm less
abrasive to critics. A refreshing exception was James Pattison,
who pointedly reminded us that "humanitarian intervention
is *only one part* of the doctrine of the responsibility to protect,
but that . . . it *is* part of the responsibility to protect."[24]

While chapter 4 explores the important conceptual and
rhetorical shift from humanitarian intervention to R2P, it is
important here to at least have a few basics. With the exception of Raphael Lemkin's advocacy for the 1948 Genocide
Convention, no idea has moved faster or farther in the international normative arena. It was formulated in a 2001 report by
ICISS,[25] and friends and foes alike point to the commission's
central conceptual contribution to reframing sovereignty as
contingent rather than absolute. Unlike many other blue-
ribbon panels, this one was demand- and not supply-driven;
and so its recommendations have had a public policy impact
rather than, as Gareth Evans has quipped, been "consigned
directly to bookshelves or hard drives and forever thereafter
unread and unremembered."[26]

ICISS coined "R2P" to move beyond the pitched battles of

the title of this book, "humanitarian intervention." It sought to switch the optic toward "an evaluation of the issues from the point of view of those seeking or needing support, rather than those who may be considering intervention." As such, the commission shifted the Security Council's moral frame of reference from state to individual security. The intergovernmental agreement on the occasion of the UN's sixtieth anniversary in 2005 is appropriately regarded as a turning point in the norm's crystallization, which 10 years later UN secretary-general Ban Ki-moon maintains reflects a "consensus [that] spans all regions,"[27] albeit not quite "an international Magna Carta" – Anne-Marie Slaughter's hyperbole.[28]

Beginning with the international response in northern Iraq in 1991, the moniker "humanitarian intervention" led to circular tirades about the agency, timing, legitimacy, means, circumstances, consistency, and advisability of using military force to protect human beings. Two events were seared in diplomatic imaginations – doing too little too late in Rwanda's 1994 genocide and purportedly too much too soon in Kosovo.

The central insight and main tactical advantage of R2P is that state sovereignty is conditional: it entails duties, not simply rights; and it permits a conversation about the limits of state power even with the most ardent defenders of sovereign inviolability. After centuries of largely looking the other way, sovereignty no longer provides a license for mass atrocities in the eyes of legitimate members of the international community of states. It is important to indicate that I have consciously left "humanitarian intervention" in the title of this book. As Ramesh Thakur has noted: "the term has a long historical pedigree and to that extent it is fair enough to use it when analysing the concept in its historical entirety, as even people closely associated with ICISS have done."[29]

Every state has a responsibility to protect its own citizens from widespread killings and other gross violations of their rights. If any state, however, is manifestly unable or unwilling to exercise that responsibility, or actually is the perpetrator of mass atrocities, its sovereignty is abrogated. Meanwhile the responsibility to protect civilians in distress devolves to other states, ideally acting through the UN Security Council.

Why was the secretary-general trying to soft-soap the use of military force? In brief, because of the anguished hue and cry about R2P as a ruse for western imperialism, which can be viewed as disingenuous but certainly resonates in parts of the global South. The result, as Simon Chesterman summarized some time ago, is "the overwhelming prevalence of inhuman-itarian nonintervention."[30] Will Libya be an aberration? Is assertive liberal interventionism of the 1990s ancient history? At that time "sovereign equality looked and smelled reaction-ary," writes the secretary-general's current special adviser on the R2P, Jennifer Welsh. "But as the liberal moment recedes, and the distribution of power shifts globally, the principle of sovereign equality may enjoy a comeback."[31] Let's hope that Libya and future events prove her wrong. At the very least, many efforts since the 1990s reinforce Jarat Chopra's and my 1992 assertion that "sovereignty is no longer sacrosanct."[32] In practice and theory, R2P matters.[33]

It is also worth noting in concluding this section that, for many audiences, "humanitarian" retains great resonance. One searches in vain, however, for a solid definition of the term in international law. The International Court of Justice (ICJ) was provided an opportunity in the *Nicaragua v. United States* case, but it engaged in a tautological evasion of sorts by stating that humanitarian action is what the International Committee of the Red Cross (ICRC) does. The *Oxford English Dictionary* – whose 1819 edition had the first citation and invoked displeasure at the neologism – is not much help when stating that "humanitarian" is "having regard to the interests of humanity or mankind at large; relating to, or advocating, or practising humanity or human action."[34] A second definition notes that the term is "often contemptuous or hostile."[35] In any case, the definition of "humanitarian" as a justification for intervention normally requires a high threshold of suffering. It refers to the threat or actual occurrence of large-scale loss of life, massive forced migration, and widespread abuses of human rights – in brief, acts that shock the conscience.

To understand more fully the contentiousness of humanitarian intervention, we delve into the key concepts underpinning the international system enshrined in the UN Charter – sovereignty and its corollary, nonintervention in the domestic affairs of states, and human rights.

State sovereignty and nonintervention: two sides of the Westphalian coin

Sovereignty has, for the past several centuries, been the foundation of interstate relations and world order. The concept – defined as the independent and unfettered power of a state in its jurisdiction – lies at the heart of customary international law and the UN Charter. It remains both an essential component of the maintenance of international peace and security and a defense for weak states against the strong. At the same time, the concept has never been as inviolable, either in law or in practice, as a formal legal definition might imply. In his 1992 *An Agenda for Peace*, UN secretary-general Boutros Boutros-Ghali pronounced that the theory of sovereignty never matched reality.[36] In exploring why Westphalian sovereignty is routinely ignored or violated, Stephen Krasner has noted straightforwardly that "organized hypocrisy is the normal state of affairs."[37]

Sovereignty has routinely been violated by the powerful. In today's globalizing world, it is generally recognized that cultural, environmental, and economic influences neither respect borders nor require entry visas in both powerful and powerless countries.[38] The principle of state sovereignty is well entrenched in legal and political discourse, but territorial boundaries have come under stress. Not only have technology and communications made borders permeable, but the political dimensions of internal disorder and suffering often can result in wider international disorder.[39] Perspectives on the range and role of state sovereignty have, particularly over the past two decades, evolved quickly and substantially.

The purpose of this discussion is to set out the scope and significance of state sovereignty as a foundation on which to explore contemporary debates about intervention. The literature on this subject is vast and contentious. As Leiden University's Nico Schrijver accurately summarizes:

> Few subjects in international law and international relations are as sensitive as the notion of sovereignty. Steinberger refers to it in the *Encyclopedia of Public International Law* as "the most glittering and controversial notion in the history, doctrine and practice of international law." On the other hand, Henkin seeks to banish it from our vocabulary and Lauterpacht calls it a "word which has an emotive quality lacking meaningful specific content," while Verzijl notes that any discussion on this subject risks degenerating into a Tower of Babel. More affirmatively, Brownlie sees sovereignty as "the basic constitutional doctrine of the law of nations" and Alan James sees it as "the one and only organising principle in respect of the dry surface of the globe, all that surface now . . . being divided among single entities of a sovereign, or constitutionally independent kind." As noted by Falk, "There is little neutral ground when it comes to sovereignty."[40]

A quick review of the basics will be useful for less specialized readers. State sovereignty denotes the competence, independence, and legal equality of states. The concept is normally used to encompass all matters in which each state is permitted by international law to decide and act without intrusion from other sovereign states. These matters include the choice of political, economic, social, and cultural systems, and the formulation of foreign policy. The scope of the freedom of choice of states in these matters is not unlimited; it depends on developments in international law (including agreements made voluntarily) and in international relations.

The concept of sovereign rule goes back centuries in the context of regulated relationships and their legal traditions among such disparate territorial entities as Egypt, China, and the Holy Roman Empire. However, the current foundations of international law with regard to sovereignty were shaped by agreements concluded by European states as part of the Treaties of Westphalia in 1648.[41] After almost 30 years of war, the supremacy of the state was enshrined within the system of independent and equal units as a way of establishing peace and order. The 1933 Montevideo Convention on the Rights and Duties of States spells out four core elements: a permanent population, a defined territory, a functioning government, and the ability to enter into relations with other states. Cuba, for example, did not meet all of the criteria between 1901 and 1934, as the Platt Amendment's provisions were included in its constitution, effectively ceding authority over the country's foreign relations to the United States.

Robert Jackson and Carl Rosberg's analysis of state sovereignty in Africa contrasts the *de facto* and *de jure* attributes of statehood. The Montevideo Convention's definition includes both empirical (population and effective government) and juridical (borders and independence) components.[42] A number of states in Africa – such as the Democratic Republic of the Congo and Somalia – and elsewhere fail to exhibit sovereignty, especially an adequate display of authority over their entire territory. These states thus fail to meet Max Weber's widely used definition of the state: the existence of an administrative apparatus with a monopoly on the legitimate use of force within its territorial borders.[43] Thus, some states are *de jure* but not *de facto* sovereign.

The post-1945 system of international order is enshrined in the UN Charter. Following decolonization, what had been essentially a western world order became generalized. There were no longer "insiders" (the metropoles exerting dominance) and "outsiders" (the colonies depending on decisions by imperial masters), because virtually every person on earth was now a citizen of a sovereign state.

In accordance with UN Charter Article 2(1), the world organization is based upon the sovereign equality of all its members, be they Vanuatu or Venezuela, China or Chad. Legal equality is also the basis on which intergovernmental organizations (IGOs) function. In 1949, the ICJ observed that "between independent States, respect for territorial sovereignty is an essential foundation of international relations."[44] Thirty years later, the court referred to "the fundamental principle of state sovereignty on which the whole of international law rests."[45]

As a hallmark of statehood, territorial sovereignty is the basis of the international system. An act of aggression is unlawful for two reasons: it undermines international order, and states have exercised their sovereignty to outlaw war in the UN Charter. In addition, the failure or weakening of state capacity brings about a political vacuum and leads to human tragedies and international insecurity, as exemplified by the cases of Bosnia and Rwanda during the 1990s, as well as Iraq and Afghanistan, or Yemen and Syria at present.

In sum, sovereignty is a key constitutional safeguard of international order. Despite the pluralization of international relations resulting from the proliferation of nonstate actors (NSAs) – which is evidenced by globalization, democratization, and privatization worldwide – the state remains the fundamental guarantor of human rights locally as well as the building block of international society.

Equality in legal status is customarily viewed as protection for weaker states in the face of pressure from more powerful ones. Addressing the UN General Assembly in 1999, immediately after Secretary-General Annan's clarion call to respect human rights, Algeria's president Abdelaziz Bouteflika, then also president of the Organization of African Unity (OAU), dubbed sovereignty "our final defence against the rules of an unjust world."[46]

Sovereignty is not, however, a *carte blanche*, because there are widely accepted limits in international law. First, the UN Charter contains collective international obligations for the maintenance of international peace and security. According to Chapter VII, sovereignty is not a barrier to Security Council action in response to "a threat to the peace, a breach of the peace or an act of aggression." The use of force is permitted either in self-defense or with a mandate from the Security Council. In other words, the UN Charter's language recognizes that sovereignty yields to the demands of international peace and security.

Second, sovereignty may be limited by customary law and treaty obligations. States are legally responsible for their international obligations, and therefore sovereignty cannot be an excuse for not performing duties to which they have agreed. UN membership presupposes a restriction of the sovereignty of members. Specifically, Charter Article 1(2) stipulates that "All Members, in order to ensure to all of them the rights and benefits resulting from membership, shall fulfill in good faith the obligations assumed by them in accordance with the present Charter." Furthermore, under "Purposes and Principles," this same article obliges member states to achieve international cooperation in solving economic, social, cultural, or humanitarian problems, and in promoting and encouraging respect for human rights and for fundamental freedoms. This article further recognizes the UN as a center for harmonizing the actions of states in the attainment of these common ends. Thus, the Charter elevates economic, social, cultural, and humanitarian problems, as well as human rights, to the international sphere. By ratifying the Charter, a national government under scrutiny can no longer claim that such matters are *exclusively* domestic.

Sovereignty thus carries with it responsibilities for states to protect persons and property, and to discharge government functions within their territories. The range of responsibilities has significantly changed since the signing of the Charter in June 1945. An expanding network of obligations in the field of human rights has created a dense set of state obligations to protect persons and property, as well as to regulate political and economic affairs. Sovereignty cannot shield internal violations of human rights that contradict international obligations.

Similarly, Article 2(7) of the Charter clearly delineates inviolable sovereignty: "Nothing contained in the present Charter shall authorise the United Nations to intervene in matters that are essentially within the domestic jurisdiction of any State or shall require the Members to submit such matters to settlement under the present Charter." While sovereignty is the fundamental building block of the world organization, it is nonetheless subject to widely accepted limits beyond those of self-defense and Chapter VII enforcement mentioned earlier, namely human rights. The words *"essentially* within the domestic jurisdiction of States" refer to those matters that are not regulated by international law. But the ICJ has concluded that "the question whether a certain matter is or is not solely within the domestic jurisdiction of a State is an essentially relative question; it depends upon the development of international relations."[47] The court has concluded that terms like

"domestic jurisdiction" were not intended to have a fixed con-
tent regardless of the subsequent evolution of international
law.[48]

Contemporary economic, cultural, and environmental factors have also altered what passes for "normal." Interference
in what would previously have been regarded as internal
affairs – by other states, the private sector, and nonstate actors
– has become routine. However, our preoccupation here is
not with these routine intrusions but with the clash between
the norm of state sovereignty and egregious human suffering. In Kofi Annan's opening remarks at the 1999 General
Assembly: "States bent on criminal behaviour [should] know
that frontiers are not the absolute defence."[49] In this respect,
events beginning in the early 1990s clearly broke new ground
because sovereignty no longer was an unquestioned justification for any and every action by state authorities.

For the first 45 years, the Charter regime privileged state
sovereignty over human rights, with the significant exception
of white minority rule in Rhodesia and apartheid in South
Africa. But the balance shifted in the 1990s. In a number of
cases, the Security Council endorsed the use of military force
with the primary goal of assisting and protecting populations
caught in the throes of war.[50] In short, the sovereignty of
individuals can trump that of states. As UN secretary-general
Boutros Boutros-Ghali emphatically asserted at the beginning
of the decade, "The time of absolute state sovereignty . . . has
passed."[51]

The end of East–West tensions reduced the fear that taking
international protection seriously would menace the interests
of the superpowers or their allies and result in a conflict whose
negative consequences would dwarf any possible human
rights benefits. At the same time, the proliferation of complex humanitarian emergencies and the inappropriateness of
the classical tenets of UN conflict management highlighted

the tensions between the neutrality of traditional peacekeeping and the consequences of peace enforcement. As Ramesh Thakur tells us, "the norm of nonintervention has softened as that of human rights has hardened."[52]

We turn our attention to that tempering because intervention consists of various forms of nonconsensual action that directly challenge state sovereignty. Hence, nonintervention is the necessary and logical corollary of state sovereignty, or the other side of the Westphalian coin and its accompanying world order.

The principle of noninterference in affairs that fall within the domestic jurisdiction of states anchors the system of international relations and obligations. Jurisdiction broadly refers to the power, authority, and competence of a state to govern persons and property on its territory. Prescriptive jurisdiction relates to the power to make law within and outside its territory, and enforcement jurisdiction concerns the power to implement the law within its territory. Jurisdiction exercised by states is then the corollary of their sovereignty and is founded on territorial sovereignty but extends beyond it. Jurisdiction is prima facie exclusive over a state's territory and population, and the mutual duty of nonintervention in domestic affairs protects both the territorial sovereignty and the domestic jurisdiction of all states.

Therefore, actions do not amount to intervention if they are based on a genuine request from, or have the unqualified consent of, a target state. Consent, if it is to be valid in law, should emanate from the legal government of a state and be freely given. Forms of interference that fall short of coercion do not amount to intervention. In fact, a central purpose of routine foreign policy is to persuade other states, friends and foes alike, to change their behavior and policies. Carrots and sticks are the common bill of fare of diplomacy.

Of course, wider and looser notions of intervention exist.

Foreign aid and military assistance, for instance, normally have strings attached. The nature of asymmetric power in the international system virtually guarantees that weaker states will agree to actions that they might not have had they been economically or militarily stronger.

However, should such decisions be classified as "intervention"? There would be little analytical traction if such routine economic activities as foreign direct investment and aid were so considered. With interdependence and globalization rising in virtually all parts of the world, anxiety levels among many governmental officials have also increased because there are substantial new vulnerabilities, including cultural "invasion" and other aspects of so-called soft power about which they can do virtually nothing.

As always, there are gray areas of "consent" not only for economic but also for military measures. Some observers note, for example, that a "request" for military intervention – like Indonesia's on behalf of East Timor – may involve so much arm twisting, including substantial economic pressure from international financial institutions, as to effectively constitute coercion. Various terms have been coined for what amounts to coerced consent, including the poetic "coercive inducement."[53] Intervention may be better framed, in effect, as a matter of factual intrusiveness rather than merely an absence of consent to ensure that a so-called request is not actually spurious. As with many definitions, readers may wish to think of consent as a continuum rather than an absolute concept.

Notwithstanding these subtleties, the actual expression of consent is a critical dividing line for any discussion of humanitarian intervention, as is a legitimate decision from the UN Security Council. And given the legacy of colonialism, it is not surprising that these are benchmarks against which developing countries far more than many of their western counterparts customarily measure the legitimacy of international action. Heightened sensitivities to increased influences – economic, social, and cultural – about which they can do little, have often led to even greater sensitivities toward western human rights norms that both governmental and nongovernmental leaders may also view as imposed, but which they are in a better position to resist.

Obviously, the use of armed force against another state without its consent constitutes intervention, but clearly so do such nonmilitary measures as political and economic sanctions, arms embargoes, and international criminal prosecution. Intervention's distinctive character lies in the use of "forcible" or "non-forcible" measures against a state, without its consent, because of its internal or external behavior.[54] Although intervention has frequently sought to preserve the vital interests – legitimately or illegitimately perceived – of intervening states, there is also a history of intervention justified on the grounds of grave human suffering.

Human rights and individual sovereignty

The Charter contains a seeming contradiction between the intervention-proscribing principle of state sovereignty (especially in Article 2) and the intervention-prescribing principle of human rights (especially in Articles 55–6). This clash is particularly evident when push comes to shove over humanitarian intervention. Individuals have become holders of rights under a growing corpus of human rights and international humanitarian law treaties and conventions – especially the 1948 Universal Declaration of Human Rights and the two 1966 covenants on civil and political rights and economic, social, and cultural rights, the International Committee of the Red Cross's Geneva Conventions of 1949 and Additional Protocols of 1977, and the two conventions prohibiting torture (1975) and genocide (1948).[55]

The cluster of norms inhibiting, if not prohibiting, humanitarian intervention includes nonintervention, state sovereignty, domestic jurisdiction, pacific settlement of disputes, nonuse of force, and, in the case of UN-authorized use of force, impartiality. At the same time, a clear challenge to traditional interpretations of sovereignty emerges from the changing balance between states and people as the source of legitimacy and authority. The older version of the rule of law of states is being tempered by the rule of law of individuals. A broader concept of sovereignty, encompassing both the rights *and* the responsibilities of states, is more widely advocated now than even a decade ago.

UN secretary-general Kofi Annan raised the issue most sharply in mid-September 1999 in his much lauded and attacked article in *The Economist* about the "two concepts of sovereignty." He helped launch an intense debate about the legitimacy of intervention on humanitarian grounds because he juxtaposed two versions of sovereignty – one oriented around states, and the other around people. For Annan and others, sovereignty is not becoming less relevant; it remains the essential ordering principle of international affairs. However, "it is the people's sovereignty rather than the sovereign's sovereignty."[56] The hostile reaction by many government officials was, not unexpectedly, different from that of human rights advocates.

Another way of approaching the increasing importance of popular sovereignty is "sovereignty as responsibility," explicitly associated with the work of Francis M. Deng, the former representative of the secretary-general on internally displaced persons, and his collaborator Roberta Cohen. First articulated in the late 1980s, this doctrine stipulates that when states are unable to provide life-supporting protection and assistance for their citizens, they are expected to request and accept outside offers of aid.[57] Should they refuse or deliberately obstruct access to their displaced or other-affected populations, and thereby put large numbers of them at risk, there is an international responsibility to act.

Sovereignty, then, means accountability to two separate constituencies: internally to one's own population and internationally to the community of responsible states in the form of compliance with human rights and humanitarian agreements. Proponents argue that sovereignty is not absolute but contingent. When a government massively abuses the fundamental rights of its citizens, its sovereignty is temporarily suspended or abrogated.

A third variant on this theme revolves around the concept of human security.[58] Traditionally, security concerns the relations between states; but for a growing number of governments and analysts, the security of individuals is becoming a foreign policy priority in its own right. For some, human security means freedom from pervasive threats to people's safety and lives – hence, humanitarian intervention enters when mass murder or displacement takes place. For others, human security also includes the empowerment of individuals to take control of their own destinies. This more expansive vision is identified with the work of Amartya Sen, which infused the Commission on Human Security's report but is too sweeping for this discussion of humanitarian intervention.[59]

Although the state remains the principal provider of security, it is seen in instrumental terms – as a means to an end rather than an end in itself. In the face of repressive or weak states, advocates of the narrower version of human security argue that international actors have a responsibility to come to the aid of populations at risk. Ultimately, in the words of Lloyd Axworthy, who as Canada's foreign minister was one of the architects of ICISS as well as a most visible spokesman for human security: "peace and security – national, regional and international – are possible only if they are derived from people's security."[60]

These approaches have something in common: the basis for sovereignty's shifting from the absolute rights determined by a small elite of state leaders to internal forms of governance based on international standards regarding democracy and human rights. Advocates suggest that, on a scale of values, the sovereignty of a state does not stand higher than the human rights of its inhabitants.[61]

It would be short-sighted, however, to ignore or underestimate a widespread residual sentiment among observers who charge that humanitarian intervention is simply the latest phase of Eurocentric domination. Human rights, in this view, are the contemporary western equivalent of Christianity's earlier "standard of civilization."[62] Nevertheless, from many quarters the view is emerging that, at least, sovereignty is no longer as sacrosanct as it once was. Sovereignty as the supreme power of a state has always been limited, originally by divine law, respect for religious practices, and natural law; and subsequently, limitations have resulted from the consent-based system of the law of nations.[63] "The doctrine of national sovereignty in its absolute and unqualified form, which gave rulers protection against attack from without while engaged within in the most brutal assault on their own citizens," writes Ramesh Thakur, "has gone with the wind."[64] We now examine the collective impact of winds that have been blowing for some time.

Change and continuity in the international system

Limits to sovereignty are more and more widely discussed and accepted – its erosion by economic, cultural, and environmental factors, for example, or by customary law and voluntarily agreed treaty obligations. Yet Annan's assertion of the importance of popular sovereignty and R2P's accompanying normative advances constitute far more direct and radical challenges.

Simultaneously, three other threats to more traditional notions of state sovereignty arose in the 1990s and are relevant for our consideration of humanitarian intervention: a reinvigorated notion of self-determination; a broadened conception of international peace and security; and the collapse of state authority. In spite of significant change, the international system reflects substantial continuities: in particular, the centrality of state decision-making and the lack of any overriding central authority. But situating the nature of changes and continuities is the task of political analysis and judgment, which is the task here.

For almost half a century, self-determination – which had emerged after World War I with the dissolution of the Ottoman and Hapsburg empires – was limited to the initial processes of decolonization. However arbitrary and dysfunctional, existing borders were sacred. And it was unthinkable that an area of a state would secede, even with the consent of its citizens. The charter of the African Union's (AU) predecessor, the Organization of African Unity, was clear: colonial borders, generally agreed to have been drawn arbitrarily, had to be respected, or chaos would ensue. *Uti possidetis, ita possideatis* ("as you possess, so may you possess") was accepted as the necessary trade-off for maintaining international order in a world in which two-thirds of the member states had only recently attained independence. The fear was that even hinting that borders were anything except fixed in perpetuity risked opening floodgates of instability.

The end of the Cold War, however, witnessed the softening of two norms that were virtually unchallenged during the previous four decades: the sanctity of borders and the illegitimacy of secession. These clear waters became muddied when the Soviet Union became a "former superpower." Russia inherited the Union of Soviet Socialist Republics' (USSR) legal status, including a permanent seat on the Security Council, but 14 other states were created by the implosion of the former Soviet Union. Shortly thereafter, Yugoslavia broke up into six independent states, with Serbia and Montenegro later forming the Federal Republic of Yugoslavia. In 1993, Czechoslovakia had its "velvet divorce," and, later in the decade, Eritrea seceded from Ethiopia. In 2006, Montenegro declared independence from Serbia referendum, making it the seventh republic of the former Yugoslavia; Kosovo followed suit in 2008, although its status remains the subject of contention, recognized by only some states in 2011. South Sudan became the UN's 193rd member state.

That weakening of the norms related to respecting borders and forbidding secessions created new tensions. Contemporary politics in developing countries is deeply conditioned by the legacy of colonialism. As European states ruled so many Asian and African countries without their consent, respect for state sovereignty is the preemptive norm *par excellence* of ex-colonial states. It is difficult for representatives of developing countries to take at face value altruistic claims by the West about so-called humanitarian intervention. What may appear as narrow legalism in the North – for instance, that Security Council authorization is a prerequisite for humanitarian as for any other type of intervention – often appears in the South as a necessary buttress against new forms of arrogance and imperialism, against the prerogatives of the rich and the powerful.

The second challenge to earlier notions of inviolable sovereignty is the broadening interpretation of threats to international peace and security, the Charter's only enshrined license to override the principle of nonintervention. The collective security system was grafted onto the experience of World War II. The focus in 1945 was principally on acts of aggression. Collective efforts by the United Nations to deal with internal problems of peace and security, and even gross violations of human rights including genocide, therefore went against the grain of the claim to sovereign status as set out in the world organization's Charter.

State actions approved or authorized after the Cold War's end by the Security Council have routinely expanded the notion of what is considered a threat to international peace and security and the basis for its decisions to authorize out-side intervention. This process actually began during the Cold War, with the council's coercive decisions in the form of eco-nomic sanctions and arms and oil embargoes against white minority rule in Southern Rhodesia and in South Africa. In both cases, the Security Council described the recourse to Chapter VII action as responses to "threats to international peace and security." What motivated state decision-making were the human costs resulting from aberrant and racist domestic policies. A truly ugly affront to civilization with minimal transboundary consequences was nonetheless packaged as a threat to international peace and security. The Charter, like most constitutions, is a living document, and this evolution in what was considered a legitimate basis for international action seemed logical and justified.

The evolution of bona fide threats to international peace and security accelerated in the 1990s. For instance, while recalling Article 2(7), 1991 Security Council resolution 688 nonetheless condemned "the repression of the Iraq civilian population in many parts of Iraq, including most recently in Kurdish populated areas." This resolution was criticized by the abstainers (China and India) and voted against by Cuba, Yemen, and Zimbabwe, but it marked the beginning of an important momentum for council action over the coming decade. The council repeatedly condemned attacks on civilians in Bosnia and Herzegovina, Sierra Leone, and Kosovo, which constituted grave violations of international law. It reaffirmed that persons who commit or order the commission of grave breaches of the Geneva Conventions and the Additional Protocols are individually responsible for such breaches.[65] Similarly, the establishment of international tribunals with criminal jurisdiction and of the International Criminal Court (ICC) signaled that atrocities committed against human beings by their own governments – including war crimes, crimes against humanity, and genocide – trumped claims of state sovereignty.[66]

Interventions of the 1990s were justified, at least in substantial part, on humanitarian grounds in countries whose internal politics were framed as threats to international peace and security. In most cases, the dire humanitarian situation was explicitly mentioned in the Security Council's resolution – the most extreme case being Somalia in 1992, when the word "humanitarian" appeared 18 times in resolution 794. In a session devoted to Africa in January 2000, even the AIDS pandemic was framed as falling within the Security Council's mandate. In short, states have broadened considerably the range of interpretations of "international peace and security," the concept that circumscribes the council's terms of reference to justify its involvement and decisions.

The third challenge to traditional interpretations of sovereignty has arisen because of the incapacity of certain states to exercise effective authority over their territories and populations, a topic that is treated more in depth in chapter 3. For some states, sovereignty is a legal fiction not matched by actual capacity. They are, in the striking image of Robert Jackson, "quasi-states."[67] As the display of actual control over territory is a prominent dimension of sovereign status, is it far-fetched to say that failed states violate the substantive UN membership requirement in Charter Article 4 that they "are able to carry out" their obligations?

This perspective is important in light of the growing awareness that state capacity and authority are essential conditions for the protection of fundamental rights. This realization does not invoke nostalgia for authoritarian rule and dictatorships, but rather recognizes that a modicum of state authority and capacity is a prerequisite for the maintenance of domestic and international order and justice.

The absence or disappearance of a functioning government can lead to the same kinds of human catastrophe as a cohesive repressive state. Comparing Qaddafi's Libya with the lawlessness of the country today is an ironic illustration. Resounding features of so-called failed states are anarchy, chronic disorder, and civil war waged without regard to the laws of armed conflict. These features, individually or collectively, inhibit or prevent a state from acting with authority over its entire territory. The failure of state sovereignty is most obviously in evidence when insurgents occupy and control large portions of the territory, inhibiting the state from carrying out its responsibility to protect lives and property and to maintain public order.

The political vacuum leads to nonstate actors taking matters into their own hands and is usually accompanied by the forced displacement of populations. These issues also create consequences for other states, international organizations, and civil society. In lending support to the intervention by ECOWAS in Liberia, Zimbabwe went so far as to take the position that "when there is no government in being and there is just chaos in the country," domestic affairs should be qualified as meaning "affairs within a peaceful environment."[68] Ironically, that same criterion has not yet been applied to its author, Robert Mugabe.

The nature of conflict in the post-Cold War era is an

essential variable in understanding the shift toward military intervention for human protection purposes. The transformed nature of warfare also has profound implications for civilian humanitarianism, which has likewise undergone considerable transformation. We return to these issues in chapter 3.

Deciding the extent to which international norms regarding humanitarian intervention and world politics have changed is, in many ways, a problem of definition and baselines. In spite of normative changes, globalization, and massive technological and communications advances, an overwhelming continuity in the discussion of humanitarian intervention – indeed, of any topic in world politics and international organization – is that decision-making is still conducted by states.[69]

Nothing has altered the pithy characterization by Adam Roberts and Benedict Kingsbury in their 1993 overview in *United Nations: Divided World*: "international society has been modified, but not totally transformed."[70] The UN does not exist in isolation from the world that it is attempting to serve. Many scholars and practitioners resist the notion that there has been a fundamental change in world politics. Essentially, they are right in claiming that the more things change, the more they stay the same. Certainly the fundamental units of the system, sovereign states, are here to stay. They are still organized to pursue their perceived national interests in a world without any meaningful overarching authority.

The world thus still essentially reflects what Hedley Bull and virtually all political scientists call "anarchy."[71] The absence of a central global authority does not mean, however, that states will not recognize binding rules and obligations or that they will refuse to build cooperative institutions to help write the rules and foster respect for them. Bull's singular contribution was to spell out the conditions for international society. Nonetheless, and in spite of the construction of a seemingly ever-denser web of international organizations, there is nothing like a world government in the offing. Although it would be wrong to ignore the extremes – ranging from fractious political authority in failed states to the supranational integration of the European Union (EU) – there remains a fundamental continuity: state sovereignty remains the core of international relations. In short, the United Nations confronts the same constraints today as diplomats and politicians have since time immemorial, and certainly since the beginning of modern efforts at multilateral cooperation in the nineteenth century.[72]

CHAPTER TWO

"Humanitarian" Interventions: Thumbnail Sketches

This chapter takes seriously the necessity to examine a wide range of examples to provide a better sense of history rather than to generalize merely from recent cases. There are brief discussions of the examples of colonial "humanitarian" interventions as well as those between 1945 and 1990 when the UN Charter regime was circumscribed by the East–West conflict.

With the dissolution of the Soviet Union, the United Nations became a more central player in the realm of international peace and security. It launched or authorized a number of peace operations, ranging from noncontroversial classic peacekeeping, in which consent by the warring parties is a prerequisite for deployment, to humanitarian interventions employing coercion for human protection purposes.

The chapter then highlights four crises where there has been mixed evidence of the imperative to come to the rescue. It concludes with the dramatic shift undertaken in response to the seismic political shift of the "Arab Spring" in the Middle East in early 2011. The Security Council's authorization of force to protect civilians from the rogue Libyan dictatorship suggests a potential rebirth for humanitarian intervention after a decade of inaction in the wake of mass atrocities. The council's inconsistent responses, however, to armed conflicts in Libya, Côte d'Ivoire, and Syria suggest that there is still far to go in realizing even-handed implementation.

The use of scare quotes in the chapter heading should

suggest to the reader that not everything dubbed "humanitarian" is indeed deserving of the label. Catalyzed in particular by the work of ICISS is the realization of the value of examining critically the facts on the ground to determine whether the "H" adjective is truly justified or merely slick propaganda. But we are getting ahead of the story. First, let us take a look at examples of what at least some observers would consider humanitarian interventions.

The nineteenth and early twentieth centuries

References to humanitarian intervention began to appear in the international legal literature after 1840, based on two interventions.[1] The first took place in Greece, where England, France, and Russia intervened in 1827 to stop Turkish massacres of populations associated with the insurgents. The second was in Syria, where France intervened in 1860 to protect Maronite Christians, and this was subsequently approved by other European countries and Turkey. In fact, there were at least five prominent interventions undertaken against the Ottoman Empire between 1827 and 1908. The others were intervention by Austria, France, Italy, Prussia, and Russia in 1866–8 to protect the Christian population in Crete; Russian intervention in the Balkans in 1875–8 in support of insurrectionist Christians; and interference by European powers from 1903 to 1908 in favor of the oppressed Christian Macedonian community.[2] By the 1920s, the rationale had broadened to include the protection of nationals abroad.

Intervention was invoked against a state's abuse of its sovereignty by brutal and cruel treatment of those within its power, both nationals and non-nationals. Such a state was regarded as having made itself liable to action by any other state or states that were prepared to intervene. One writer in 1921 depicted humanitarian intervention as "the reliance upon force for the justifiable purpose of protecting the inhabitants of another state from the treatment which is so arbitrary and persistently abusive as to exceed the limits of that authority within which the sovereign is presumed to act with reason and justice."[3]

Intervention of any sort was surrounded by controversy, and many looked, and continue to look, askance at the earliest cases of so-called humanitarian intervention.[4] Critics argue that humanitarian justifications usually mask the exercise of raw power motivated by strategic, economic, or political interests. Furthermore, there can be no doubt that even when aims were less objectionable, the paternalism of intervening powers – who were self-appointed custodians of morality and human conscience as well as the guarantors of international order and security – partially undermined the credibility of interveners. Ramesh Thakur points out that developing countries "are neither amused nor mindful at being lectured on universal human values by those who failed to practice the same during European colonialism and now urge them to cooperate in promoting 'global' human rights norms."[5]

One noted legal authority concluded in 1963 that "no genuine case of humanitarian intervention has occurred with the possible exception of the occupation of Syria in 1860 and 1861."[6] The scale of the atrocities in that case may well have warranted intervention – more than 11,000 Maronite Christians were killed, and 100,000 made homeless, in a single four-week period. But by the time the 12,000-strong European force arrived, the violence was largely over.

By the end of the nineteenth century, many jurists argued that a doctrine of humanitarian intervention existed in customary international law, but a considerable number of legal scholars disagreed. Contemporary analysts disagree about the significance of these writings, with the most bullish positing that the doctrine was clearly established in state practice prior to 1945 and that only the parameters, not the existence, of the doctrine are open to debate. Critics reject this claim, noting inconsistency in state practice – particularly in the twentieth century – and that a substantial number of scholars had earlier rejected the proposition that there existed customary law.

Clearly humanitarian intervention evolved substantially before the appearance of the current generation of international institutions. Historians point to the first restrictions on recourse to war in the Kellogg–Briand Pact in 1928. Since 1945, the threat or use of force against the territorial integrity and political independence of states has been prohibited by UN Charter Article 2(4), with exceptions granted for the collective use of force under Chapter VII and for individual or collective self-defense in the event of an armed attack. Yet questions remain. In 1946, for example, the eminent legal scholar Hersch Lauterpacht argued that intervention was legally permissible when a state was guilty of cruelties against its nationals in such a way as to deny their fundamental human rights and shock the conscience of humankind.[7]

The Charter regime and the Cold War

The adoption and entry into force in 1945 of the UN Charter had a fundamental impact on earlier interpretations of the legality of intervention. Not only did it set out the circumstances under which intervention was permissible, it also changed the terms of the debate by employing the term "the use or threat of force" instead of "intervention."

As "intervention" had often been used as a synonym for the threat or use of force, a host of questions arose then, and remain. Did the Charter's prohibition on the unilateral threat or use of force prohibit intervention altogether, or was intervention subsumed by the system of the collective use of force? Was there an interpretation of the term "intervention" that would render the concept an exception to the Charter's prohibition on the use of force against the territorial integrity and political independence of a state? Does the Charter prohibit the use of force without the authorization of the Security Council even under exceptional circumstances?

As the Charter explicitly permits the use of force in self-defense and allows the Security Council to authorize it to confront threats to international peace and security, a recurring aspect of diplomatic debates is the deployment of force to protect human beings and their fundamental rights. The sparks during the debates of the 1990s were not the first. Various interpretations of the legality of humanitarian intervention were fiercely debated, particularly in the late 1960s.[8]

The ideological competition of the Cold War lent a particular character to discussions. With much of the world aligned with one of the two superpowers, both sides sought to avoid intervention in both internal and international armed conflicts, in order to avoid a larger confrontation. The reality of the Security Council veto also increased the likelihood that interventions would either not occur at all or be undertaken without a council mandate. In fact, interventions during the Cold War were far more likely to be undertaken by a single state (for example, the United States in Vietnam, the Soviet Union in Afghanistan, and South Africa and Cuba in Angola), whether directly or by proxy, than they were to be multilateral.

On two occasions during the Cold War, the International Court of Justice ruled on cases that involved assessing the legality of interventions for which humanitarian purposes had been declared: the United Kingdom in the Corfu Channel and the United States in Nicaragua. In both cases, the ICJ opined that nonintervention involves the right of every state to conduct its affairs without outside interference, and that international law requires territorial integrity to be respected. The world court rejected intervention that impedes a state from pursuing what sovereignty permits it to decide freely

– namely, its political, economic, social, and cultural system, and the formulation of its foreign policy.

More specifically, in the case of *Nicaragua v. United States*, the ICJ reiterated the attributes of humanitarian aid or assistance, which are also relevant to military intervention for human protection purposes. The court took the view that, if the provision of assistance is to escape condemnation as an intervention in the internal affairs of a state, it must be "limited to the purposes hallowed in practice, namely to prevent and alleviate human suffering, and to protect life and health and to ensure respect for the human being without discrimination to all in need," and that it be "linked as closely as possible under the circumstances to the UN Charter in order to further gain legitimacy." These criteria should be applicable in extreme situations, for which the need to "prevent and alleviate human suffering, to protect life and health, and ensure respect for the human being" constitutes a humanitarian crisis threatening international or regional peace and security. The ICJ rejected the notion of the use of force to ensure the protection of human rights; "where human rights are protected by international conventions, that protection takes the form of such arrangements for monitoring or ensuring the respect for human rights as are provided for in the conventions themselves. . . . In any event . . . the use of force could not be the appropriate method to monitor or ensure such respect."[9]

Such a conclusion should be interpreted with care and is not definitive, certainly in light of subsequent events. The protection of human rights by international conventions presupposes a stable system ensuring respect for human rights. What is to be done in cases in which state or nonstate misconduct makes a mockery of human rights protection? Furthermore, in extreme situations where the Security Council is unable to act, political and moral imperatives may leave no choice but "to act outside the law."[10] Readers need only recall images of bodies floating in rivers in Rwanda or children with bloated bellies fleeing the Janjaweed in Darfur to look somewhat askance at the conclusions of 15 ICJ judges ruling in the comfort of their chambers in The Hague.

In evaluating 10 cases of intervention between 1945 and 1990, the Research Directorate of ICISS came to an important conclusion about the UN's Cold War period: that the rhetoric of humanitarianism had been used most stridently in cases where the humanitarian motive was weakest, including protecting one's own nationals. The use of the "H" adjective to mask other motivations indicates the scope for abuse. This was true when Washington sought, on supposedly humanitarian grounds, to help the Contras in Nicaragua, as well as when Moscow assisted comrades in Budapest in 1956 and Prague in 1968. More or less the same could be said for seven cases that were conducted for claimed humanitarian purposes or that resulted in humanitarian benefits during the Cold War: Belgium in the Congo (1960); Belgium and the United States in Stanleyville (1964); the United States in the Dominican Republic (1965); France and Belgium in Shaba Province (1978); France in Central Africa (1979); the United States in Grenada (1983); and the United States in Panama (1989). Great powers have a history of intervening against weak states. The debate about what justifies humanitarian intervention is crucial; but with or without the right, major powers will intervene.

Before discussing cases of the post-Cold War era, three interventions of this earlier period are worth mentioning here because of their humanitarian implications. The reality of the 1990s represents a sea change in views, and it contrasts starkly with the experience of the 1970s. Ironically, three interventions with very substantial humanitarian payoffs were not even partially framed or justified by the interveners in such terms. At that time, the notion of humanitarian intervention was simply too far from the mainstream of acceptable international relations. World order was firmly grounded on the inviolability of state sovereignty, and therefore states were more attuned to their own political interests and far less to humanitarian imperatives.

Specifically, India's invasion of East Pakistan in 1971, Vietnam's in Kampuchea (later Cambodia) in 1978, and Tanzania's in Uganda in 1979 were unilateral efforts geared to overthrow menacing, destabilizing regimes; and they were all explicitly justified as self-defense. India's ended up creating the state of Bangladesh after millions of refugees had fled; Tanzania's led to the overthrow of the despot Idi Amin Dada and a halt to atrocities; and Vietnam's ended the Khmer Rouge dictatorship that had resulted in the deaths of approximately a quarter of the Cambodian population. In retrospect, all three are frequently cited as evidence of an emerging norm of humanitarian intervention. Yet none was approved by the Security Council – and Vietnam's was actually condemned.

The UN in the post-Cold War era

The Soviet Union's implosion in 1991 profoundly changed the dynamics of world politics, and more specifically the role of the United Nations as a broker of international peace and security. Cooperation among the permanent five veto-wielding members of the Security Council (the United States, the United Kingdom, France, China, and Russia) increased, as exemplified by the number of vetoes invoked and resolutions passed during the post-Cold War versus the Cold War period. During the East–West conflict, vetoes (mostly by the Soviet Union) stymied the council on 212 occasions. From the fall of the Berlin Wall in 1989 until mid-2015, the veto has been invoked some 30 times, mostly by the United States.[11]

There is a parallel with the number of resolutions passed during the same periods. From 1946 to 1986, the council passed 593 resolutions (or about 15 per year);[12] in less than half that length of time, between 1987 and 2010, this figure climbed to 1,373 (or about 60 per year).[13] In the last five years, the Security Council has passed an average of about 57 a year.[14]

With the thawing of the Cold War and the dissolution of the Soviet bloc, peacekeeping operations increased exponentially. From the launch of the first peacekeeping operation in 1948 until 1978, the UN deployed 13 missions. For almost a decade thereafter, the Security Council approved no new operations with UN blue helmets because the political realities of the East–West split rendered launching such operations politically impossible. New operations resumed in 1988, when the Soviet Union dramatically altered its foreign policy position toward the world body. Since 1988 the UN has undertaken 54 peace operations.[15] In mid-2015, for instance, the world body had its troops in 16 countries with approximately 107,000 soldiers, military observers, and police – a larger overseas presence than that of any country except the United States. The UN's peacekeeping budget alone amounted to some $8.5 billion during the 2014–15 fiscal year; however, even the record-breaking expenditure on UN peacekeeping operations worldwide was the equivalent of only one month of US expenditures to rebuild Iraq in the years following the Bush administration's invasion of the country.[16]

Peacekeeping operations – as we saw earlier, called "Chapter VI and a half" because this UN invention was not in the Charter but seemed to fall between the peaceful settlement of disputes and enforcement – were deployed during the Cold War period, but they always adhered to the constraints of the international system's imperatives of state sovereignty and nonintervention. They were premised on consent and the nonuse of force and essentially responded to the realities of interstate conflict in a bipolar world.

Peacekeeping missions in the late 1980s, however – as exemplified by those undertaken in Central America – were still premised on traditional operating principles but began to engage in activities that fell within the domain of sovereign jurisdiction, such as election monitoring and weapons collections from insurgents. More significant, however, was the UN's authorization of operations under Chapter VII of the Charter in the context of state repression and domestic armed conflict that allowed for the use of force, or "all necessary means" in the code of Security Council language, for the purpose of ensuring international peace and security.

These operations were another qualitatively different step away from earlier UN operations. It is to the hard cases of humanitarian intervention that we now turn.

Humanitarian interventions beginning in the turbulent 1990s

Many saw the end of the Cold War as leading to the rebirth of the United Nations, and the changed politics bore witness to an urge to sort out the problems of civil strife that suddenly seemed out of control.[17] Throughout the 1990s there was an unpredictable and diverse pattern of UN involvement stretching from Iraq to Bosnia, Somalia to Haiti, Kosovo to East Timor.

Within the General Assembly, the tensions between intervention and state sovereignty initially focused on the delivery of humanitarian assistance.[18] Already in 1988, resolution 43/131 was a contentious milestone acknowledging that nongovernmental organizations – that is, nonstate actors – had an essential role in responding to deadly domestic disasters. The resolution maintained that humanitarian aid could and should be provided to affected populations who needed access to essential supplies. By implication, states were obliged to grant such access. A number of governments objected on the grounds that NGOs might interfere in what they considered to be strictly internal affairs.

Barely two years later, UN actions in the Persian Gulf established precedents for humanitarian intervention. In the wake of the First Gulf War, the Security Council passed resolution 688 in April 1991. It declared that the international repercussions of Saddam Hussein's repression of Kurdish and Shiite populations – resulting in the deaths of at least 30,000 and the flight of some 2 million Kurds and 100,000 Shiites – constituted a threat to international peace and security. It insisted that Iraq allow access to international relief organizations so that they could care for the beleaguered groups.

The council had previously taken a broad view of its duty to protect human rights, as in Rhodesia and South Africa, but this 1991 resolution provided for a far more powerful and immediate enforcement of human rights. While the transboundary consequences weighed heavily in the support by the council's non-western members, nonetheless the definition of international peace and security was continually expanding to include very domestic actions. The invasion of Kuwait was reversed, and subsequently the precedent of ending the Persian Gulf War was cited to protect the Kurds. The use of military force was a dramatic ratcheting-up over the earlier forms of intervention in comparable decisions, such as economic sanctions against the white minority regimes in southern Africa. While resolution 688 did not specifically invoke Chapter VII, authorize the "use of all necessary means," or mandate Operation Provide Comfort and the "no-fly zones" in northern and southern Iraq, the resolution's language permitted the Allies to justify their intervention to respond to an overwhelming humanitarian crisis.

In its wake, the General Assembly passed resolution 46/182; the most relevant section reads: "The sovereignty, territorial integrity and national unity of states must be fully respected in accordance with the Charter of the United Nations. In this context, humanitarian assistance should be provided with the consent of the affected country and in principle on the basis of an appeal by the affected country." Leading the charge behind the scenes was Bernard Kouchner, the founder of Médecins Sans Frontières (MSF) – the radically pro-individual and anti-sovereignty NGO established in the midst of the Nigerian civil war – and later France's minister of humanitarian and then foreign affairs.[19] Somewhat surprisingly in light of the war that had preceded and precipitated it, this resolution gives weight to the consent of the state in which the affected populations are located. The implications of the resolution were wide-ranging, but the debate in the General Assembly focused on military intervention. The views of developing and developed countries, however, remained polarized.

The result of the negotiated consensus of 1991 is open to interpretation, and its subsequent application is equally controversial. Consent may reflect less the wishes of a government and more the severe international pressure – as was arguably the case with Indonesia over the island of East Timor in 1999. Moreover, the government of a state requesting assistance may be disputed – as was arguably the case in Haiti with the government-in-exile of Jean-Bertrand Aristide after the 1991 military coup headed by General Raoul Cédras. Behind the consensus is an assumption that the state has a government exercising effective territorial control and allowing it to offer or refuse consent. Where no such government exists, the requirement for consent, by definition, cannot be met, as was the case in Somalia in 1992 where more than a dozen factions vied for power, producing more than 1.5 million displaced persons as well as 90,000 deaths due to

Table 2.1 Authorizations for military interventions in the 1990s			
Country	Chapter VII authorization and UN mission	Chapter VII authorization with delegation	No initial Security Council authorization
Liberia, 1990–7			ECOMOG
Iraq, 1991–		Coalition	Coalition
Former Yugoslavia, 1992–	UNPROFOR	IFOR & SFOR	
Somalia, 1992–3	UNOSOM II	UNITAF	
Rwanda, 1994–6	UNAMIR II	Opération Turquoise	
Haiti, 1994–7		MNF	
Sierra Leone, 1997–	UNAMSIL		ECOMOG
Kosovo, 1999–		KFOR	NATO
East Timor, 1999–	UNAMET	INTERFET	

violence and an additional 200,000–350,000 due to famine. Furthermore, some observers point out that the phrase "in principle" may, in practice, mean that consent may be subordinated to the necessity to counter an overwhelming human tragedy, or indeed, perhaps consent should come from citizens rather than governments.

Using the absence of consent and prominence of humanitarian criteria to justify humanitarian intervention, nine cases from the 1990s are depicted in Table 2.1. The cases are also categorized according to the nature of their authorization under three categories: those authorized by the Security Council under Chapter VII of the Charter with a

UN mission; those authorized by the council under Chapter VII that were delegated to multinational coalitions; and those not initially authorized by the Security Council.[20] The details of those operations are too complex to run through in the space allocated here, but secondary treatments are readily available.[21]

Trends from the early post-Cold War years

More useful is a brief discussion of three trends from the 1990s concerning the motives, justifications, and state interests emanating from these cases of humanitarian intervention: the increased legitimacy of intervention, high-intensity military action, and coercion from sanctions and international judicial pursuit.

First, all humanitarian interventions in this period were, according to virtually everyone's definition, more legitimate than earlier cases. Rather than remaining on the sidelines, the Security Council authorized coercion. Unlike earlier examples, in which the rescue of nationals and self-defense were the prominent justifications, the conscience-shocking and widespread humanitarian elements of the cases in the 1990s were explicitly recognized as justifications for international action. Instead of single-state military operations, the interventions of the 1990s were more multilateral than their predecessors.

Second, the decade ended as it began, with multinational coalitions undertaking extremely high-intensity military interventions. The years in between witnessed considerable skepticism about the utility of military force for humanitarian purposes. Particularly traumatic were experiences in Somalia, where UN troops and US soldiers were murdered by warlord Mohamed Aidid's militias, and the Balkans, where some 400 military personnel under UN command and control were taken hostage and chained to bridges by Serbian forces in order to prevent NATO air strikes. But the level of fire power went far beyond what had been the norm in earlier UN peace operations.

Third, it was a decade of profound change for two other forms of intervention as well: namely, coercion in the form of economic sanctions and international criminal prosecutions. These "non-forcible" coercive measures are not treated in depth elsewhere in this volume, and so considerable attention is given to them here.

David Cortright and George Lopez have labeled the 1990s "the sanctions decade" because the Security Council imposed 12 sanctions regimes, several more than in the previous 40 years combined.[22] As well as being used more frequently, sanctions were also applied more widely, including against nonstate actors such as the National Union for the Total Independence of Angola (UNITA) and the Khmer Rouge in Cambodia.[23]

This frequent resort to sanctions occurred even though most observers criticized their political inefficacy, and others lamented their humanitarian consequences.[24] In Haiti, for example, sanctions crippled the economy and increased child mortality, malnutrition, and disease, while at the same time fostering conditions for the elite to profit from smuggling. And after all was said and done, and after deprivation and suffering for civilians was inflicted, the arrival of the US 82nd Airborne Division was required to change the government.

The painful human suffering from sanctions came into sharpest focus in Iraq, where in the range of 150,000 excess deaths among children were associated with the sanctions regime. This figure was established by taking three-quarters of the average of the highest and lowest estimates of excess child deaths offered. Other more alarmist analysts, including the authors of a report from the Iraqi government at the time, argued that sanctions caused half a million excess deaths among children.[25] Whatever the exact number, the view that sanctions represented a kinder and gentler alternative to deadly force was unsustainable. Ultimately, the UN Charter's call to use non-forcible before forcible measures may lead to less than optimal humanitarian results. Some advocate moving toward "smart sanctions," designed to target regime leaders while minimizing the impact on the general population,[26] while others call for the application of deadly force sooner rather than later.

International criminal prosecution was another type of intervention that, for the first time since the immediate aftermath of World War II, was employed to bring to justice those who had committed crimes against humanity. Previously, senior officials (including retired ones) of a state could not be tried in courts in another country for acts committed in their own state and in the exercise of their official duties.[27] Although the Genocide Convention specifically calls for punishing perpetrators "whether they are constitutionally responsible rulers, public officials or private individuals," state practice over decades overwhelmingly supported the notion of sovereign immunity. This is one reason why states avoided labeling the Rwandan bloodbath "genocide." A number of legal decisions in the 1900s suggest considerable erosion of these operating procedures.

The fight to establish limits to impunity received a boost with the establishment of the International Criminal Tribunal for the former Yugoslavia (ICTY) and for Rwanda (ICTR) in 1993 and 1994, respectively. Subsequent violence in Burundi, the DRC, East Timor, and Sierra Leone led to calls for additional ad hoc tribunals, as, two decades later, for the Khmer Rouge's atrocities of the 1970s. While the tribunals for the former Yugoslavia and Rwanda are entirely international, those for Cambodia, East Timor, and Sierra Leone are a mix of local and foreign judges and an international prosecutor. The death of Slobodan Milošević in the dock in The Hague instead of in a luxury suite on the Riviera in 2006 made it seem as if a new era had perhaps dawned in the 1990s, especially when Charles Taylor was captured shortly thereafter and indicted for his crimes in West Africa.[28] The ICTR's 2008 prosecution of a chief architect of Rwanda's 1994 genocide, Colonel Théoneste Bagosora, marked another milestone for international criminal justice, as did the 2011 arrest and extradition of Ratko Mladić, chief of staff of the Bosnian Serb Army, after 16 years of evading arrest for genocide, crimes against humanity, and war crimes. At a minimum, dictators and military commanders have been served notice that on occasion there could be international juridical consequences for abusive conduct and their responsibility for mass atrocities.

Dissatisfaction with early institutional shortcomings of both the ICTY and the ICTR demonstrated to many observers the need for a permanent court. The Rome Statute on the International Criminal Court was signed in 1998, when 120 states participating in the United Nations Diplomatic Conference of Plenipotentiaries on the Establishment of an International Criminal Court adopted the statute, which entered into force only four years later after the requisite 60 ratifications. Any individual who commits a crime under the statute after July 1, 2002 can be prosecuted.

While some important states (including the United States) still are not party to the statute, widespread international agreement on the independence of the prosecutor and the court's jurisdiction over internal conflicts and disturbances suggests that criminal prosecution could become a common, rather than an ad hoc, form of intervention as a response to large-scale atrocities. For instance, Security Council resolution 1564 established the International Commission of Inquiry on Darfur, which concluded that "the Government of Sudan has not pursued a policy of genocide," but also recognized that "in some instances individuals, including Government officials, may commit acts with genocidal intent."[29] The commission identified perpetrators and asked the ICC to prosecute unnamed Sudanese war criminals. Indeed, even the United States called upon the ICC for an interpretation regarding the violence in Sudan. In 2010, the ICC issued an arrest warrant for Sudanese president Omar al-Bashir and charged him with war crimes and later three counts of genocide in Darfur. The following year, its chief prosecutor sought an arrest warrant for another sitting head of state, Libya's Qaddafi, after the UN Security Council referred the case to The Hague-based court in the wake of his regime's brutal repression of protestors. His death made this indictment moot, although his son Saif is in Libyan custody, but the ICC claims jurisdiction.

Second guessing

The Security Council's willingness to authorize military actions in response to matters thought previously to fall within the domestic jurisdiction of states was not without dissenters. The 1990s witnessed the appearance of serious second thoughts about humanitarian intervention, in particular. Euphoria after the First Gulf War and the rescue of the Kurds in 1991 gave way just three years later to the nihilism of the nonresponse to Rwanda's genocide, mass rape, and millions of forcibly displaced persons. The last year of the millennium conjured up, depending on one's point of view, optimism or pessimism about humanitarian intervention because of the visible but costly international efforts in Sierra Leone, Kosovo, and East Timor.

Therefore, it is important to parse two trends that should be highlighted in summarizing the impact of precedents in this turbulent decade. The first relates to the expansion of what constitute "threats to international peace and security." The second relates to the UN's organizational limitations and the concomitant use of multinational forces and dependence on "coalitions of the willing" for the application of deadly force.

First, the most basic transformation in the use of Security Council powers is that civil wars have been routinely described as threats to *international* peace and security and therefore the basis for Chapter VII enforcement. As we learned at the end of the last chapter, this development was virtually inconceivable during the Cold War, when the Security Council did not consider similar conflicts as constituting such threats. Already by 1995, however, the Appeals Chamber of the ICTY summarized that it is the "settled practice of the Security Council and the common understanding of the United Nations membership in general" that a purely internal armed conflict may constitute a "threat to the peace."[30] In fact, when the Security Council considered the civil war in Angola, it was even prepared to locate such a threat within a specific rebel movement.

Substantial flows of forced migrants clearly now are viewed as a threat to international peace and security. This enabled the council to justify Chapter VII actions to create safe areas and havens in Iraq, the Balkans, and Rwanda. The Security Council's determination that "serious" or "systematic, widespread and flagrant" violations of international humanitarian law *within* a country threatened international peace and security undoubtedly represents a considerable stretch for those who are familiar with the convictions of the framers of the UN Charter. Moreover, resolutions establishing separate international criminal tribunals were also based on domestic abuses – a stance strongly supported by the ICRC and other humanitarian agencies.[31] Therefore, a gradual shift has occurred away from strict reliance on the transboundary implications of a humanitarian situation as the determining factor in an "international" threat to justify international coercion.

The ever-widening definition of international peace and
security is artificial and unsustainable, and is ultimately a
slippery slope, according to critics. For example, in 1995 the
independent Commission on Global Governance proposed
"an appropriate Charter amendment permitting such intervention but restricting it to cases that constitute a violation of
the security of people so gross and extreme that it requires
an international response on humanitarian grounds."[32]
But this recommendation became moot a few years later
because so many precedents had been set that mass murder
and ethnic cleansing clearly qualified as "threats to international peace and security" that could trigger Security Council
action. A Charter amendment is thus no longer required to
permit timely decisions about such conscience-shocking
events.

The restoration of democracy within a country demands
more leeway still. Operation Restore Democracy in Haiti can
be seen as a high watermark of council activism in the 1990s.
The unprecedented authorization called for the use of force to
remove one regime and install another. The most enthusiastic
proponents have argued that this foreshadows the emergence
of a more general norm of intervention in support of democracy, a proposition that finds limited support in the amended
Charter of the Organization of African States.[33] Some scholars argue that the absence of democracy may itself constitute a
threat to international peace and security, an extreme form of
the "democratic peace" theory that authentic democracies do
not fight each other. Depending on definitions, at least one-
third of the world's states could be deprived of the protection
of Article 2(7) of the UN Charter,[34] clearly a source of apprehension for many repressive governments.

The ECOWAS intervention in Sierra Leone further
supports the argument that an international norm of "pro-
democratic" intervention is developing. While it can be

viewed neither as a literal interpretation of Chapter VIII nor as involving a threat to international peace and security, the council's *post hoc* approval of ECOWAS's intervention may certainly be interpreted as an example of pro-democratic intervention. Three other cases of pro-democratic intervention are not discussed in detail here because they do not fall under the humanitarian heading defined at the outset. Outside military efforts in Guinea-Bissau (by Senegal, Guinea, and ECOWAS), in the Central African Republic (by MISAB), and in Lesotho (by South Africa and Botswana under Southern African Development Community agreements) suggest that democratic governance is in the forefront of African "interventions." One analyst notes: "While in theory, Western nations purport to have the strongest democratic traditions, in *practice*, this emerging norm is taking firmer root in Africa than in any other region."[35]

Some consider these expansions in a less positive light. Ambiguous resolutions and conflicting interpretations of them, most notably in the operations against Iraq throughout the 1990s and in the Kosovo War in 1999, may have undermined the substantive provisions of the Charter's collective security system and contributed to facilitating actions in advance of Security Council authorization, or indeed without it.[36]

The second trend, and a source of concern in expanding the council's activities, stems from the absence of any real UN operational capacities to meet the growing demands for the responsibility to protect civilians. The result has been a delegation of authority to "coalitions of the willing." The provisions in Charter Article 43 concerning Security Council military enforcement presume the existence of agreements with member states to make forces available to the council "on its call." Those who are not deeply steeped in UN history may be surprised to learn that such agreements have never been concluded, and that Chapter VII has never been applied according to the strict terms of Article 42. Yet, the Security Council has repeatedly authorized states to use "all necessary means" (or similar language as code words for overwhelming military force), and this appears to be accepted as a legitimate application of its Chapter VII powers. Similar language is relevant for the delegation of authority to regional organizations under Chapter VIII as well.

Security Council enforcement was limited to situations in which states had the political will to bear substantial financial and human costs. For humanitarian interventions, the division of labor resulting from the experience of the 1990s highlights the chasm between peacekeeping and peace enforcement. Some argue that these challenges can be accommodated by a more robust form of traditional UN peacekeeping. But the evidence suggests that demilitarizing refugee camps and creating safe havens that are truly safe requires the deployment of combat-capable troops willing to employ deadly force rather than scaling up blue helmets.

Distinctions that were fuzzy in Boutros Boutros-Ghali's 1992 *An Agenda for Peace* became clearer in his 1995 *Supplement to "An Agenda for Peace"*.[37] They subsequently became clearer still in recommendations from the 2000 Panel on UN Peace Operations: the UN should concentrate on peacekeeping and civilian administration, while others should undertake robust military deployments.[38] Many of the same themes returned in the 2015 Report of the High-level Panel on United Nations Peace Operations.[39] The loose, or sometimes nonexistent, connections between UN authorization and member state enforcement can be problematic. As Victoria Holt argued, "Of the four organizations outside the UN which can offer intervention forces – NATO, the EU, the AU and ECOWAS – none has an easily identifiable concept of operations for civilian protection."[40] The delegation of authority by "subcontracting" to coalitions of the willing or to regional arrangements has thus been a solution while raising concerns about the use of council authority to give legitimacy to the foreign policy objectives of only powerful states.

In spite of these serious second thoughts, the use of military means to foster humanitarian ends remains a serious public policy option in most capitals. Future cases of mass murder, displacement, and rape will require the deployment of boots on the ground. Martha Finnemore summarizes the changes since the nineteenth century as follows: "States now entertain claims from non-white, non-Christian people who previously would not have registered on their consciousness, and, when they intervene, they will do so now only multilaterally with authorization from an international organization."[41]

Are we in the midst of a revolutionary expansion of what constitutes a "threat to international peace and security" and a period of increased readiness to rescue strangers? The reader of 2015 headlines might be confused by mixed evidence, but the widespread revulsion against the executions and forced marriages by ISIS and Boko Haram suggested that humanitarian sentiments retain a strong appeal and mobilization device.

The DRC, Uganda, Zimbabwe, and Darfur: nothing new?

Overzealous military action for insufficient humanitarian reasons – the voiced concern of many developing countries whose diplomatic representatives have often sought to fight the normative and operational advance of humanitarian intervention – is no danger. Rather, the real threat to international society comes from doing nothing and overlooking massive suffering in the DRC, slaughter in northern Uganda, massive forced displacement and human rights abuses in Zimbabwe, and slow-motion genocide in Darfur.

The conflict in the DRC, often described as Africa's "First World War," is the deadliest on the planet since World War II.[42] The simultaneous domestic and international conflict – directly involving nine African countries and some 20 armed groups – is fueled by the looting of the country's rich deposits of copper, zinc, and diamonds, as well as ethnic violence and tribal warfare.[43] Exact numbers are disputed, but some observers point to what may be the numerical equivalent of nearly seven Rwandas since 1998, largely from the famine and disease that accompany armed conflict. An estimated 2.6 million people remain internally displaced, and another 500,000 have fled into neighboring countries.[44]

In spite of the landmark election of July 2006, another refugee exodus took place at the end of 2009 with some 120,000 fleeing violence in the western province of Equateur over natural resources. An ongoing humanitarian catastrophe, some 45,000 excess deaths occur each month mostly due to easily treatable illnesses and food shortages – with nearly half these fatalities being children under the age of 5, according to a mortality survey by the International Rescue Committee.[45]

The government lacks consolidated authority over some parts of its vast territory, and thus armed groups and thugs continue to perpetrate human rights abuses and operate with impunity. The DRC has the dubious honor of being labeled the "rape capital of the world," with estimates of sexual attacks reaching as high as 400,000 women per year. In 2009, western media revealed another dimension to the mass sexual violence – it crosses the gender divide, with male rapes sharply increasing as a means of subjugating rival communities. Violence and political instability have persisted beyond the November 2011 elections.

The UN's foray into the war-torn country began in 1999 after a tenuous brokered peace agreement among the warring factions. Although expanded from the original UN Mission

in the Democratic Republic of the Congo's (MONUC) deployment, the renamed UN Organization Stabilization Mission in
the Democratic Republic of the Congo (MONUSCO), authorized under Chapter VII of the Charter, consists of a mere
20,000 uniformed personnel to secure peace and security in
a country that is the size of Western Europe.[46] Moreover, as a
report from the International Rescue Committee noted, the
resources available to the mission have been "absolutely inadequate for the scope of Congo's needs." According to Human
Rights Watch (HRW), "attacks on civilians and human rights
abuses continued with disturbing frequency in 2010," leading that respected organization to conclude that the mission's
new name "made little difference in the struggle to protect
civilians."[47] The lack of political will to address the human
catastrophe unfolding daily has rendered the DRC the world's
most enduring "forgotten emergency."[48]

Until the fragile peace initiated after a 20-year civil war
between the Ugandan government and the Lord's Resistance
Army (LRA) in late 2006, the situation in northern Uganda
amounted to a "secret genocide," according to Olara Otunnu,
a former foreign minister and UN under-secretary-general
and special representative for children and armed conflict.[49]
Although the government of Uganda's president Yoweri
Museveni was generally favored in the media and by international financial institutions as a new model for Africa,
his regime's decade-long effort to subjugate some 2 million
people (from the Acholi, Lango, and Teso regions) in 200
refugee camps was a hidden side of Museveni's "success."
Ninety-five percent of the Acholi lived in these camps, where
as many as 1,500 children died each week, while the rate of
HIV infection may have been as high as 50 percent. "The
genocide in northern Uganda is a burning test for the United
Nations' declaration on the 'Responsibility to Protect,'"
declared Otunnu. Failing to take the urgent action deemed

essential to protecting civilians, the international community of states reneged on its World Summit promise.

One possibly more encouraging development was the ICC's indictment of Joseph Kony, leader of the LRA, whose arrest warrant was issued in July 2005.[50] President Obama signed the Lord's Resistance Army Disarmament and Northern Uganda Recovery Act, which committed US assistance to African efforts to disable the LRA and capture Kony in late 2011 – militarily, this ultimately amounted to 100 troops in support roles. The issue came into the spotlight, however, after the March 2012 online release of Invisible Children's video "KONY 2012," which was viewed almost 100 million times in its first week.[51] The viral nature of the awareness campaign captured Congressional attention, and the Senate unanimously passed a resolution condemning the LRA, Joseph Kony, and their war crimes; and supporting ongoing US backing of African-led troops. The AU also cited the video in its decision to seize the moment when it mobilized 5,000 troops for a manhunt in the same month.[52] The campaign roused interest and rhetoric, but efforts to capture and try Kony for his 12 counts of crimes against humanity and 21 counts of war crimes remain futile; Kony remains at large three years later.[53]

As head of Zimbabwe's government since 1980, Robert Mugabe's image as anticolonial guerrilla hero has been replaced by that of an aging tyrant refusing to abdicate his throne. He has unleashed violence against political opponents and implemented policies to consolidate his personal position that have led to the country's economic decline since 1998. Since 2000, Mugabe has implemented land reform and resettlement programs to redistribute white-owned farms, mostly to his cronies. Frenzied and chaotic implementation led to a sharp decline in Zimbabwe's agricultural exports and hard currency reserves, which has continued unabated ever since. Mugabe's decision to print hundreds of trillions of Zimbabwean dollars led to hyperinflation and chronic oil and food shortages. In 2005, the government launched Operation Murambatsvina, an urban demolitions campaign that forcibly displaced hundreds of thousands of people, virtually all supporters of the opposition. As a result, some 3.5 million people fled abroad, and at least 1 million were internally displaced.[54] While many have returned, some 22,500 refugees remain scattered in the region, especially in South Africa.[55]

Whereas at least inadequate regional and UN peacekeeping forces were deployed in the DRC and Darfur (as we see next), international efforts to resolve the crisis in Zimbabwe were abandoned after merely weak sanctions and weaker diplomacy.

Zimbabwe provides yet another illustration of anemic political will, both regional and international, to confront tyrants, and suggests how difficult it is to induce governments to act against other states, even those whose policies result in high-profile calamities.

We devote somewhat more detail to Sudan, where firm numbers are also hard to come by concerning the catastrophe in the western part of Darfur. The UN under-secretary-general of humanitarian affairs estimated already in April 2008 that at least 300,000 black Africans had died as a result of conflict, hunger, and disease; countless women left behind had been raped; and more than 2.7 million people had been forcibly displaced.[56] As for next door in the DRC, these numbers have not prompted robust Security Council action. The collective yawn since early 2003 in the face of Darfur's disaster could be even more destructive of the fabric of international law than the 800,000 deaths in Rwanda. At least in 1994 there was an attempt to maintain the fiction that no such horror was under way. The Clinton administration, for instance, dared not use the "G" word, which would have implied the necessity to act.[57]

New York Times columnist Nicholas Kristof conscientiously and continually called attention to the tragedy. He cryptically lamented that "the publishing industry manages to respond more quickly to genocide than the UN and world leaders do."[58] The US Congress condemned Darfur unanimously, voting 422 to 0 in July 2004 that Khartoum was committing "genocide,"[59] while then secretary of state Colin Powell actually used the dreaded term in a speech in September of that year,[60] which coincided with views of such private groups as Physicians for Human Rights.[61] In the same month, European Union parliamentarians urged Sudan to end actions that could be "construed as tantamount to genocide."[62]

Invoking the term genocide, however, has not changed the underlying political dynamics in the least. Military overstretch and the prioritization of strategic concerns to the virtual exclusion of humanitarian ones is the sad reality of a post-9/11 world. The sloppy and disingenuous use of the "H" word by Washington and London in the aftermath of the invasion of Iraq has played into the hands of those Third World countries that wish to slow or reverse normative progress.

Rather than military action to halt the killing and displacement, the reinforced apprehension across the global South about any western pressure in hapless Sudan helped lead to the deployment of 7,000 largely ineffective African Union soldiers and additional investigation.[63] In February 2006, with the United States presiding, the Security Council decided to start planning to absorb the AU troops in a UN force. The council, however, was obviously not in a hurry to put boots on the ground; three years after the killing and displacement began, it remained unclear which countries (other than the United States, which categorically said "no") would put their troops in harm's way. In April 2006, when the council managed to agree only on targeted sanctions against four individuals, the chasm between the magnitude of the suffering and the international response could hardly have been greater. In addition to the mass killing and displacement, continued insecurity left some 750,000 people beyond the reach of aid workers, rendering them vulnerable to starvation and disease.[64]

The tenuous peace agreement negotiated in 2006 served as the basis for a UN peacekeeping force, not an intervention, although two of the three main rebel groups refused to respect the agreement, and normally such consent is a prerequisite. The charade continued as states courted the central government, responsible for the tragedy in the first place, to seek its permission.

On August 31, in resolution 1706, the Security Council finally approved a military force of up to 17,300 troops and an additional 3,300 civilian police to replace or absorb the feeble 7,000-member AU force. The council, however, continued to equivocate about consent, "inviting" the government to approve the operation. The members had apparently forgotten – or, as is their custom, chose to ignore – that the essential element of R2P is the international responsibility to act with *or* without the approval of the host country and belligerents. The equivocation resulted because the council supposedly acted under UN Charter Chapter VII – the deployed military contingent would be authorized to use force to protect civilians, UN staff, and relief workers. Paradoxically, while using enforcement measures, the council still called for the consent of Khartoum.

The next twist in the story involved Khartoum's threat to disband the AU force if it were to be incorporated into a UN force. At the end of his tether and his term as UN secretary-general, Kofi Annan posed three questions: "Can we, in conscience, leave the people of Darfur to such a fate? Can the international community, having not done enough for the people of Rwanda in their time of need, just watch as this tragedy deepens? Having finally agreed just one year ago that there is a responsibility to protect, can we contemplate failing yet another test?"[65] While the secretary-general was asking what appeared to be rhetorical questions whose replies should have been negative, they actually received affirmative responses.

In 2008, the joint AU/UN Hybrid Operation in Darfur (UNAMID) replaced the AU force. Despite some 23,000 uniformed personnel on the ground, not much has changed for civilians. In June 2011, HRW issued an alarming report aptly titled *Darfur in the Shadows*. With the collapse of the 2006 peace agreement in December 2010, renewed fighting "has resulted in scores of civilian casualties, destruction and looting of property, and the displacement of up to 70,000 people." President Bashir, whom the ICC has charged with war crimes and genocide, remains a staunch impediment to UN efforts to protect civilians. As the HRW report asserted: "the Sudanese government continues to restrict UNAMID peacekeepers and humanitarian organizations from accessing large swathes of territory in Darfur, seriously undermining efforts to protect and monitor civilians affected by the fighting."[66]

Violence in Darfur has ebbed and flowed – but the totals are appalling, as it is commonly thought that since 2003 upwards of 300,000 people have lost their lives and more than 2.5 million people been displaced. The worst of the mass killings had eased by 2015, although a report by Human Rights Watch evoked the atrocities committed earlier and detailed campaigns involving war crimes and crimes against humanity in 2014 by the so-called Rapid Support Forces.[67] The Bashir government severely constrains the movements of UNAMID peacekeepers, many of whom have been held hostage and 145 of whom have lost their lives. In 2014, just as UNAMID was approaching full strength, UN Security Council resolution 2173 reduced the number of peacekeepers to just under

16,000. In 2015, the UN secretary-general opened talks with Sudan to withdraw the entire force. Under increased pressure from Sudan and shifting international priorities, the ongoing drawdown reflects a political stalemate in the Security Council regarding the best strategies for promoting stability and protecting civilians in the region.

It is appalling that the Security Council remains unable to act robustly in the face of Khartoum's intransigence. The odds of actually deploying military force to halt atrocities remain close to zero, especially after the January 2011 referendum that led to the breakup of Africa's largest state. The uncertainties and hostility between north and south as the UN's 193rd member state took its seat suggest continuing danger to international peace and security with little appetite for outside military intervention, however great the threat to civilians.

Part of the reason for the feeble attention to Darfur is that international attention has also shifted back to the south, as the Khartoum government recognized the results of a referendum that paved the way for the UN's newest member state in July 2011, South Sudan. Virtually from the end of independence celebrations, however, Sudan and South Sudan have resorted to force to try to resolve their border and economic issues. The two states exchanged military blows over contested oil fields, prompting the African Union to call on the states to withdraw troops from the disputed area and for the Security Council to issue a Chapter VII decision.

Just two years into its statehood, South Sudan's president Kiir was challenged by his deputy, casting the country into renewed ethnic conflict that spread from the capital. Two years later, in mid-2015, more than 2 million had been displaced as a result of the violence, and UN Mission in the Republic of South Sudan (UNMISS) complexes have been repurposed as encampments given the overwhelming need. But even the UN shelters are fraught with violence, from within and without; the groups that are warring outside, sleep together inside. Further, government forces and allied militias have launched attacks on the camps.[68] A UNMISS human rights report in the midst of the violence cited targeted government attacks: burning of entire villages, mass abductions and killings, women subjected to gang rape, and the forcible recruitment of child soldiers.[69] The release of this report prompted the Unity State Cabinet to call for the removal of Mary Cummings, UNMISS state coordinator, from the country. South Sudan quickly announced that Unity State had acted outside its mandate, and that Cummings could stay, but this is little relief to Toby Lanzer, previously the UNMISS humanitarian coordinator, who had been expelled just one month earlier. Renewed civil wars, ongoing ethnic violence, competition for oil, government attacks, and attempted suppression of crimes leave little respite for civilians. Lamenting the culture of impunity, HRW program director Iain Levine called South Sudan's recent fourth anniversary an "unhappy birthday."[70]

In short, the civil war within South Sudan complicates an already difficult political landscape. UNMISS – some 11,000 soldiers and 1,200 police – has a Chapter VII mandate to protect civilians but it is not only inadequate for that purpose but also has no mandate to protect the territory of South Sudan.

This reality suggested that Alex Bellamy's interpretation of the "watering down" of R2P by the World Summit was on target. He argued that the consensus at the summit was reached mainly by placing an emphasis on the host state's primary responsibility to its citizens rather than on the obligation of outsiders to come to their rescue; and by emphasizing the requirement for Security Council agreement rather than action by any coalition of the willing when the just cause threshold was crossed.[71] From the outset, Khartoum cleverly linked even feeble western activism in Darfur to US and UK action in Iraq – a conversation stopper. As David Rieff wrote, "In Europe or the US, sending NATO forces to Darfur may seem like fulfilling the global moral responsibility to protect. But in much of the Muslim world, it is far likelier to be experienced as one more incursion of a Christian army into an Islamic land."[72] The 2011 intervention in Libya by US, UK, and French forces with the blessing of Arab leaders, however, has revealed that the Muslim world may sometimes be more on board with R2P than presumed.

Libya, Côte d'Ivoire, and Syria

International military action against Libya in March 2011 was a turning point in the post-9/11 intervention slump. The Security Council's willingness to authorize "all necessary measures" against the rogue Libyan regime as it mowed down protestors initially seemed to have signaled the dawn of an era of R2P implementation before the lack of post-intervention peacebuilding led to the *de facto* partition of the country in which warring militias have become the only law in the land.

Nonetheless, it is worth examining this case of humanitarian intervention that began after nine members of the 22-member Arab League called on the world body to implement a no-fly zone against Libya. Along with France and the United Kingdom, the United States implemented council resolution 1973 to protect civilians with air strikes. While President Obama asserted that he "refused to wait for the images of slaughter and mass graves before taking action"[73] against the Libyan dictator, he was firm about the US's limited role in the operation to "days not weeks."[74] With American troops still tied down in Afghanistan and Iraq, ground troops were out of the question. Within less than two weeks of the March 19 start of the no-fly zone, ironically the seventh anniversary of the Bush administration's invasion of Iraq, the shared

France–UK–US command for the operation was handed over to NATO, supplemented with military support from the region (Qatar and the United Arab Emirates). Qaddafi proved far more difficult to oust than initially expected; and the stalemate between the regime and rebel forces tested the willingness to stay the course. In October 2011, insurgents with outside military support finally eliminated the rogue dictator. That regime change was an unstated objective, however, also complicated consideration by the Security Council of action elsewhere in the region (especially Syria).

If action in Libya was swift and robust, Côte d'Ivoire lagged for several weeks. The wake of the country's first election in ten years in December 2010 brought renewed violence when Laurent Gbagbo refused to step down from his decade-long rule when he lost to his opponent Alassane Ouattara, who was internationally recognized as the winner. The UN Operation in Côte d'Ivoire (UNOCI) refused to withdraw in the face of Gbagbo's demands that it leave the country as it attacked peaceful protestors and prompted the flight of thousands. For three months, the UN Security Council dragged its feet. By taking no decisive action to seriously change the situation on the ground, the result was refugees, massacres, full-scale civil war, and a ruined economy. It was not until March 30, in the context of robust action against Libya, that the council authorized UNOCI in resolution 1975 to "use all necessary measures" to implement its mandate in protecting civilians and in self-defense. Heavy fighting broke out between the opposing factions in late March; and the UN mission, with the assistance of French forces, attacked pro-Gbagbo military installations. Ultimately, the violence was brought to an end by Ouattara's troops with French assistance in an assault on Gbagbo's residence.

In Syria's abattoir, meanwhile, inaction rather than intervention was the international default setting, resulting in the largest humanitarian crisis in recent memory. As of mid-2015, some 250,000 deaths and massive displacement (probably 12 million people, or half of Syria's population) delineated clearly the limits of normative advance in the face of tough geopolitical calculations.

Given these recent scars on the current international conscience, the three cases merit further probing and comparison.

So, why Libya, and why not Syria?

Contemporary controversies about military humanitarianism typically vacillate between two genuine concerns: between the international legality of a humanitarian intervention, on the one hand, and its feasibility, on the other. Since the signing of the UN Charter in 1945, legality is usually interpreted as spelled out by Article 2 (the sovereign equality of states and the principle of nonintervention) and by Chapter VII that sanctions war – with or without humanitarian justifications – only in the cases of self-defense or of threats to international peace and security when the Security Council so decides.[75]

Debates about humanitarian intervention thus are contested for fairly obvious reasons. They also have a ring of *déjà vu*. Diplomatic debates continue to revolve around the trade-offs between legality and feasibility, but UN mandates too rarely are associated with the physical capacity to deliver. The five permanent members can block resolutions before they are tested for efficacy, and even categorical language can readily be ignored by important powers. At the same time, states that are able and willing to intervene do not necessarily garner international support and UN approval before acting. Importantly, there often is an inverse relation between the feasibility of an intervention and its legality.

Much ink and toner customarily are devoted to parsing legality and legitimacy, but feasibility is the essential variable, which is measured by the existence of sufficient political will and military capacity to make a difference. Together, they ultimately determine whether, when, and where to protect and assist vulnerable populations. However shocking to the conscience a particular emergency, and however hard or soft the applicable public international law, when adequate political will and a military capacity exist, humanitarian space will open and civilians will be assisted and protected. Libya was unusual: the moral, legal, political, and military dimensions dovetailed under the responsibility to protect. Rather than speaking truth to power, R2P's value-added in Libya was speaking truth *with* power. In Syria, only the moral dimensions of R2P have to date been apparent. As a result, civilians are slaughtered or forced to flee.

Security Council paralysis over Syria illustrated the distinction between international legality and legitimacy. The bloodshed and suffering inflicted by the Bashar al-Assad regime are far worse than Qaddafi's. It certainly was not the contents of the R2P norm that explained action in Libya and inaction in Syria but, rather, geopolitics and collective spinelessness. Aidan Hehir's label of "the permanence of inconsistency" is an accurate description for the politics of R2P in the two cases – or indeed, for the politics of anything.[76]

Why Libya and why not Syria? In addition to the politics in the Security Council (specifically, Moscow's and Beijing's unrelenting support of the regime in Damascus and the accompany exercise of the double veto), Syria also confounded easy generalizations and looked distinctly more complicated, chancy, and confused than Libya. Whereas the latter's relatively cohesive opposition movement was run from inside and spoke with one voice, the former's was based outside as well as inside the country, dispersed geographically, and divided politically. The visible but fractious central opposition group in exile, the Syrian National Council, was divided among the

Muslim Brotherhood (itself split into more and less tolerant factions) and two other Islamist organizations, the National Action Group and the Syria National Movement. Indeed, successive attempts to cobble together a more unified opposition invariably ended in acrimony and failure.

Inside Syria, some 100 rag-tag groups of fighters and unarmed protesters agree on little except that Assad must go. Inchoate and unable to coalesce into a unified force, they have no common ideology; and they lack a clear chain of command to coordinate operations, protests, or arms supplies. It was not until September 2012, in fact, that the loosely knit and western-backed Free Syrian Army moved its headquarters from Turkey. Whereas three-quarters of the Libyan population lived in areas that had broken away from the regime and fallen immediately under rebel control, in Syria the opposition is unable to maintain control over major population concentrations. In fact, the opposition is incapable even of exerting control over fighters who increasingly are committing crimes similar to those of the regime.

Moreover, instead of virtually an entire country (other than those on his payroll) being mobilized against Qaddafi, a substantial number of Syrians support the regime or are sitting on the fence waiting to see who ultimately will end up on top. The Assad government has sufficient firepower and support among minorities to keep fighting and maintain control over the central government. Instead of Libya with virtually a single ethnic group (Arabized Berbers, virtually all Sunni Muslims), Syria's diversity is striking. Arabs constitute 90 percent of the population, but there are substantial numbers of Kurds, Armenians, and others. In terms of religion, Sunni Muslims are about three-quarters of the population, and another 15 percent are Alawites (an offshoot of Shiite Islam), Druze, and other Muslim sects; and in addition to possible inter-Muslim divides, there is a likely cleavage with the Christian 10 percent of the population. Unlike the largely desert-like Libya with a few isolated cities, Syria's numerous urban areas mean that surgical airstrikes are implausible, and that significant civilian deaths from military action are guaranteed. Rather than Libya's small mercenary army, which quickly defected or departed, the Syrian armed forces for the most part remain well equipped, disciplined, and loyal.

As hinted earlier and will become clearer in chapter 4, the World Summit Outcome actually amounts to "R2P lite" and is distinct from the original ICISS conception in an essential way. The September 2005 summit made Security Council approval a *sine qua non* rather than merely the most desirable outcome of the preferred decision-making process. As a result, the baby of potential international action was tossed out with the holy water of UN Charter legality and legitimacy.

We should recall that Canada had originally convened ICISS precisely because Rwanda and Kosovo, in polar opposite ways, had demonstrated the futility of being held hostage to Security Council procedures – especially the veto power – in the face of mass atrocities.[77] Instead of doing too little too late (in Rwanda) or too much too early (according to some, in Kosovo, where sanctions were not allowed to run their course and NATO literally jumped the gun), an alternative concept was required. How could the international community of states finesse stooping to the lowest common denominator in the Security Council?

ICISS was composed of card-carrying internationalists who, of course, stressed the central role of the UN Charter and urged the one entity in the world organization where decisions are made, the Security Council, to act swiftly and authoritatively to halt mass atrocities. But when it does not or cannot – as has been the case in Syria from the outset – the World Summit decision leaves humanitarians and victims exactly where former UN secretary-general Kofi Annan was in September 1999 when he shocked his diplomatic audience in the General Assembly Hall. Its highest official could not lightly dismiss the UN's constitutional provisions, but he also could not justify legalism and doing nothing with bodies floating on Rwanda's Great Lakes. He was compelled to probe state self-satisfaction. He wondered about a dramatic counterfactual: what if there had actually been a state or a group of states willing to act without the Security Council's blessing in April 1994 amidst the ongoing mass murder?

In UN diplomatic circles, answers to that bone-chilling inquiry remain equivocal. However, a resounding affirmative answer would have come from all of the 800,000 dead Rwandans – or from millions of murdered Sudanese or Sri Lankans, Syrians, or Congolese.

The responsibility to protect is a principle and not a tactic. Friends and foes both point to the commission's central conceptual contribution and value-added: reframing sovereignty as contingent rather than absolute. That principle remains intact in Syria even if international action is woefully absent.[78]

In fact, the transformation of international attitudes is nothing short of remarkable if we contrast the deafening silence that greeted the 1982 massacre by Hafez al-Assad of some 40,000 people in an artillery barrage of Hama with the steady stream of hostile condemnations and actions against his son's murderous machinations. The UN's Joint Office on the Prevention of Genocide and R2P called for a halt to crimes against humanity. The Human Rights Council (HRC) has condemned the Assad regime by a crushing vote in 11 resolutions and published a report detailing extensive crimes. The United States, the European Union, and other states have imposed sanctions. The Arab League condemned the actions, formulated a peace plan, and sent human rights monitors. And even the usually supine UN General Assembly condemned the violence and supported the peace plan with a two-thirds majority; and on three subsequent occasions, it even more overwhelmingly (only 12 of 193 states voted against the resolutions) condemned Assad's unbridled crackdown and mass atrocities and specifically called for his resignation.

Dilemmas remain all too palpable as Libya – a weak state with no history of democracy and plenty of evidence of feuds and bitterness in addition to some 200,000 militia – hurtles headlong into a new era without the kind of post-intervention support that the West handsomely financed for Kosovo. Instead of 60,000 NATO troops to provide some breathing room in Kosovo, there were no outside boots on the ground after the air war – no western country was anxious to get bogged down, and in addition the Libyan people and their successive interim and fighting governments demanded independence and resisted any suggestion of outside peace-keepers.[79] We should be perfectly clear: military force is not a panacea, and its use is not a cause for celebration. That said, and despite substantial ongoing transitional problems in Libya, at least concerted international action in 2011 halted Colonel Qaddafi's onslaught of mass atrocities.

Meanwhile Syria continued to hemorrhage until the use of chemical weapons in August 2013 led to threats of force and ultimately accelerated international diplomacy to dismantle them. Assad's deployment was a tactical blunder. The threat of US air strikes – despite the lack of support worldwide among populations and parliaments – catalyzed a frenzy of diplomacy, Russian engagement, and a hasty but seemingly successful agreement to dismantle Syria's stock of weapons of mass destruction (WMD) under the auspices of the UN and the Organization for the Prohibition of Chemical Weapons. Just how far international pressure had pushed the regime became obvious because the transport of WMD through rebel territory became the major concern rather than Assad's intransigence or obfuscation.

In terms of crimes against humanity and war crimes, what could be more abhorrent and less discriminating than the use of chemical weapons? While they could and should have justified an R2P response, they did not. Again, geopolitical calculations trumped the protection of civilians.

While of little solace to Syria's victims and their families, clarion calls have reaffirmed the R2P principle; or, as Ramesh Thakur wrote, "it would be premature to conclude that R2P can be branded 'RIP.'"[80] In comparison with Libya, the "why not?" in Syria was clear: the politics in the country and at the UN were totally different – demonstrated by several actual or threatened double vetoes from Russia and China – as well as the geography and the demography; the military challenge was far tougher; and the potential costs by 2013 already appeared to outweigh the benefits of coercion as insurgent atrocities gradually replicated those of the regime, and in 2015 Russia began its own military offensive.

And so, why Côte d'Ivoire?

While the world was mesmerized by the Arab Spring in the Middle East in late 2010 and early 2011, in West Africa another crisis was brewing, the response to which falls somewhere between the rapid and robust reaction to Libya, and the anemic one to Syria. The installation of Alassane Ouatarra and the surrender of former president Laurent Gbagbo followed a half-year of dawdling as Côte d'Ivoire's disaster unfolded.

In the aftermath of robust action against Libya, the council decided in resolution 1975 to authorize "all necessary means" to implement its mandate in protecting civilians and in self-defense.

That decision was the third time in March 2011 alone that the Security Council had menaced the loser of the elections. However, the empty resolution-rattling ended early in April.

Driven more by French domestic politics than by R2P, Paris approved robust military action by its 1,650-strong Licorne contingent as UNOCI's avant-garde.

The "why?" for international action in Côte d'Ivoire can be located in the fact that it was justifiable and doable even if it took longer than it should have; even so, the benefits outweighed the costs for the intervening and neighboring countries. Washington had no dog in this fight, but its diplomatic engagement with regional and international partners helped unleash French ground troops in combination with the modest UN peacekeeping contingent, which ended the violent electoral standoff and protected civilians.

Posing counterfactual questions is invariably unsatisfying, but nonetheless the following two queries are important. Was it necessary to enable war crimes and crimes against humanity, a million refugees, and a ravaged economy? Although Gbagbo was indicted by the ICC where he appeared in December 2011, should he not have been inscribed on the court's docket earlier and put in custody in The Hague?

African-centric focus of the ICC

While responses to halt mass atrocities in the early twenty-first century have been uneven, so have the ICC's efforts to end impunity – the court's workload has been almost exclusively African. This fact has led to serious rumbling from governments and regional organizations on the continent. While 34 African countries are states parties and initially were enthusiastic about the ICC's potential for the region, the pursuit of sitting heads of state made for awkward and embarrassing public diplomacy, especially in the cases of Sudan and Kenya.[81]

Sudan's Omar al-Bashir was the first sitting president to be indicted by the ICC following his role in the genocide in Darfur. Government bombing campaigns, coordination with proxy militias, looting and burning of villages, and systematic executions of men and raping of women resulted in more than 300,000 deaths and 2.5 million displaced; for his part, Bashir is charged with crimes against humanity, war crimes, and genocide. And while the role of the ICC is to secure justice for the victims of crimes, he has exploited his position as head of state to subvert these efforts and engender an adversarial relationship between the country and the ICC. The Sudanese National Intelligence and Security Director cheekily warned that ICC action against Bashir might alienate the country and incentivize abandoning its "moderate and civilized" disposition.[82] Following the issuance of Bashir's arrest warrant in March 2009, the Sudanese government canceled the licenses of a dozen humanitarian aid organizations, accusing them of channeling information to the ICC, and in effect cutting off significant food, water, and medical services to 2 million internally displaced persons (IDPs).[83] A second arrest warrant was issued in July 2010, though Bashir still remains at large and even welcomed in parts of Africa and China.[84]

After Kenya's 2007 election, in which incumbent President Kibaki retained his seat, charges of election fraud prompted widespread ethnic violence. Within two months about 1,200 people were killed, 3,500 injured, and 350,000 displaced as a result of homes being looted and burned, victims being forcibly prevented from fleeing, and those who had taken refuge in buildings being burned alive. Evidence gathered by the Kenyan Commission of Inquiry into the Post-Election Violence suggested that these attacks constituted a coordinated effort directed by a network of leaders.[85] The ICC charged Uhuru Kenyatta with murder, forcible transfer of population, rape, persecution, and other inhumane acts in July 2012.[86] As a party leader, he described his charges as an effort by the international community to undermine "the democratic will of the people of Kenya" and a threat to Kenyan sovereignty.[87] He ran for election and won the presidency in 2013, and this narrative informed his compliance with ICC proceedings. Though he appeared before the court when summoned, Kenyatta temporarily transferred his presidential power to his deputy before doing so – appearing in a personal capacity rather than as a representative of the Kenyan people, simultaneously making a display of both national pride and compliance with international law. Amidst charges of bribery and threats, his government was sufficiently uncooperative with the investigators that all charges against Kenyatta were withdrawn in December 2014 due to a lack of evidence.[88]

The ICC offers the potential to put an end to criminal impunity and to act as a deterrent, but it evokes many of the same concerns about violations of sovereignty and Western political designs as other interventions, particularly when cases target heads of state. To bolster the appearance of one-sided justice, all nine situations currently under investigation in the ICC are African. President Kenyatta requested an amendment to Rome Statute Article 27, which stipulates that status as a government official "shall in no case exempt a person from criminal responsibility under this Statute," and he was not alone in challenging the procedures of the court.[89] At the 2013 Assembly of States Parties, the African Union requested a special segment during which they discussed "Indictment of sitting Heads of State and Government and its consequences on peace and stability and reconciliation."[90] Given the increasing distance between the ICC and the AU, Alex de Waal concedes that "it is inconceivable that another African state will refer a case to the ICC in the foreseeable future, and most unlikely that any will cooperate with the ICC in executing arrest warrants. Africa may well become a jurisdiction-free zone as a result, scarcely a victory for human rights."[91]

Toward new wars and new humanitarianisms

The repeated failure to come to the rescue and to implement civilian protection even-handedly mocks the value of the R2P norm, and ultimately threatens the UN's credibility. Before we tease out the implications of inaction and inconsistency for the world organization, however, we need to explore further the phenomenon of new wars and new humanitarianisms, as well as the intellectual history of ideas pertaining to humanitarian intervention that have penetrated international public policy discourse.

CHAPTER THREE

New Wars and New Humanitarianisms

As we saw in the last chapter, the collapse of the bipolar system enhanced the prospects for great power cooperation and multilateral action through the Security Council, thereby generating an enhanced role for the United Nations in the realm of peace and security. The end of the Cold War, however, also precipitated other dramatic and less salubrious changes, especially in parts of the developing world.

We learned that peacekeeping was a UN invention to carve out a role for the world body in the context of the East–West conflict, which had in many ways paralyzed the Security Council and certainly had impeded it from acting coercively. The Third World served largely as a ground for proxy wars between the United States and the Soviet Union, with both superpowers channeling military and economic aid to their favored respective allies. Peacekeeping was developed to fit the realities of a world in which sovereignty and nonintervention were more privileged Charter values than human rights, and warfare was largely of the interstate variety. Actions against a government's wishes in a civil war would have violated traditional notions of domestic jurisdiction.

With the end of the Cold War, however, the vast sums of aid that once propped up many Third World regimes, especially in sub-Saharan Africa, were no longer available for leaders to bolster coercive state capacity and to repress internal dissidents. These regimes also had less to distribute as patronage among their clients – a necessity in light of their feeble legitimacy among the populations over whom they ruled.

Increasing globalization and the integration of many aspects of the world economy, moreover, has compounded the fragility of these quasi-states. Spurred by technological revolution and economic liberalization, globalization essentially entails the "deterritorialization" of political, economic, and social space. Such processes have also eased the flow of arms across borders and facilitated cross-border illegal activity, often the source of funding for powerful nonstate actors. For example, organized crime syndicates – engaging in illegal trade in arms, money laundering, as well as drug and human trafficking – reap the benefits of increased globalization, garnering an estimated $1.5 trillion a year.[1] These pernicious actors are emerging alongside multinational corporations as economic powers and eroding the state's monopoly of violence in many parts of the globe.[2] For example, war-torn Afghanistan generates some 90 percent of the world's supply of opium, with profits accruing to warlords who have long carved up the country into rival fiefdoms.[3] Narcotics also fuel a decades-long conflict that typically has killed some 3,000 people annually in Colombia, which produces about half of the global cocaine supply.[4]

While trade in illicit commodities provides a lucrative source to finance violence, such natural resources as gold, copper, and timber also play an important role in mobilizing funds for wars, as the label "blood diamonds" illustrates. Angolan independence group and political party UNITA garnered $3.7 billion in revenue from diamonds – some of which were purchased by DeBeers, the world's primary marketing corporation for them – while timber exports to the European Union alone earned Charles Taylor $3.6 million within six months of his initial offensive in Liberia.

Neoliberal reforms have made borders more porous

and have also diminished state capacity in many developing countries. Trimming public sector expenditures and implementing other austerity measures added to the fiscal dilemmas of many Third World leaders. These measures not only contributed to instability by further eroding the patronage base of many illegitimate rulers; they also had the adverse effect of diminishing access to education and social services and in many places increasing unemployment and inequality, thereby fueling the "grievance" factor that many attribute to civil wars.[5]

Thus, the forces of globalization have contributed to instability across the global South. Throughout the 1990s, a number of "weak" states further deteriorated, such as the Democratic Republic of the Congo and Haiti. Some collapsed into civil war – Liberia, Rwanda, Somalia, and Sierra Leone. And some maintained a "durable disorder"[6] – for example, Colombia and Sudan.

The frequency of state-versus-state conflict has decreased relative to the upsurge in violence within states – in the turbulent 1990s, for instance, 94 percent of wars resulting in more than 1,000 battle-related deaths (the generally agreed, social scientific definition to qualify as a bona fide war) were civil wars.[7] However, civilians do not fare better in intrastate wars than they do in interstate wars.[8] The battlefields of these wars do not feature conventional front lines; instead, violence gravitates toward resources and trafficking for which borders are largely meaningless.

Beginning in the 1990s and continuing today are varying degrees of fragmentation: the wars in western Africa (in Nigeria, Liberia, Mali, Sierra Leone, and the Côte d'Ivoire) and central Africa (the DRC, the Central African Republic (CAR), Rwanda, Burundi, and Sudan), the splintering of societies and states in central Asia (Afghanistan, the Caucasus, and Kashmir), and the growing unrest in South America

(Colombia and other Andean countries such as Peru and Bolivia on the brink). Once the bulwark of authoritarian stability, Arab countries also feature domestic turmoil, most notably Iraq, Syria, Libya, and Yemen.

While interstate elements may be part of the mix of these conflicts, these new wars are fought locally (in neighborhoods, villages, and other subnational units), even if modern technologies make external connections easy. James Rosenau coined a term for the dual processes of integration and fragmentation associated with globalization: "fragmegration."[9] The culmination of fragmegration was the appearance virtually overnight of such transnational terrorists as Al Qaeda, ISIS, and Boko Haram. The media-savvy groups, which broadcast beheadings and brutal attacks on ethnic and religious groups, place still more complicated challenges on the international agenda of the post-post-Cold War landscape.

Often they precipitate grave humanitarian crises, or what are commonly called "complex emergencies." These crises are characterized by massive bloodshed and displacement, and often disease, malnutrition, and starvation. In Rwanda, some 800,000 people (a tenth of the total population) were slaughtered in a period of a few weeks, while as many as 250,000–500,000 women were raped, and half the population forcibly displaced; in Bosnia-Herzegovina, there were some 100,000 deaths,[10] with 20,000–50,000 rapes, and 2.7 million people left in need of assistance; in Somalia, 4.5 million people required assistance, and 1.5 million risked starvation, while anywhere between 200,000 and 350,000 people died of famine precipitated by scorched-earth tactics; in the DRC today, as many as 45,000 people die each month of conflict-related disease and malnutrition. These disasters clearly pose significant quantitative and qualitative challenges for those seeking to come to the rescue, whether they be soldiers or civilian humanitarians.

This chapter highlights some of the resulting structural features of the violence resulting from fragmegration, revealing why both traditional peacekeeping and humanitarian principles often do not track well as antidotes for today's threats. Changes in the nature of warfare and the impact on contemporary humanitarian action are a critical part of the story of military intervention to help and protect human beings caught in the throes of armed conflicts. As the challenges in delivering aid to war victims and protecting them have changed, some civilian humanitarians have come to recognize the need to adapt their operating principles and styles. This has led many actors, public and private as well as governmental and nongovernmental, to support what some still consider an oxymoron, humanitarian intervention or even the sharp end of the R2P stick, military force for human protection purposes. At the same time, measuring the costs and benefits of soldiers' coming to the rescue is itself fraught.

New wars

"New wars" is widespread in the contemporary vocabulary of practitioners and analysts who seek to capture fragmegration's violent results in the twenty-first century. This notion has been speeded along by scholarly analyses from Mary Kaldor and Mark Duffield and more popular depictions from journalist Robert Kaplan.[11] The simplistic shorthand can, however, lead to misunderstandings. It is not so much that totally new elements have appeared as that elements thought extinct or tangential have come to the fore or been combined in ways that were heretofore unremarkable or largely unknown. Hence, change often is so quantitatively great, or the elements are combined in such previously unfamiliar ways, that many wars can effectively be dubbed "new."

More concretely, in comparing the older and newer varieties

of armed conflict and random violence, there are four essential changes that must be discussed. First, the locus of war no longer coincides with state borders – in areas of fragmented authority, in fact, borders are often meaningless. Second, instead of states and their militaries being the main agents, nonstate actors are playing an increasing role. Third, the economies of war are no longer financed principally from government tax revenues but increasingly from illicit activities, aid, and plunder. Fourth, instead of informed combatants being the main victims, civilians are increasingly paying the lion's share of the costs.

The higher the number of altered characteristics and the greater the amount of change, the "newer" the armed conflict could be considered. The very newest are also the most treacherous terrains for humanitarian intervention at the same time as they are the ones begging for outside militaries to halt the carnage and abuse of rights. Each of the four changes should be dissected to determine how, precisely, the new landscape differs from the old.

The first and least disputed contemporary characteristic concerns the newness of the locus of war. The bloodiest wars of the first half of the twentieth century – including World Wars I and II – were waged by large and powerful states across borders for prolonged periods of time in order to gain territory, wealth, and influence. Other conflicts pitted a major power against a less powerful unit that resisted through decolonization struggles or the manipulating of rivals. However, whether it is France in Indochina, the United States in Central America, or the United Kingdom in the Falklands/Malvinas Islands, interstate frameworks (and especially clearly delineated borders) distinguished belligerents and largely defined armed conflicts.

The new wars are departures because belligerents have minimal power, and often even that is contested by multiple internal armed opposition movements that pay no attention to internationally recognized borders. Many are in countries whose central governments are constituted mainly by UN membership and that maintain control only over the national capital or the main exports. In brief, these battlegrounds bear limited resemblance to western counterparts in the Westphalian order; one might even repeat that these wars do not look like stereotypical wars.[12] They depart from conventional sovereign states in terms of authoritative control over populations and resources. At a territorial level, they suffer from an "unbundling," a negation of their exclusive authority as states.[13] The horrifying images of drug-crazed child soldiers who hack off the limbs of terrorized civilians in Sierra Leone capture some of the horror, as does the thought of seeking agreement from the 40 or so armed opposition movements in the DRC, the new record holder for rape as a tactic for subjugation.

Social science since Max Weber has emphasized the state's legitimate monopoly on violence and its authoritative position in society. But it is worth recalling that much of the recent discussion of wars has instead focused on feeble relatives, on "weak" and "failed" states, which have been the main places where humanitarian intervention either has taken place or where many unsuccessfully called for it.

"Weak" describes states that do not measure up to western role models in international political prestige, wealth, military prowess, and national unity.[14] Such states may lack the capacity to pursue national interests and be largely without an effective leader or bureaucracy.[15] They may lack the financial resources, technology, skill, population, or political capital to fulfill goals. They may not have the authority to make credible and binding decisions.

"Failed" states are feebler still. Gerald Helman and Steven Ratner coined the term in 1992 as Somalia imploded and

caught the attention of decision-makers.[16] While "weak" con-
notes various types of vulnerability and a range of capacities,
"failed" implies fatal flaws in central authority – after almost
25 years, Somalia is still without anything resembling a cen-
tralized government. Not all weak states actually fail (for
example, Chad), and some collapsed ones are able to make
a strong comeback (for example, Lebanon until the massive
influx of Syrian refugees).[17] While some analysts contest the
validity of the term, it highlights how fundamental flaws may
destine a state to come apart at the seams.

Hedley Bull speculated in 1977 about a possible future
return to violent subnational contests over authority. In fact,
the gradual development of international society among states
that is so crucial to international order seems to have been
jolted in the late twentieth century with patterns of unraveling state authority accompanied by huge humanitarian
needs. What disturbed Bull was a potential "new medievalism,"[18] and this ugly reality has led scholars to draw parallels
between today's wars and those that accompanied European
state formation. Jessica Matthews notes that ongoing power
shifts among states, markets, and civil society resemble the
dynamics of the Middle Ages.[19] Mohammed Ayoob, drawing
on Charles Tilly's work, goes so far as to argue against those
who try to halt humanitarian emergencies by pointing out that
armed conflict was an essential ingredient of eighteenth- and
nineteenth-century European state-making, and that similar
kinds of humanitarian disasters are the invariable byprod-
uct of comparable processes at work in much of the Third
World.[20] It is hard to make an omelette, so the saying goes,
without breaking eggs.

What is far less familiar, however, is the current central
challenge to international peace and security, as Kalevi Holsti
reminds us: "[T]he major problem of the contemporary society
of states is no longer aggression, conquest and the obliteration

of states. It is, rather, the collapse of states, humanitarian emergencies, state terror against segments of local populations, civil wars of various types, and international terrorist organizations."[21] Traditional humanitarian thinking may be skewed by unhelpful assumptions about progress because, in responding to challenges of what is a pre-Westphalian order in certain parts of the globe, the principles and tactics that have worked well in the past for humanitarians dealing with interstate wars are undoubtedly of less utility in many of today's civil wars. As a practical matter, the deinstitutionalization of sovereign central authorities means, at a minimum, a vastly diminished role for international law.

The dramatic shift away from state-centric perspectives is crucial for students of international relations. For the past century, war has fundamentally been filtered through the lenses of state belligerents, which James Rosenau has dubbed "sovereignty-bound."[22] It should be clear that these lenses no longer provide a clear focus, because organized violence and humanitarianism are not beholden only, or even mainly, to state authorities. Hence, the second defining characteristic of current armed conflicts consists of the rise of a multitude of unconventional political units with dramatic security implications.

Some nonstate actors in effect usurp the roles of states. Stephen Stedman and Fred Tanner use the expression "pseudo-states" to denote crafty belligerents who manipulate the presence of refugees to attract and exploit humanitarian resources for their political agendas.[23] In another apt image, Beatrice Hibou refers to criminal NSAs as "parallel states."[24]

While neither historically new nor completely absent from the margins of earlier interstate armed conflicts, the presence and scale of nonstate actors as political authorities and belligerents, along with the inability of agencies in a growing number of crises to guarantee humanitarian action, are new phenomena. Four groups of NSAs are of particular concern. The first consists of armed belligerents, whether they are local militias, paramilitary groups, former members of the military, or the followers of warlords. The second group is composed of those whose primary economic interests are served by violence. Ranging from mafia, criminal gangs, and illegal businesses to opportunistic profiteers, they may seek to sustain war and a humanitarian crisis that promote an economic atmosphere conducive to their own profits.[25] The third group of "spoilers" consists of hybrids that blend military and economic agendas, including both mercenaries and a distinctly new creation: private military companies.[26] The fourth group consists of the various terrorists who have threatened civilian populations and governments from West Africa to the Levant.

The third altered, salient characteristic of contemporary armed conflicts concerns idiosyncratic economies in war zones. Many readers will be familiar with Carl von Clausewitz's celebrated dictum that war is the continuation of politics. But David Keen argues that today "war may be the continuation of *economics* by other means."[27] Economic conditions and structures of new wars allow some individuals to pursue war and profit thereby. While states are failing or rebuilding, unusual economic opportunities abound. Local balance sheets have always been important in fueling war, and certainly captains of industry from Krupp in the Third Reich to Halliburton today have been more than willing to help the national cause and simultaneously enrich corporate and personal coffers.

However, the local economy plays a quantitatively and qualitatively different role than previously in contemporary wars.[28] The society as a whole suffers, while isolated individuals benefit. With cash, arms, and power flowing into their hands, warring factions have no incentive to proceed to the bargaining table; instead, their interests are served by pro-longing war.

In conventional theory, the control of territory is essential to maintaining authority, but the political economies of many contemporary wars impel actors to concentrate their energies instead on controlling commerce for a few key resources like diamonds or tropical timber. Much spoiler behavior – before, during, and oftentimes after wars – can be explained by economic interests. For example, "taxing" for protection is a prime tactic for sustaining and enriching local actors. In short, new wars present several overt means of enrichment (protection and plunder) while they also hold the prospect of an infusion of fungible resources (an aid economy). If war is profitable, why end a good thing?

The fourth change that attracts our attention is the prevalence of civilian casualties. Military force is used against civilian populations in a variety of ways. At the most extreme is the intentional targeting of selected civilian populations – or genocide, the attempt to destroy entire populations. But extermination of noncombatants is not the only viable ugly strategy. Forcibly moving populations can also accomplish many of the same heinous aims, which has helped usher in the new and disheartening term "ethnic cleansing." In the wars of the 1990s and 2000s, NSAs often operated without concern for humanitarian responsibilities and targeted populations, thereby producing an elevation in the proportion of civilians killed in combat as well as the toll from less direct but war-related fatalities (e.g., famine). Although humanitarians have made progress in garnering greater protection for civilians through legal means, there appears to be a correlation between the growing institutionalization of the laws of war among states and the growth in violations perpetrated by NSAs in new wars.

Historically, civilians certainly were not unknown targets,

with one recent analyst estimating that over the last three centuries they constituted about half of all war-related deaths.[29] This estimate would strike most observers as too high, but in any case what is unusual is the extent to which civilians are now at the center of military strategy. In World War I (1914–18), 8.3 million soldiers and 8 million civilians were killed,[30] but the approximate 1:1 ratio of civilians to combatant casualties did not last. Despite being fundamentally an inter-state conflict, World War II (1939–45) brought huge numbers of civilians into the fray – the German air blitz of London, the Allied fire-bombing of Dresden, atrocities perpetrated in Japanese-occupied Nanking and Manila, the Holocaust inflicted on European Jewry and other minorities, and ultimately the use of the atomic bomb by the United States on the residents of Hiroshima and Nagasaki. In the end, 23 million soldiers and more than 57 million civilians lost their lives.

In retrospect, the 1:2.5 soldier–civilian ratio of casualties in World War II seems modest today, because civilians have continued to represent an increasing percentage over this century. The Carnegie Commission, which was set up to find a way to prevent such violence, found that 90 percent of those killed in the new wars of the 1990s were civilians, who had comprised only 15 percent of such fatalities at the turn of the century.[31] Mary Kaldor agrees that civilians accounted for 10–15 percent of total combat deaths at the start of the twentieth century, 50 percent during World War II (falling at the middle of the century), and 80 percent in new wars in the late 1990s.[32] Holsti's data depict a slightly sharper increase – only 50 percent of casualties were civilians in World War II, but in recent wars the figure is near 90 percent.[33] Virgil Hawkins goes even further and argues that civilians now constitute 95 percent of total combat deaths.[34]

Researchers continue to debate the precise percentages, and many call into question the actual numbers.[35] However, no one questions that the crucial distinction involves the motives for targeting civilians.[36] The painful reality is clear: the "total war" model associated with the twentieth century's two world wars was based upon the range of weapons permitted to be used against other soldiers. Those ugly numbers are surpassed by wars with a different kind of "totality," all-encompassing in the sense of routinely targeting civilians. Not only local populations, but also journalists and agency staff are increasingly targets. There are tactical and strategic reasons for taking aim at them. Tactically, humanitarian agencies may undermine NSAs by presenting an alternative source of vital resources to war-ravaged populations. Strategically, NSAs may also view attacking humanitarians as a means of signaling the seriousness of threats to outside military forces and governments.

The debate about danger turns around the extent to which one believes that Afghanistan and Iraq, or the Central African Republic and Syria are aberrations or rather the "model" for the future. While some commentators have argued that fatalities have not actually increased all that dramatically if one takes into account the growth in the volume of humanitarian aid workers, journalists, for instance, would certainly see Iraq as quite a "new" level of threat. In late May 2006, covering the war assumed its place as the deadliest conflict for reporters in modern times. In a little over two years following the start of the war in March 2003, 73 persons covering that conflict had lost their lives – more than the 66 killed in Vietnam and the 68 in all theaters during World War II.[37] According to Reporters Without Borders, 204 journalists alone (excluding other media staff) have been killed in Iraq since 2003.[38]

Aid workers would certainly not disagree about the increased danger, as the number of fatalities among them in Afghanistan and Iraq illustrates. A review of aid workers killed in recent years attests to a disconcerting upswing: from

1992 to 2001, 204 UN civilian personnel were killed, and more than 250 were assaulted or robbed.[39] Over the course of 2005 in Afghanistan, 31 aid workers were killed, up from 24 the previous year.[40] A decade later, in 2014, fatalities reached 54, making Afghanistan "the deadliest country in the world for aid workers."[41] Meanwhile, in Sri Lanka, Action Against Hunger confirmed the deaths of 17 of the organization's aid workers in the town of Muttur in 2006. These staff were not even involved in war-related efforts, but in post-tsunami relief work. However, the degree to which aid workers are increasingly in harm's way must be placed in the context of their mushrooming numbers in the field. Because of the increase in humanitarian budgets, the heightened danger is less than would appear from the absolute numbers of violent accidents, which doubled between 1997 and 2005. Indeed, "the annual number of victims per 10,000 aid workers in the field averaged five in the first half of the period and six in the second." The number of aid workers who lost their lives (434) approached the total of UN soldiers killed in action during the same period.[42]

According to the April 2011 UN Office for the Coordination of Humanitarian Affairs (OCHA) report, *To Stay and Deliver*, the number of attacks against aid workers actually tripled over the first decade of the twenty-first century, resulting in an average of more than 100 deaths per year. Unsurprisingly, war-torn Afghanistan, Somalia, and Sudan were the most dangerous, with fatalities in these countries inflating global trends.[43] A record high number of violent incidents against civilian aid workers was reached in 2013, resulting in 155 fatalities.[44]

In the past, the humanitarian mantle afforded meaningful physical protection, but the danger of the new wars has prompted humanitarians to push for legal protection. In the early 1990s, the Security Council began to note the increased violence directed toward aid workers. During humanitarian operations in Somalia in 1993, the council passed resolution 814 to respond to "acts of violence against persons engaging in humanitarian efforts." The next year, the UN also adopted a convention criminalizing attacks on such international personnel.[45]

Perhaps the grimmest examples can bring home the point about why the continuation of humanitarian business as usual is not an option. Following US action in Afghanistan, the videotaped beheading of the *Wall Street Journal*'s Daniel Pearl in January 2002 was gruesome enough. But the ceremonial murder in November 2004 of CARE's Iraq country director, Margaret Hassan, was an undoubtedly calculated way to shake humanitarians to the core. Living in the country for 30 years and being married to a Muslim Iraqi did not make her less vulnerable, but rather a perfect symbolic target to send a message about insecurity.

Yet another gruesome "advance" was marked in 2014, when ISIS distributed via social media the real-time executions of UK and Japanese aid workers. After the beheading of the American James Foley, one commentator remembered when Islamic extremists wanted to persuade journalists and aid workers instead of killing them. Since militant terrorists now communicate their atrocities directly to readers and viewers, they no longer need to bother with first-hand reporting or with wooing reporters.[46] Joel Simon, executive director of the Committee to Protect Journalists, summarized in announcing the release of its 2015 report that today is "the most deadly and dangerous period for journalists in recent history."[47]

Humanitarian symbols no longer provide adequate protective armor for humanitarian workers. Indeed, the bombing of ICRC's Baghdad headquarters in September 2003 – just after the attack on UN headquarters, which also housed some humanitarian organizations, during the previous month

– was carried out by a local white ambulance appropriately displaying a red crescent (rather than a red cross as it does in primarily Christian countries).

Paradoxically, positive normative developments to ensure access to and protection of victims exist side by side with growing numbers of civilian victims – among local populations as well as among those who come to their rescue or to report on the tragedy. The extent of this paradox reached new heights during the 1990s when atrocities with large numbers of civilian victims erupted – in Iraq, Somalia, Bosnia, Rwanda, Kosovo, and East Timor – and ultimately led to a dramatic shift in international political norms about intervention. The parallel growth of norms and victims encapsulates the tragedy of the new humanitarian order.

Humanitarian intervention is often necessary because of the treacherous and unfamiliar terrain of the new wars – internal armed conflicts waged primarily by nonstate actors who subsist on illicit and parasitic economic behavior, use small arms and other low-technology hardware, and prey upon civilians, including aid workers and journalists. New wars have ignited and cooled in many regions. And humanitarian intervention has played a role in helping – and, according to some critics, hindering – conflict resolution. But, as one might suspect, the new contexts have also led to problems in pursuing humanitarian strategies and using humanitarian tactics developed for earlier armed conflicts.

New humanitarianisms

Humanitarianism is a highly contested concept among scholars and practitioners alike,[48] described by Antonio Donini as in the eye of the beholder.[49] Humanitarian action (both succor and protection), however, is not a western phenomenon. Kith and kin have long sought to extend helping hands, symbolized by the biblical tale of the Good Samaritan. But Michael Barnett's "The Empire of Humanity," or the institutionalization of such action, is the creation of the last century and a half.[50] As such, the space within which humanitarians operate is more contested than in the past.[51]

Contemporary civil wars, usually characterized by large-scale killing and displacement, challenge the traditional operating principles of independent humanitarians – independence, impartiality, and neutrality. Anxiety and doubt have arisen as belligerents fail to respect international humanitarian law, attack aid personnel, block relief convoys, use food aid to fuel their war efforts, and "tax" humanitarians working in war zones.

At a minimum, humanitarians confront formidable problems in war-torn societies. The scale of human suffering ranges from enormous to overwhelming. During the first decade of the post-Cold War era (1989–99), wars (mainly civil but some international) killed more than 1.5 million people and wounded many more.[52] More than fatalities and wounded, the number of people forcibly displaced by armed conflicts perhaps gives a better indication of the amplitude of the challenge for those coming to the rescue. Although the numbers of displaced persons have varied, at the end of the 1990s approximately 1 in 135 of the world's population required international assistance and protection as a result of wars at the peak of the flows. The sheer volume represents a staggering burden for humanitarians, not to mention for war-torn societies themselves. And the depressing numbers have continued to grow, although estimates vary wildly.[53]

The end of the Cold War resulted in no transformation of international institutions but, rather, new armed conflicts, along with the eruption of crises formerly held in check by East–West tensions; and it also resulted in the proliferation of humanitarian agencies and the opening of resource floodgates.

Before proceeding to a discussion of trends in humanitarian budgets, it would be useful to consider the origins of most data, which emanate from the Organisation for Economic Co-operation and Development (OECD). A non-UN body now composed of 34 member states committed to democracy and market economies, it began as the Organisation for European Economic Co-operation to help administer the Marshall Plan in 1948 after the rejection by the Soviet Union and its satellites. In 1961 it became the OECD and remains a "club" for high-income countries for the purpose of coordinating various economic activities. The Development Assistance Committee (DAC) is an OECD sub-unit, consisting of 34 states that focus on international development priorities and on maximizing efficiency of development investments. One of its central tasks is to report country data, including humanitarian aid, as part of measuring the total annual flows of what is called "official development assistance" (ODA).

The end of the Cold War, and the unraveling of the artificial stability it maintained, resulted in a sharp increase in humanitarian crises, and corresponding aid donations. The budgets of humanitarian organizations registered a five-fold increase from about $800 million in 1989 to some $4.4 billion in 1999, with an additional quadrupling to $16.7 billion in 2009. After peaking at just over $20 billion in 2010, the figures drifted downward to $19.4 billion in 2011 and $17.9 billion in 2012, but then increased dramatically to $22 billion in 2013 and perhaps $24 billion in 2014.[54] While the number of UN organizations has not grown, their budgets have (accounting for about two-thirds of total DAC humanitarian disbursements). As many as 37,000 international NGOs form what Linda Polman calls "the crisis caravan," but only a handful of the 4,000 humanitarian ones are truly significant.[55]

Since the early 2000s, governments have disbursed more than $110 billion for humanitarian assistance. In 2010 and

2011, they provided some $14 billion per year, $13.2 billion in 2012, and $16.4 billion in 2013; and private voluntary contributions reached a peak of $6.3 billion in 2010 (roughly $4 billion in 2012 and $5.6 billion in 2013), up from $3.0 billion in 2007.[56] More recently, UN peace operations have added another $8–10 billion annually, with most missions deployed carrying large humanitarian allocations. Whereas 16 mainly western states pledged their support to Bosnia in the mid-1990s, a diverse group of 73 attended the 2003 pledging conference in Madrid for Iraq, and 92 responded to the December 2004 tsunami. OECD governments almost doubled their assistance between 2000 and 2010, from $6.7 billion to $11.8 billion, which stood at $14.1 billion in 2013. Meanwhile, the contributions from non-DAC donors between 2011 and 2013 increased from $0.8 billion to $2.3 billion, representing about 15 percent of total official humanitarian aid, double the percentage from 2011.[57]

Estimates of aid workers – including cleaning personnel and drivers in field offices to CEOs in headquarters – many total close to 300,000 people.[58] But Peter Walker and Catherine Russ are undoubtedly closer to the mark: "We have no idea." They estimate some 30,000 professionals (both local and expatriate) worldwide.[59]

The global bottom lines of some $18–22 billion in aid contributions in recent years, with personnel spread across the planet helping 75–100 million people, would strike most observers as a substantial business. The culture of humanitarian cooperation is actually one of humanitarian competition. Alexander Cooley and James Ron point to "the scramble" for resources, which means a "contract culture" that is "deeply corrosive" of the humanitarian soul.[60]

Although there are more resources than ever, only some crises are given attention, while others are neglected. The practice of donor earmarking of funds for specific tasks or crises has contributed to the uneven distribution of assistance. For example, during the crisis in Kosovo in 1999, aid poured abundantly into the region; however, while "the donor response [to the UN's Consolidated Appeals Process] for the former Yugoslavia was $207 per person; for Sierra Leone, it was $16, and $8 for the Democratic Republic of the Congo."[61] In another telling comparison, one analyst noted that "the money spent by the US Army/OFDA [Office of Foreign Disaster Assistance] on Camp Hope in Albania, which housed just over 3,000 people for two months, was roughly the same amount as the UN's entire annual appeal for Angola."[62]

In addition to massive crises and inadequate resources, humanitarians must grapple with a host of challenges in delivering aid to those in need. There are numerous illustrations of direct and indirect attempts to thwart the efforts of aid workers from conflict zones around the world. In Liberia, for instance, warlord Charles Taylor – afterward put on trial in The Hague for war crimes – demanded 15 percent of aid entering territory that he controlled. Estimates of the percentage of aid looted, diverted, and extorted in Somalia reach as high as 80 percent, while at least half of all food aid in Bosnia was used to feed and supply combatants.[63]

As discussed earlier, aid diversion empowers those responsible for the bloodshed, while feeding killers in militarized camps threatens civilian refugees and IDPs, and further enables violence. Paying a "tax" to those who control access allows humanitarians to assist victim, but simultaneously funds continued violence by belligerents. Moreover, by working with spoilers, humanitarian organizations may grant legitimacy to otherwise illegitimate actors. Formal relations with spoilers implicitly acknowledge their authority, and a relief role bolsters their claims of legitimacy.

In this context, humanitarians confront formidable dilemmas because their traditional operating principles frequently lead to unexpected outcomes. Observers have pointed to a major break in the late 1980s and early 1990s; and the labels to describe the experiments that emerged on the increasingly complex terrain included "new humanitarianism" and "political humanitarianism."[64] They were attempts to distinguish today's from yesterday's variety. When practitioners debate the 1990s, during which humanitarian intervention became widespread, they usually point to a radical shift in the social purpose and organizing principles of humanitarian action. Regarding social purpose, the traditional goal was to save lives at risk through short-term assistance to belligerents and victims alike. Many agencies, however, redefined the scope of their activities. Whereas they formerly saw their niche as temporary assistance, many have begun to design projects both upstream and downstream. They abandoned apolitical and short-term approaches in favor of both eliminating poverty and consolidating peace processes.[65]

The shift from emergency relief to attacking root causes and post-conflict peacebuilding represents the pursuit of a far more ambitious agenda. No longer satisfied with saving individuals today to place them in jeopardy tomorrow – the infamous "well-fed dead" is a memorable framing about aid in the former Yugoslavia by the late Fred Cuny,[66] who was executed in Chechnya in April 1995 – many humanitarians now aspire to attack the structural conditions that endanger vulnerable populations. Rather than provide band-aids, they wish to use assistance and protection as levers. Many aid agencies desire to spread development, democracy, and human rights and create stable, effective, and legitimate states.[67]

Humanitarian principles have changed. Independence, impartiality, and neutrality make sense if the objective is to provide relief and gain access to affected populations. Independence demands that aid should not be connected to any of the parties directly involved in the conflict or who have a stake in the outcome, including donors who fund particular activities. Thus, to guarantee independence and also the perception of independence, many agencies either refuse, or limit reliance on, government funding to which strings are attached. Impartiality demands that assistance be based solely on need, without discrimination among recipients because of nationality, race, religion, or other social characteristics. If necessary, aid agencies should be prepared to provide assistance to all sides of a conflict. Neutrality, like impartiality, involves refraining from taking part in hostilities or from any action that knowingly either benefits or disadvantages the parties to an armed conflict. Neutrality is both an end and a means because it helps relief agencies gain access to populations at risk.

However, unanticipated and unintended negative consequences have meant that reciting the humanitarian mantra is of little avail. The principles worked well as guidelines when combatants were from state militaries and usually respected the laws of war and humanitarian space. In the wake of the Rwandan genocide, it became clear to many humanitarians – and to donors who paid the bill – that even the best efforts were producing unexpected and pernicious results. What economists call "negative externalities" – an especially striking example was in strengthening the position of the *génocidaires* who controlled the camps in what was then Zaire – were not the result of minor design flaws or a modest lack of professionalism. A radically changed context required a radically new approach.

Humanitarian principles are supposed to be insulated from politics, but there has been a long-standing recognition that humanitarian activities have political consequences and are inextricably part of politics. However, what was once implicitly political is now explicitly so, and what was once taken for granted is now problematized. Furthermore, agencies actually find these principles dysfunctional in some war-torn areas. In particular, access to populations in zones of violence often requires working alongside and associating their activities with those of militaries. As humanitarians have attempted to promote human rights, they have found that neutrality can be an obstacle. Can one be neutral toward war criminals? Humanitarian organizations, which once treated "politics" as a dirty word, have become more willing to engage with politically.

Once a state ceases to maintain political authority or have a monopoly on violence, borders lose meaning as the locus of war. The legality as well as the actuality of access are in doubt and may have little or nothing to do with the authorities who occupy central government offices in the national capital – the usual interlocutors for outside humanitarian agencies. The focus on people or resources, more than on territory or formal boundaries, creates challenges for humanitarians when they respond to conflicts that cross borders but are legally dependent on the consent of territorially bound authorities.

UN organizations are bound by their constitutions to deal with member states, and NGOs have usually operated in a similar fashion, even if their terms of incorporation were not linked to states. Finding victims, securing access to them, and delivering relief to victims have led to the creation of humanitarian space in law and practice – that is, room to maneuver and help in providing protection and relief to war-ravaged populations. Humanitarian space was guaranteed by states (including belligerents) in many interstate conflicts of the twentieth century and by the Geneva Conventions.[68] But in most new wars, victims do not have this luxury. Belligerents often do not provide consent, allow the passage of relief, or respect international agreements – they are often unaware of them and are not signatories. Hence, the most elementary struggle is for aid agencies to actually carve out secure space in which to operate.

Beginning with northern Iraq in the early 1990s, the Security Council authorized making room within safe areas without the consent of belligerents – indeed, oftentimes against their expressed wishes.[69] The concept of opening humanitarian space inside war zones without such approval developed gradually. The dynamics of contemporary armed conflicts and, specifically, the need to engage nonstate actors did not appear with sufficient regularity to generate support for new international humanitarian legal mechanisms and operational principles until late in the twentieth century. With the exception of the 1977 Additional Protocols to the Geneva Conventions, the Cold War had hamstrung the development of legal measures for the international humanitarian system to address the violence produced by NSAs.

As agencies deployed in areas lacking state authority and encountered menacing NSAs, access to victims became problematic, along with the security of aid staff. In situations where the state is under stress or is essentially nonexistent, agencies have always been on dubious legal ground, and this uncertainty not only carries over, but is also multiplied for arrangements with NSAs. There are only a few references to NSAs in international humanitarian law – basically in common Article 3 to the Geneva Conventions and Article 1 of Additional Protocol II. Negotiations previously centered on state authorities. However nebulous or cumbersome the follow-through, at least the channels, or the official interlocutors, were clear. To the extent that wars no longer follow the contours of interstate borders and shift onto more uncertain political, economic, and social terrain, agencies have no choice but to widen the range of actors with whom they negotiate access to affected populations.

The evolution of new humanitarianisms illustrates that the

crises of the 1990s not only shocked agencies but also provoked policy reactions. Seminal events included the following. Somalia witnessed "Black Hawk Down," the gruesome deaths of 18 US Rangers, and a humanitarian mission that was too close to the parties but without sufficient military muscle to end hostilities. The "fig leaf" of humanitarianism in Bosnia led to the phenomenon of keeping people alive to be potentially massacred later and the lesson that aid without military protection can be meaningless. The manipulation by belligerent "victims" in the refugee and IDP camps inside Rwanda itself and next door in what was then Zaire exposed the difficulties of relying upon good intentions in militarized camps. And the use of force in Kosovo without UN authorization undermined legitimacy in some eyes.

These traumas in particular shed light on three themes that especially characterize the new humanitarianisms and for which the collective learning curve has been especially steep. The first is politicization. From the founding of the international humanitarian system up through the final stages of the Cold War, humanitarian action was essentially predicated upon state consent and support. Indeed, much as in previous periods, state interests were implicit in shaping agency decision-making. For example, the UNHCR's forcible repatriation of refugees during the 1980s violated the principle of *non-refoulement* – that endangered populations not be returned to menacing states or those that could not afford protection.[70]

However, in order to cope with the causes and scope of crises common in the 1990s, the system had to depart from the interstate logic that had framed its existence. The specific actions and policies of certain agencies such as MSF and UNHCR were instrumental in pushing the political envelope of humanitarianism by making choices that would reverberate throughout the international humanitarian system. Working with NSAs, and sometimes even without the consent of belligerents, occurred with increasing frequency during this period and thus brought to the surface the politics upon which the system hinges. The myth of depoliticized humanitarianism was dispelled – first by the political strings of states and later by the challenges of a lack of consent from credible, powerful nonstate authorities.

The second trend concerns militarization. The dramatic increases in the numbers and kinds of civilian fatalities and human rights abuse heightened humanitarian calls for an injection of military resources to protect victims and ensure access to them. In the context of war zones where belligerents target aid workers and serve as gatekeepers, there may simply be no alternative to coercive protection.

Sometimes, as in Kosovo, this led to securitization or a sense that displacement and human rights violations were enough of a threat to international security to elicit a forceful response. The notion that the international community of states has a responsibility to protect is predicated upon military resources being available to ensure access and protect human rights. However, as the case of Kosovo also demonstrated, military utilization may lag behind humanitarian action. Thus, the major strand of militarization of the new humanitarianisms signals that aid agencies are more likely than in the past to call for the use of force, but military forces may also be less available when and where they are needed.

The third is the marketization that we encountered earlier. The aid economy and the influx of massive outside resources skews the local economy in various ways – inflation and property values, salaries, and mores all take a beating. And what remains of the local economy plays into the hands of spoilers who also respect the rules of the marketplace – why negotiate or make peace when war is so profitable?

But what about the relative costs and benefits of applying

such a tool to rescue civilians? Crassly, when and where is it worth it?

Measuring the costs and benefits of military humanitarianism

Throughout these pages, readers have encountered an enormous variety of views about the pluses and minuses of using outside military force to protect human beings who are caught in the crosshairs of armed conflicts. Moreover, there has been anything but consistency in the views of participants over time. The ICRC, for instance, as the custodian of the laws of war (also called "international humanitarian law"), has traditionally kept its distance from soldiers. However, in the chaos of Somalia it experimented with hiring "technicals" – local armed guards who mounted automatic weapons on jeeps and were often associated with a particular faction. Its president during the tumultuous 1990s, Cornelio Sommaruga, was a member of ICISS and insisted that his fellow commissioners set aside the expression "humanitarian intervention," even if he supported the notion of "military intervention for human protection purposes" (the expression finally adopted in the report). Prize-winning journalist David Rieff was an enthusiastic proponent of armed intervention in the Balkans and Rwanda, but by the end of the decade he did an about-face. Disillusioned with what he found in war zones, he proposed returning to the "good old days" of neutral and impartial aid without the use of military humanitarianism.

Two kinds of criticism are worth discussing because they illustrate the problems surrounding a decision about whether the use of military force in a particular humanitarian crisis is justified. The first relates to the ability of a coalition, with or without UN authorization, to stay the course and provide the chance for a country to recover somewhat and even stabilize after a humanitarian intervention. The most tragic recent example is post-intervention Libya, where virtually no international sustenance followed the massive air war and eventual regime change. The unwillingness not only to provide security with boots on the ground but even the most basic assistance reflects the "model" of the precipitous departure of the United States from Somalia after the degrading deaths of 18 Rangers in October 1993. More than two decades later, the country is still fragmented and embroiled in conflict. Even the country's capital lacks a central governmental authority, as Mogadishu remains a battlefield with AU troops vying to wrestle control of the city from Al Shabab, Islamist rebels linked to Al Qaeda. Somalia's anarchy has spread to the surrounding high seas, as pirates pose a threat to international shipping through violence and hostage-taking.[71]

Despite a US-led intervention in 1994, Haiti to this day is also an impoverished and conflict-ridden country with gross human rights violations. The inadequacy of institution building – that is, the creation of a viable governmental apparatus and judicial system to enforce the rule of law – set the country up for renewed violence and rendered it utterly unprepared to cope with the massive earthquake of January 2010, which resulted in anywhere between 46,000 and 85,000 deaths and about 900,000 displaced persons, according to the US Agency for International Development (USAID);[72] and the country remains feeble despite publicity and help from former US presidents Bill Clinton and George W. Bush. Temporarily seen as a UN "success story," East Timor reverted to chaos and violence in 2006, prompting the return of Australian military forces that had previously assisted in stabilizing the country but departed with the onset of post-conflict reconstruction. The International Stabilisation Force of 400 Australian and 75 New Zealand troops remained, finally withdrawing in 2012.

The infusion of military force is doubly problematic because it may be dangerous at the outset and because humanitarian intervention does not end with the termination of an emergency. Even if lives are no longer at immediate risk, often suffering has not ended, while destructive forces may remain largely intact and capable of perpetrating violence in the future. No longer satisfied with saving individuals today only for them to be in jeopardy tomorrow, many humanitarians now aspire to transform the structural conditions that endanger populations.[73] With the expansion of humanitarian work to include development, democracy promotion, establishing the rule of law and respect for human rights, and post-conflict peacebuilding, a longer-term commitment is increasingly viewed as essential.[74] As few states are willing to make such a commitment, some skeptics ask, "Why start in the first place?" At a minimum, the original ICISS recommendation that R2P include the responsibility to rebuild seems prescient, and its absence in the 2005 World Summit decision is a shortcoming that ignores this reality.

A related line of criticism of the use of the military in humanitarian crises is that any deployment of soldiers is bound to reflect the grand strategies of powerful states. If so, their presence creates an opportunity to help and protect war victims but also poses a danger that might overwhelm the humanitarian enterprise. The use of military force necessarily clashes directly with the traditional humanitarian principles of independent, neutral, and impartial provision of relief to victims of conflict and natural disasters. As such, relief-oriented actors who dishonor that definition are on a slippery slope to a kind of corruption. In its most extreme form, which many see in Afghanistan and Iraq, humanitarians who collaborate with the military can be seen to embody colonialism and imperialism.

The second consideration is whether the application of

military force does more harm than good, which requires applying consequentialist ethics. Instead of the moral absolutes that many humanitarians espouse as part of their worldview, situational ethics are of the essence, or what the late pioneer of forced migration studies Myron Wiener called "instrumental humanitarianism."[75] The devil lies in the details, as folk wisdom would have it. The real difficulty is to determine whether using the military will help bring about a better outcome than the alternatives. The various controversies involved in determining the least-bad result include consideration of the consequences at different levels; whether we should think in terms of the consequences of individual acts or of rules governing domains of actions; the appropriate time horizon for evaluating consequences; and the uncertainty that surrounds any action and its possible impacts.

There is now recognition that humanitarian relief will almost always have negative and unintended consequences – David Kennedy's "dark sides of virtue"[76] – and the use of the military is even more likely to mean that someone must be disadvantaged. As it is impossible to know all the effects of aid or of military force, the issue therefore is whether, on balance, it does more harm than good, and whether the prospects for success are at least 50:50.[77] Accordingly, many humanitarian agencies increasingly refer to consequentialism as they evaluate their efforts. The overwhelmingly negative outcomes in Rwanda and Bosnia are driving the soul-searching, along with donors' desire for evidence of effectiveness and impact. If acting on the moral obligation to help those in need leads to feeding those killers mingling with victimized populations in refugee camps or prolonging war by, for example, offering a portion of food aid to combatants in exchange for access to victims, or if the use of military force is not guaranteed to help, how can such acts be judged ethical?

Further, there are significant quantitative problems

regarding the actual measurement of costs and benefits. Establishing a bottom line for determining the benefits to civilians in a targeted country resulting from coercive intervention by external military forces requires determining the economic costs of the military intervention itself, along with the casualties, fatalities, and political impact of such an intervention. Determining the civilian benefits of intervention in a targeted country requires determining the difference before and after an intervention in terms of such factors as displacement (numbers of refugees, IDPs, and besieged populations), suffering (hunger, disease, and human rights abuse), and the state of the local polity (its ability to exercise sovereignty).

Any reader who has tried to attach values to social scientific questions will immediately realize the challenge of such an exercise. The lack of data – or a common understanding of what number-crunchers would call "stylized facts" – itself sometimes poses close to an insurmountable problem.[78] Armed forces are not forthcoming about data; nor do all countries employ comparable accounting and reporting methods. Humanitarian agencies are hardly better. Moreover, reliable statistics about the actual costs of delivering goods and alternatives are sketchy and not comparable among sources or sectors.

And finally, an enormous source of ambiguity arises in attaching a value to human life itself. Even such stalwart defenders of humanitarian action as Ian Smillie and Larry Minear acknowledge how painful making ethical decisions has become: "In recent years, the moral necessity of humanitarian action is no longer self-evident and has become a matter of debate."[79] "'Moral calculus' is not a highly developed form of mathematics," note Marc Lindenberg and Coralie Bryant. "It is hard to know whether one hundred lives saved is worth the price of having inadvertently helped to prolong a conflict by a month. It is even harder to document the numbers of lives lost and saved in such situations."[80] In short, how can analysts measure impacts within affected areas without assigning a specific monetary value to a human being? For some critics, every life has an infinite value; and if so, cost–benefit analyses are beside the point. But for most analysts it is necessary to assign values, and they must be willing to cross this philosophical and moral minefield.

I favor the image of Olympic diving as an additional element behind any judgment, because an evaluator needs to consider the degrees of both difficulty and execution to fairly assess the overall utility and success of a particular humanitarian intervention.[81] Factors entering into the judgment include: how dangerous and chaotic a particular humanitarian situation is, how physically challenging a specific terrain, and how ambitious a concrete mandate.

Taking into account the above considerations, my own judgment is that northern Iraq in 1991, Haiti, East Timor, and Kosovo are at one end of the spectrum, with the benefits to civilians (in terms of lives saved, improved access, and fewer rights violations) worth the economic, military, and political costs. At the other end would be pre-Dayton Bosnia, because the high economic and political costs and low effectiveness of the military forces were not commensurate with the civilian benefits. Indeed, the half-hearted military intervention there perpetuated violence in some areas such as the "safe zones," where the concentration of Bosnian Muslims facilitated mass slaughter. The most notable example is Srebrenica – one of the so-called safe zones under the protection of UN troops – where Serbian forces systematically killed some 8,000 Bosnian Muslim men and boys.

In between, I would place Rwanda closer to the successful end of the spectrum after July 1994 – ironically, because the military expenditures were nonexistent earlier and rather trivial over a concentrated period of a few months. Most of the bloodshed had already unfolded as powerful states stood by. Thus, while the benefits to civilians resulting from the eventual intervention in terms of humanitarian assistance and eventual repatriation were considerable, overall the international community of states failed to halt or abate one of the worst genocides of the post-World War II period.

Somalia would be closer to the failure end, especially because of the backlash against multilateralism in the United States, in the wake of the degrading deaths of 18 US rangers there in October 1993. This tragedy directly informed its delayed and minimal response to the massive bloodshed in Rwanda, including its refusal to label it "genocide," and influenced US decision-making in subsequent crises. Of course, Rwanda and Somalia – or any of the other cases for that matter – could be pushed closer to either end of the spectrum by a shift in subjective appreciation or an emphasis (or de-emphasis) on particular data or priorities.

The 2011 intervention in Libya by US and NATO forces successfully ended Qaddafi's dictatorship. However, the Security Council's authorization of air strikes without boots on the ground improved the situation for civilians in the short term, but the chaos and effective partition of the country that ensued without adequate post-intervention assistance made many nostalgic for the days of the deposed dictator. Uncertainty about the short- and longer-term benefits of using military force properly makes many dedicated humanitarians truly uneasy. If I were unkind, I would argue that those uncomfortable with the contemporary political temperature should stay out of the humanitarian kitchen. It is not going to get cooler or easier in this "space." Politics – including double standards and inconsistencies – are a fact of humanitarian or any other life.

Modesty is a virtue for aid workers *and* social scientists, as the preceding discussion of costs and benefits should demonstrate. Many would have us believe in the humanitarian "imperative," the obligation to treat affected populations similarly and react to crises consistently; but such a notion flies in the face of politics, which consists of drawing lines as well as weighing options and available resources in order to make tough decisions about doing the greatest good or the least harm. A more accurate description of likely efforts to save strangers is the humanitarian "impulse" – sometimes we can act and sometimes cannot.[82] Humanitarian action is desirable, not obligatory. The humanitarian impulse is permissive; the humanitarian imperative would be peremptory.

Moral hazard

An economic concept drawn largely from the insurance business, "moral hazard" refers to the risk that a policy may encourage risky or fraudulent behavior because the insured expects to be rewarded with a payout. For example, a car owner with an insurance policy may drive faster or run more risks because she knows that, in the case of an accident, the insurance company will pay for repairs. The car owner may even seek out a fraudulent accident in order to get a new car. The concept presents a potentially troubling debit for the humanitarian intervention ledger.

When applied to humanitarian interventions, critics argue that a more favorable climate for outside intervention can encourage risky or fraudulent behavior because insurgents believe that they will be saved by international intervention. Critics point to two kinds of moral hazard. First, insurgents could calculate a lower cost of rebellion because of a potential intervention and thus take greater risks than they would have taken without the possibility for outsiders coming to their rescue. Second, insurgents could hypothetically encourage the forgery of evidence for a chemical weapon attack or doctor photos to exaggerate state violence. In these circumstances, moral hazard could make armed conflicts worse or even start when they should not have done so.

This line of criticism has been popularized by Alan Kuperman for conflicts in the Balkans and Libya.[83] He also has suggested that applying concepts from economics could reduce the moral hazard of humanitarian interventions. He explored cost-sharing, randomization, and regulation – all policies used in the insurance industry – which could reduce moral hazard in relationship to the responsibility to protect. For example, interveners could "cap the insurance payout" by only protecting civilians and excluding rebels. Alternatively, restrictive regulations could specify that no intervention would occur if rebels provoke violence from the state, or reward rebel groups that are nonviolent. Such regulations might reduce moral hazard, but they are not necessarily new. Humanitarians have long wrestled with how to provide aid, particularly to refugees, without inadvertently assisting rebel combatants. Further, it is virtually impossible to forecast the moral hazard of an intervention because doing so requires data that are absent or sketchy, in addition to answers to counterfactuals ("what if?") that are impossible to formulate with any certainty in a crisis (but easy afterwards when 20–20 academic hindsight helps).

Moral hazard is a useful thought experiment that extends our understanding of unintended consequences. Kuperman's proposals resemble cautionary ones from R2P proponents: intervene only when state retaliation is grossly disproportionate; provide pure humanitarian aid; and ensure protection of civilians from violent backlash.

A more fundamental problem with the application of moral hazard to the use of military force for human protection purposes is that the concept assumes that mass atrocities are triggered by rebels. This is clearly not the case for humanitarian interventions in which a government was the primary perpetrator and acted first or refused to protect threatened populations. This assumption misses the wider picture of why a group would pick up arms in the first place. "Rebel" groups often have legitimate grievances to levy against state authorities that perpetuate human rights abuses, inequality, and economic or political exclusion. To suggest that all groups that lodge such claims are fraudulently manipulating the international moral compass amounts to "blaming the victim." Clearly it is essential to consider and mitigate the unintended consequences of humanitarian interventions, but moral hazard is more often used to defend the status quo than to better understand the dynamics of armed conflicts and mass atrocities.

The role of new thinking

Whatever the morality and law affecting humanitarian space, politics and military capacity ultimately are more important in determining when, where, why, and how to protect and assist affected populations.[84] The 2011 international action in Libya was unusual in that moral, legal, political, and military dimensions came together under the R2P rubric.[85] However shocking to the conscience a particular emergency and however hard or soft the applicable public international law, when political will and a military capacity exist, humanitarian space will open in which war victims will receive relief and protection.

Setting aside for a moment the problems of measuring the costs and benefits, what remains clear is that the transformation of war discussed at the outset of this chapter requires the transformation of humanitarianism. Not everything is new under the sun; but, in many arenas, there is certainly much novelty. While the extent of change in contemporary wars and the wisdom of alternative humanitarian strategies and tactics can be debated, the newness of thinking during the turbulent 1990s and beyond is much less contested. Without it, we would have to respond affirmatively to Fiona Terry's rhetorical question about humanitarian actions: are we "condemned to repeat"?[86] It is to essential ideational and normative developments that we now turn.

CHAPTER FOUR

New Thinking:
The Responsibility to Protect

Transformations in the nature of contemporary war and of
accompanying human disasters have also changed ways of
thinking about sovereignty and human rights. Here we delve
into relatively recent normative efforts to grapple with this
fundamental tension, focusing on the ground-breaking work
of the International Commission on Intervention and State
Sovereignty.

An imaginative way to reconcile sovereignty and human
rights emerged from ICISS's 2001 report, *The Responsibility
to Protect*. The immediate stimuli were the divergent reactions
– or rather, the nonreactions – by the Security Council to
Rwanda and Kosovo (where intervention was a unilateral
NATO mission, launched without prior Security Council
authorization). In 1994, intervention was too little and too
late to halt or even slow the murder of what may have been as
many as 800,000 people in the Great Lakes region of Africa.
In 1999, the formidable North Atlantic Treaty Organization
finessed the council and waged war, for the first time in its
50 years of existence, in Kosovo. But many observers saw
the 78-day bombing effort as being too much and too early,
perhaps initially creating as much suffering as it relieved. In
both cases, the Security Council failed to act expeditiously
and authorize the use of deadly force to protect vulnerable
populations.

These realities prompted convening the commission, but
two essential intellectual efforts had broken new ground and

provided underpinnings for ICISS's efforts. First is the normative work by Francis M. Deng and Roberta Cohen on the issue of internally displaced persons. Their conceptualization of "sovereignty as responsibility" lies at the heart of what became known as the "responsibility to protect."[1] Secretary-General Kofi Annan's own use of the bully pulpit is also an essential chapter in the story, and the acknowledgment by the 2005 World Summit (preceded by the work of the High-level Panel on Threats, Challenges and Change) of R2P has reinforced the legitimacy of humanitarian intervention as a policy option. As a result of these normative efforts, the four characteristics of a sovereign state spelled out in the 1933 Montevideo Convention – territory, authority, population, and independence – have been complemented by another: a modicum of respect for human rights.

Optimists view ICISS's *The Responsibility to Protect* as the most comprehensive attempt to date to tackle sovereignty versus intervention, reflecting "the international state of the mind," according to former *New York Times* columnist Anthony Lewis.[2] The report is more successful in reconciling the sometimes contradictory political, legal, and moral arguments relating to humanitarian intervention than the Danish and the Dutch government reports in 1999 and 2000 and the 2000 report (sponsored by the Swedish government) of the Independent International Commission on Kosovo.[3] Even bitter opponents like Mohammed Ayoob admit that conditioning sovereignty on human rights and the responsibility to protect has "considerable moral force."[4] We turn first, however, to the intellectual antecedents.

Sovereignty as responsibility

The most reliable indicator of suffering in war zones is usually the number of "refugees" – in the vernacular or according to the text of the 1951 UN Convention on Refugees, exiles who flee across the borders of their country of origin. Physical displacement is prima facie evidence of vulnerability because people who are deprived of their homes, communities, and means of livelihood are unable to resort to traditional coping capacities. With more than 50 million people forcibly displaced – some 17 million living outside their countries of origin and almost 35 million internally displaced[5] – international migration raises numerous problems for states, societies, and international relations more generally.[6] Paradoxically, forced migrants *within* their own countries are often even more vulnerable. Whereas international law entitles refugees to human rights protection and assistance, no such guarantees exist for those who are struggling to overcome an "exodus within borders."[7] Agencies seeking to help persons who have not crossed a border require permission from the very political authorities responsible for their abuse and displacement. If the state causing the problem were not doing so, there would be no need to ask its permission. Helping and protecting IDPs requires at least humanitarian intrusion, if not intervention.

Since the mid-1990s, the ratio of refugees to IDPs – that is, forced migrants who physically remain within their own countries – has been dramatically reversed. As we just saw, the number of IDPs – depending on who is counting and counted – is considerably higher and certainly double that of refugees.[8] When IDP data were first gathered in 1982, there was one IDP for every ten refugees; at present the ratio is approximately 2:1.

At the outset of the 1990s, the massive number of IDPs and the changing nature of warfare suggested to watchful observers that what had seemed a blemish on the international system was an ugly structural scar. The fastest-growing category of war-affected populations – "orphans of conflict"[9] – had, and still has, no institutional sponsor or formal international legal framework. At the same time, diminishing refugee populations continue to benefit from well-developed institutional and legal efforts by the UNHCR. Moreover, the anodyne lingo of "internal displacement" fails to convey immense human suffering. IDPs lack food, shelter, and physical and legal security. According to an early study from the Centers for Disease Control (CDC), they may have death rates 60 times higher than non-displaced populations in their home countries.[10]

In 1992, when the CDC generated that dramatic statistic, UN secretary-general Boutros Boutros-Ghali submitted the first analytical report on IDPs to the UN Commission on Human Rights (CHR) in Geneva. The commission in turn, but not without controversy, approved resolution 1992/73 authorizing him to appoint a representative to explore "views and information from all Governments on the human rights issues related to internally displaced persons, including an examination of existing international human rights, humanitarian and refugee law and standards and their applicability to the protection of and relief assistance to internally displaced persons." Nonetheless, many states were uneasy with this potential intrusion into domestic jurisdiction, while many humanitarian agencies were leery about the likely bureaucratic fallout.

Shortly thereafter, Boutros-Ghali designated Francis M. Deng, a former Sudanese diplomat and a senior fellow at the Brookings Institution, the representative of the secretary-general (RSG) on IDPs. The CHR consistently extended his mandate for two- and three-year terms until July 2004, when Deng's extension ran into UN time limits; he was replaced by Walter Kälin, a Swiss professor of international law whose title became "representative of the secretary-general on the human rights of internally displaced persons." Since 2010, Chaloka Beyani, a Zambian professor of international law at the London School of Economics, has fulfilled these responsibilities. UN secretary-general Ban Ki-moon appointed Deng as special adviser on the prevention of genocide, a position he held from 2007 to 2012.

The first framing efforts pertaining to IDPs began with Deng's early work on Africa and continued with reports from his official country missions.[11] The first full-fledged book on the topic was published in 1993 under his authorship,[12] and this was followed by two authoritative volumes with Roberta Cohen as a coauthor and coeditor in 1998.[13] Subsequently, the Norwegian Refugee Council began – with the urging of the Brookings Project on Internal Displacement (PID) headed by Deng and Cohen – to publish what remains the best data about these war victims.[14] And a host of articles and books are now in the academic and policy literatures.[15]

From the outset of his mandate, Deng sought not only to increase information about IDPs and the quality of data about their plight, but also to push out the envelope of international law. In addition to being the year of publication of both *Masses in Flight* and *The Forsaken People*, 1998 also marked the publication, following five years of difficult negotiations, of the UN's Guiding Principles on Internal Displacement.[16] This "soft" form of international law – not a convention or treaty, but a compilation of generally agreed principles – has been promulgated widely, and now constitutes the point of departure for virtually all public and private efforts. In referring to the Guiding Principles and the accompanying *Manual on Field Practice in Internal Displacement and Handbook for Applying the Guiding Principles on Internal Displacement*,[17] a team from Oxford University's Queen Elizabeth House summarized that they "are increasingly used by governments and international and national humanitarian agencies to raise awareness and to guide policy and practice in countries with IDP populations."[18]

Existing norms applicable to this category of forced migrant

– prior to and during displacement, as well as during return, resettlement, and reintegration – are conveniently brought together in a single document that guides political authorities and humanitarians. The process leading to the adoption of the Guiding Principles was a key tactical decision that finessed state reluctance. It took half a decade and involved international lawyers and experts from all over the world, regional organizations, IGOs, the ICRC, and NGOs. States were eventually brought into the process and were prepared, for the most part, to promote them or at least not to lobby too aggressively against them.

The evolution from an idea to a set of principles to guide governments, militaries, humanitarian agencies, and non-state actors was a substantial achievement in half a decade, especially because many Third World countries initially viewed any external scrutiny of domestic human rights as an unacceptable assault on their sovereignty. Countries that have actually applied the Guiding Principles to the development of laws and court decisions include Angola, Colombia, Georgia, Peru, Uganda, and Sudan. "Incorporating the Guiding Principles into domestic law does not necessarily lead to better government policies or to automatic improvements in the rights of IDPs," wrote three evaluators, "but at least there is legislation in place against which governments can be held to account."[19] And representatives of civil society in places as diverse as Sierra Leone, Sri Lanka, Colombia, India, Russia, Liberia, and the Sudan People's Liberation Movement/Army have been empowered by the Principles to seek better assistance and protection from governments and aid agencies.

Why should we analyze these efforts? For students of international organizations, the answer is: "People matter. Ideas matter."[20] For humanitarian intervention, the power of conceptualizing "sovereignty as responsibility" – and especially the need for international protection of people who remain in their country of origin and subject to the jurisdiction of their government – is a story worth telling.[21] Deng and Cohen's conceptualization had policy consequences as the direct precursor of ICISS's responsibility to protect.

Starting from scratch and without an official and assessed UN budget – the usual poverty-stricken approach to human rights in the UN system – PID's productivity and output were impressive. Beginning in 1993, the CHR regularly extended the mandate of the RSG. Deng reported annually to the CHR, and at least biannually to the General Assembly. He undertook 28 official country missions, with many more field visits. In that period, PID conducted 16 regional and country workshops and seminars, many of which were made to dovetail with the country missions. Independent research and analysis put this issue squarely on the public policy map.

Aiding and protecting IDPs through the realization of sovereignty as responsibility clashed directly with the customary prerogatives of state authorities who often believe that sovereignty means that they can do as they wish with their citizens. The contrary idea – that there are not only rights but also responsibilities, or, perhaps better, that there are limits to abuse – moved quickly in the intergovernmental arena, largely as a result of research and pressure from outside the United Nations. There are other illustrations of the same phenomenon – for example, NGOs and the signing of the Universal Declaration of Human Rights in 1948, and both women's and environmental groups and the host of conferences in the 1970s and 1990s on gender and sustainable development.[22]

Reframing sovereignty as responsibility provided a handy way to navigate around the shoals of state sovereignty. In the first decades of the twenty-first century, sovereignty remains the essential lens through which we perceive the way in which the world operates, in spite of the facts that globalization erodes the power of the state to guarantee outcomes and act independently, and that human rights norms and conventions circumscribe the autonomy of state authorities in dealing with their populations, sometimes resulting in opprobrium and sanctions. Yet this principle of the international system dominant since the Peace of Westphalia has never been as revered as its most die-hard defenders claim.

The idea that there was an international responsibility to enforce international human rights standards *inside* the boundaries of states grew from Deng and Cohen's conceptual framework that called for international access to, and protection of, the growing number of war victims who did not cross an international boundary. Their successful efforts to improve knowledge, data, and soft law have not as yet transformed the institutional structures dealing with IDPs, but some fledgling steps have been taken.

In brief, Deng and Cohen's efforts on behalf of IDPs broke new conceptual and policy ground. International discourse is different, a clear normative framework is in place, guiding principles regarding IDPs are circulating with new coalitions behind them, and individual institutions emphasize to varying degrees the particular problems of IDPs within their programs and projects. This new field was prepared for more significant planting and harvesting at the end of the 1990s, first by UN secretary-general Kofi Annan and then by the Canadian-sponsored International Commission on Intervention and State Sovereignty. Our story of ideas in action and the march of humanitarian intervention now turns to them.

Kofi Annan's two sovereignties

In trying to deride the lack of raw power, Joseph Stalin is widely reported to have asked, "How many divisions does the pope have?" Realists might well pose the same question to the secretary-general of the United Nations, often viewed as a secular pope. And the statistical answer has varied widely over the years, from 10,000 during the Cold War to between 80,000 and 100,000 from the mid-1990s and the second decade of the twenty-first century – more deployed overseas than any country other than the United States.

Those figures are somewhat misleading, however, because the UN's top official actually borrows soldiers from member states; and his real power, like the pope's, does not come out of the barrel of a gun. More than his predecessors, secretary-general Kofi Annan (1997–2006) took human rights seriously and preached about humanitarian intervention from his bully pulpit. A series of speeches in 1998–9 is widely viewed as having placed the issue squarely on the intergovernmental agenda.

The first three speeches were delivered at Ditchley Park (a conference center in England), Geneva, and The Hague. Because he starkly juxtaposed the relative value of state versus individual sovereignty, these speeches received some publicity. More significant press and media coverage began shortly before the opening of the General Assembly on September 20, 1999, when a controversial opinion piece by Annan appeared in the influential weekly *The Economist*. His black-and-white challenge to traditional state sovereignty emerges from changing the balance between states and people as the source of legitimacy and authority. The older version of the rule of law of states is thus being tempered by the rule of law based on the rights of individuals. And a broader concept of sovereignty is emerging, which encompasses both the rights *and* the responsibilities of states.

The then secretary-general's clarion call was hard to muffle. His "two concepts of sovereignty" helped launch the intense debate on the legitimacy of intervention on humanitarian grounds:

State sovereignty, in its most basic sense, is being redefined – not least by the forces of globalization and international cooperation. States are now widely understood to be instruments at the service of their peoples, and not vice versa. At the same time individual sovereignty – by which I mean the fundamental freedom of each individual, enshrined in the Charter of the UN and subsequent international treaties – has been enhanced by a renewed and spreading consciousness of individual rights. When we read the Charter today, we are more than ever conscious that its aim is to protect individual human beings, not to protect those who abuse them.[23]

Later that week, in his opening address to the General Assembly, the moral plea from the future Nobel laureate reached member states in six official UN languages. Annan argued passionately that human rights transcended narrow claims of state sovereignty, a theme that he put forward more delicately a year later at the Millennium Summit.[24]

The reactions in the General Assembly Hall were raucous and predictable, from China, Russia, and especially much of the Third World. Unilateral intervention – that is, without Security Council authorization, however many countries are involved in a coalition – for whatever reasons, including genuine humanitarian ones, remained a taboo. It is easy to underestimate the extent to which Westphalian sovereignty permeated not only the thinking of the framers of the UN Charter but also the perspectives of new states following decolonization. As Gareth Evans tells us, "sovereignty thus hard won, and proudly enjoyed, is sovereignty not easily relinquished or compromised."[25] Indeed, the chorus of complaints after Annan's remarks in September 1999 had a remarkably similar tenor to hostile reactions over the years voiced in the General Assembly and the Economic and Social Council about many aspects of human rights campaigns or initiatives by Francis M. Deng.

Annan's reframing of two sovereignties clearly helped shift the balance away from the absolute rights of state leaders to respect for the popular will and internal forms of governance based on international standards regarding democracy and human rights.[26] Advocates suggest that, on a scale of values, the sovereignty of a state does not stand higher than the human rights of its inhabitants.[27] The fact that this argument came from the world's top international civil servant resonated.

International Commission on Intervention and State Sovereignty

Readers have encountered ICISS from the outset of this book. But it is worth parsing in greater detail here its deliberations and findings.[28] We have just seen the growing salience of popular sovereignty rooted in the notions of Cohen and Deng and of Annan. This doctrine stipulates that when states are unable to provide life-supporting protection and assistance for their citizens, they are expected to request and accept outside offers of assistance. Should they refuse or deliberately obstruct access to their affected populations, and thereby place large numbers of people at risk, an international responsibility to act arises. Sovereignty means accountability to two separate constituencies: internally to one's own population and internationally to the community of responsible states in the form of compliance with human rights standards. Proponents argue that sovereignty is not absolute, but contingent. In brief, when a government massively abuses the fundamental rights of its citizens, its sovereignty is suspended or abrogated.

The ICISS mandate was to build on this emerging understanding of the problem of intervention and state sovereignty and to unearth new common ground, or political consensus, about military intervention to support humanitarian objectives. The notion was that this independent commission would seek to square the circle – to harmonize intervention and state sovereignty – much as the Brundtland Commission overcame the seemingly estranged notions of growth and environmental protection with "sustainable development."[29] Similarly, ICISS reconciled respect for human life with state sovereignty through "the responsibility to protect."

The 12-person group moved at a forced-march pace and formulated its recommendations less than a year after its establishment by then Canadian foreign minister Lloyd Axworthy. Given the supposedly wide disparity of views across the North–South divide, it was co-chaired by Gareth Evans (a former Australian foreign minister) and Mohamed Sahnoun (a respected Algerian diplomat). In addition to Evans, the "North" included Lee Hamilton (USA), Michael Ignatieff (Canada), Klaus Naumann (Germany), Cornelio Sommaruga (Switzerland), and Gisèle Côté-Harper (Canada). In addition to Sahnoun, the "South" included Ramesh Thakur (India), Cyril Ramaphosa (South Africa), Fidel Ramos (Philippines), and Eduardo Stein (Guatemala). Russia's Vladimir Lukin completed the group.

The new twist for independent commissions of this type was the behind-the-scenes role of a sympathetic government, Canada – a model to be replicated in a subsequent commission on human security with Japan in the lead. Furthermore, Ottawa ensured that the topic and the work were not relegated exclusively to coffee tables and bookshelves. Indeed, the eventual blessing by the 2005 World Summit can be traced to Ottawa's persistence and diplomacy.

Humanitarian intervention is not really a North versus South issue, but that is how it – like virtually all international issues – is analyzed in UN circles. This is the convenient, familiar, and readily available organizing principle for diplomats. Ten consultations were held in both the northern and southern hemispheres to expose the views of governments, scholars, NGOs, and journalists. The cacophony cannot be summarized except to say that what was notable, in historical perspective, is that nowhere did a substantial number of people argue that intervention to sustain humanitarian objectives was never justifiable. As a result of the horror in Rwanda, there were few policymakers, pundits, or practitioners who dared to exclude humanitarian intervention in principle.

The commission laid down two normative markers.[30] First, it aimed to alter the consensus about the use of deadly force to help victims in harm's way. Second, it emphasized that the international responsibility to intervene to halt mass killings and ethnic cleansing is located in the UN Security Council, and that any intervention should be efficient and effective.

There are two public policy angles fraught with ethical dimensions resulting from the R2P report: "core principles" and "principles for military intervention." The former is politically correct enough packaging so that Chinese, Russian, and many Third World readers may be able to stomach the latter, the real meat of the report.

The "foundations" for the report contain an innocuous list with something for everyone, but the "basic principles" behind the report merit attention:

> State sovereignty implies responsibility, and the primary responsibility for the protection of its people lies with the state itself. Where a population is suffering serious harm, as a result of internal war, insurgency, repression or state failure, and the state in question is unwilling or unable to halt or avert it, the principle of non-intervention yields to the international responsibility to protect.[31]

The first four words could have been written by Deng, Cohen, or Annan; and the remainder of the sentence is noteworthy for those who chart changes in international discourse. As hinted earlier, the recognized need to reinforce state capacity is not a misplaced nostalgia for repressive regimes but, rather, an apt recognition, even among committed advocates of human rights and robust intervention, that state authority is fundamental to enduring peace and reconciliation. Human rights can only be defended over the longer term by democratic states with the authority and the monopoly of force to sustain such norms. The remedy is thus to rebuild failed or weak states rather than to place a misguided hope in the potential of international trusteeships and transnational NGOs to protect human rights. This fact reflects a growing appreciation not only of the international legal bases of the contemporary state system, but also the practical reality that domestic authorities are best placed to take steps to guarantee respect for fundamental rights.

The responsibility to protect embraces three essential, temporal phases:

- The responsibility to prevent: to address both the root causes and the direct causes of internal conflict and other man-made crises putting populations at risk.
- The responsibility to react: to respond to situations of compelling human need with appropriate measures, which may include coercive measures like sanctions and international prosecution, and in extreme cases military intervention.
- The responsibility to rebuild: to provide, particularly after a military intervention, full assistance with recovery, reconstruction, and reconciliation, addressing the causes of the harm the intervention was designed to halt or avert.

The notion of a logical continuum of responsibility before, during, and after assaults on civilians is indisputable. Clearly, preventing the outbreak of mass violence would be preferable to intervening to stop it, although just as clearly such a notion is politically very hard to sell. A commitment to post-conflict peacebuilding is imperative if the long-term benefits of intervention are to be realized. The disintegration of Libya in the aftermath of the first textbook use of military power on the basis of R2P was preceded by earlier headlines that highlighted the reality following humanitarian interventions: the continued instability throughout Haiti; the triumph of militant Islamists in consolidating control over the capital of Somalia, Mogadishu; and the eruption of gang violence in Dili, the capital of East Timor – earlier a much-vaunted "success story" of UN involvement after the Australian-led military intervention. These cases highlight the need for what Roland Paris has correctly identified as "longer-lasting and ultimately more intrusive forms of intervention in the domestic affairs of these states."[32]

Notwithstanding the necessity for such a holistic approach across time for the R2P, there is still the fundamental significance of the choice of the title of this book – with its focus on what can make a difference at the middle stage when the need for outside coercion confronts the traditional and crucial norm of nonintervention. The challenges before and after the outbreak of lethal conflicts are indisputable, but more urgent still is the requirement to emphasize nonconsensual intervention to protect populations under deliberate attack. If we are unsure about whether states will act to prevent armed conflict or be in a position to commit themselves to longer-run investments, should we throw up our hands and refuse to take feasible steps to stop mass murder?

ICISS sought to drive a stake through the heart of the term "humanitarian intervention." The shift in language is based on several assumptions, some more sensible than others. The first, which is frankly the least solid, is the allergic reaction by many humanitarians. The self-righteous monopoly by civilian agencies about who can be considered a legitimate humanitarian is hard to stomach. On many occasions, use of the military is the only way to halt atrocities; and many members of the

armed forces have certainly contributed substantial humanitarian benefits.

However, there are two more sensible justifications in
weighing the pluses and minuses of setting aside the familiar
terminology of "humanitarian intervention." Using the "H"
word – for "humanitarian," though it may also be used face-
tiously for "hurrah," or bitterly for "hypocritical" – stakes out
prematurely the moral high ground. Trying to avoid debate
about the merits of a particular case is wrong – intellectually
as well as politically. It overlooks the self-interested dynamics
of the strong to impose their will on the weak in the name of
the so-called universal principles of the day. History counsels
caution to anyone even vaguely familiar with many purported
humanitarian interventions. An honest debate about motivations and likely costs and benefits is required, not visceral
accolades because of a qualifying adjective. Moreover, serious
discussions have become particularly relevant, because analyses of interventions in the 1990s suggest that outside assistance
can do more harm than good or can become entangled in a local
political economy that favors war rather than peace.

Moreover, there is another possible payoff from switch-
ing to the vocabulary of the responsibility to protect. Moving
away from the picturesque vocabulary of the French Doctors
Movement has the political advantage of shifting the fulcrum
of debate away from the rights of interveners to the rights of
affected populations and to the obligations of outsiders to
help. The new terminology means that the emphasis is on the
rights of those needing support and suffering from starvation
or being raped, and on the responsibility – the moral injunc-
tion does not yet, however, constitute an obligation or duty
– of others to protect such victims.

According to the ICISS report, the change in vocabulary
reflects two priorities, both seemingly sensible upon first reading. It is important that "less intrusive and coercive measures

be considered before more coercive and intrusive ones." And "prevention is the single most important dimension of the responsibility to protect."

These priorities are highly situational. In fact, more coercive measures may make sense sooner rather than later. We need only think about Haiti's painful experience with sanctions or the distressing exhaustion of options in all of the Balkan wars to make a plausible case that earlier military intervention would conceivably have been more humane than attempting less coercive measures followed by military ones. By the time that all the alternatives to military force have been explored, many of the people whom humanitarian intervention is intended to save could be dead or have fled. Furthermore, Stanley Hoffmann offers another warning: waiting could drastically up the ante by increasing the level and intensity of military force required to do the job – which not only makes a response politically less likely, but also more lethal if it takes place.[33]

Moreover, it is preposterous to argue that to prevent is *the* single most important priority; the most urgent priority is to react better when sufficient political will is present. Most of the mumbling and stammering about prevention is a superficially attractive but highly unrealistic way to try to pretend that we can finesse the hard issues of what essentially amounts to humanitarian intervention. ICISS's discourse about prevention is a helpful clarification, but it nonetheless obscures the essence of the most urgent part of the spectrum of responsibility: to protect those caught in the crosshairs of war.

For bullish humanitarians, any loss of life is deemed sufficient to warrant an intervention. For ICISS, which accurately reflects the existing international political consensus on the subject, a higher threshold of human suffering must be crossed: acts of such a magnitude that they shock the conscience and elicit a fundamental humanitarian impulse.

Intervention consists of three categories of threat or actual use of coercion: military force, economic sanctions and arms embargoes, and international criminal prosecution. After mentioning that "military intervention for human protection purposes is an exceptional and extraordinary measure," the ICISS report specifies what warrants such an unusual military response. The "just cause threshold" is reached if the following conscience-shocking harm occurs:

> large-scale loss of life, actual or apprehended, with genocidal intent or not, which is the product either of deliberate state action, or state neglect or inability to act; or a failed state situation; or large-scale "ethnic cleansing," actual or apprehended, whether carried out by killing, forced expulsion, acts of terror; or rape.

This double-barreled justification did not go as far as many might have hoped. For instance, Article 5 of the ICC's Rome Statute identifies the "most serious crimes of concern to the international community as a whole." In particular, its list of "crimes against humanity" mentions everything from murder and slavery to imprisonment and "other inhumane acts of a similar character intentionally causing great suffering." As we learned earlier, this crime was added to the list of R2P triggers by the 2015 World Summit.

The value of the lengthy ICC shopping list is questionable, but there were two strong candidates for inclusion in ICISS's shorter list of threshold conditions that did not make the cut. One was the overthrow of democratically elected regimes (favored by some African states and regional institutions) and massive abuses of human rights (favored by most western enthusiasts for outside intervention).

However, the insertion of "actual *or* apprehended" to qualify both agreed thresholds opens the door fairly wide to acting in advance of massive loss of life or forced displacement. Justifiable causes could include overthrow of a democracy or violations of human rights or, perhaps, even an environmental catastrophe like the one in Chernobyl if a state reacts as slowly as the Soviet Union did in 1986. The requirement to endure high levels of loss of life *before* any action would have undermined the logic of saving lives.

In any event, contemporary policy debates revolve around the advisability of identifying any criteria whatsoever. Pragmatists see that interventions have taken place outside the Security Council and will continue to do so. As council approval is a desirable option but not an absolute requirement, the argument goes, a set of criteria could be useful in guiding forceful action to stem mass killings and wholesale slaughter. In the post-9/11 world, ICISS commissioner Ramesh Thakur has argued that a consensus resolution about R2P criteria would make it more difficult for states to wrap themselves disingenuously in a humanitarian blanket for purely self-interested interventions.[34] At the same time, opponents argue that Security Council endorsement under Chapter VII is a sine qua non, so that intervention without it is a violation of international law. They worry that formulating a list of criteria might facilitate and regularize the practice of ad hoc intervention, which tends to be by the most powerful states.

St. Thomas Aquinas, and the contemporary moral voices of Michael Walzer and Bryan Hehir,[35] would undoubtedly be pleased with "the precautionary principles" underlying the responsibility to protect. The debate in the 1990s can actually be seen as moving beyond "whether to intervene" to "how."[36] Concepts from the just war tradition animate much of the discussion about appropriateness. ICISS's modified just war doctrine includes four elements:

1 Right intention: The primary purpose of the intervention, whatever other motives intervening states may have, must be to halt or avert human suffering. Right intention is better

assured with multilateral operations, clearly supported by regional opinion and the victims concerned.

2 Last resort: Military intervention can only be justified when every nonmilitary option for the prevention or peaceful resolution of the crisis has been explored, with reasonable grounds for believing that lesser measures would not have succeeded.

3 Proportional means: The scale, duration, and intensity of the planned military intervention should be the minimum necessary to secure the defined human protection objective.

4 Reasonable prospects: There must be a reasonable chance of success in halting or averting the suffering which has justified the intervention, with the consequences of action not likely to be worse than the consequences of inaction.

The ICISS's clear affirmation of these criteria was useful, even if they are remarkably similar to those from other work done over recent decades. In 1965, the International Law Association established a commission on human rights that, in turn, established a subcommittee that published four reports on humanitarian intervention between 1970 and 1978 and a protocol with criteria for legitimate intervention.[37] The issue was controversial and abandoned, but subsequently it was the subject of intense work by the Swedish, Dutch, and Danish governments mentioned earlier, as well as a major concern of the Lawyers' Committee for Human Rights for the George W. Bush administration and of the International Council on Human Rights Policy for NGOs.[38] The same types of criteria exist in new work by independent scholars such as Michael Ignatieff, Simon Chesterman, Nicholas Wheeler, and Fernando Tesón.[39]

As ICISS pointed out at a special meeting after September 11, 2001, the precautionary principles for humanitarian intervention are also relevant for any unilateral or multilateral military operation. Even the special challenges by the war against terrorism demand adherence to the principles that the commission gave operational meaning to as precautionary considerations for humanitarian intervention.

Since the Security Council's lack of reaction to Rwanda and inability to act in Kosovo were the main driving force, the question of "right authority" was critical. The details of the ICISS recommendations are worth spelling out in full because of the subsequent decision by the General Assembly at the World Summit to make the Security Council's imprimatur an absolutely essential element of the responsibility to protect:

- There is no better or more appropriate body than the United Nations Security Council to authorize military intervention for human protection purposes. The task is not to find alternatives to the Security Council as a source of authority, but to make the Security Council work better than it has.
- Security Council authorization should in all cases be sought prior to any military intervention action being carried out . . .
- The Security Council should deal promptly with any request for authority to intervene where there are allegations of large-scale loss of human life or ethnic cleansing . . .
- The Permanent Five members of the Security Council should agree not to apply their veto power, in matters where their vital state interests are not involved, to obstruct the passage of resolutions authorizing military intervention for human protection purposes for which there is otherwise majority support.
- If the Security Council rejects a proposal or fails to deal with it in a reasonable time, alternative options are: consideration of the matter by the General Assembly in Emergency Special Session under the "Uniting for Peace" procedure;

and action within area by regional or sub-regional organizations under Chapter VIII of the Charter, subject to
their seeking subsequent authorization from the Security
Council.

- The Security Council should take into account in all its
deliberations that, if it fails to discharge its responsibility
to protect in conscience-shocking situations crying out for
action, concerned states may not rule out other means to
meet the gravity and urgency of that situation and that the
stature and credibility of the United Nations may suffer
thereby.

A key lingering question thus hovers around authority –
who may and will act, and how. Indeed, any standardization
of criteria governing interventions to protect the vulnerable
is problematic. Individual states will not act against major
powers because more harm than good would result – the cure
would be worse than the disease. For instance, who could
rationally argue that Moscow and Beijing should be subject
to military intervention to reverse their policies and actions
in Chechnya and Xinjiang? There are good reasons not to
challenge nuclear powers, but that gives little comfort to the
victims among the latter's citizens, especially as the number
of nuclear powers continues to increase. If the Security
Council is paralyzed, action can still occur if conditions are
right. This fact was highlighted by the Kosovo Commission's
report, which concluded that "the NATO military intervention was illegal but legitimate."[40] However, we should bear
in mind that selective action or inaction damages the UN's
credibility.

The final topic examined by ICISS concerns "operational
principles." Here, there are no surprises. The shopping list
of desirable conditions includes the items on a wish list for
most practitioners, such as clear objectives, unambiguous

mandates, adequate resources, unity of command, and maximum coordination among humanitarians. There is no recommendation whose implementation would not strike most military and humanitarian staff as sensible and straight-forward, however implausible.

At the same time, there are a number of specific challenges in giving operational meaning to R2P that are distinct from the more familiar challenges of either peacekeeping or war fighting, the two distinct end points on a spectrum of international military action. The report's recommendations seek to highlight specific challenges in between – namely, how can protection be afforded to populations at risk, and how can those who prey upon them be deterred?

To date, the cumulative scorecard is not encouraging. There has been too little success in meeting the challenges of coercive protection. Moreover, there seems to be a lack of institutional adjustment and learning at the operational level, as is indicated by military doctrines. These shortcomings pose the future challenges of the responsibility to protect. One potential advantage of coercive protection is that it is politically and militarily less onerous than compelling compliance.

Yet this "do something" approach can save lives and provide the chance that a functioning sovereign state can re-emerge as the provider of protection. Rwanda furnishes a helpful coun-terfactual. There was no robust humanitarian intervention, and there was too little international follow-up. Nevertheless, security and state services have returned, in spite of the tragic events of 1994. Would it not be possible to imagine the same outcome but with slightly more robust and more timely international military responses in that fateful year that might have deterred or slowed the momentum of the genocide, prevented the flight of millions, and saved *only* a few hundred thousand lives?[41]

The essential results of the International Commission on

Intervention and State Sovereignty are twofold. First, it reformulates the conceptual basis for humanitarian intervention. It calls for moving away from the rights of interveners toward the rights of victims and the responsibilities of outsiders to act. It is primarily state authorities whose citizens are threatened who have the responsibility to protect. Yet, a residual obligation rests with the larger community of states when an aberrant member of their club misbehaves egregiously or implodes. Essentially, governments not intervening in the face of massive loss of life and displacement should be embarrassed. Their responsibility to protect includes action not only to halt mass atrocity crimes but also to prevent armed conflicts and to help mend societies.

The implications are plain. The status of state sovereignty is not challenged per se, but rather reinforced. However, if a state is unwilling or unable to exercise its protective responsibilities for the rights of its own citizens, it forfeits the moral claim to be treated as legitimate. Its sovereignty, as well as its right to nonintervention, is suspended; and the residual responsibility necessitates vigorous action by outsiders to protect populations at risk.

Second, ICISS proposes a new international default setting – a modified just war doctrine for future interventions to sustain humanitarian values or human rights. As mentioned in chapter 2, the Security Council was largely missing in action regarding humanitarian matters during the Cold War. For more than two decades, there was a *tabula rasa* – no resolution mentioned the humanitarian aspects of any conflict from 1945 until the Six-Day War of 1967.[42] The first mention of the ICRC in a council resolution was not until 1978.[43] And in the 1970s and 1980s, "the Security Council gave humanitarian aspects of armed conflict limited priority . . . but the early nineteen-nineties can be seen as a watershed."[44] During the first half of that decade, twice as many resolutions were passed as during the first 45 years of UN history. They contained repeated references, in the context of Chapter VII, to humanitarian crises amounting to threats to international peace and security, and repeated demands for parties to respect the principles of international humanitarian law.

In short, today's normative landscape for humanitarian intervention is substantially different from that dominating international relations during the Cold War. José Alvarez observes the acceleration in the usual pace for the development of an emerging customary law: "traditional descriptions of the requisites of custom – the need for the passage of a considerable period of time and the accumulation of evidence of the diplomatic practices between sets of states reacting to one another's acts – appear increasingly passé."[45]

The 2005 World Summit and since

The UN's sixtieth birthday celebration in New York was attended by more than 150 presidents, prime ministers, and princes. Anticipated as a window of opportunity to revisit the United Nations in light of changes in world politics since 1945, the September 2005 World Summit's negotiations exposed the debilitating political and bureaucratic conflicts that regularly paralyze the organization. Summit gatherings of 150 world leaders are infrequent – the previous UN one was in September 2000 and the most recent in September 2015 – and are supposed to provide a political and policy boost to the world organization. However, this "once-in-a-generation opportunity to reform and revive the United Nations has been squandered,"[46] said the lead editorial in the New York Times. Even though the overall results constituted considerably less than Kofi Annan's prior plea that "the UN must undergo the most sweeping overhaul in its 60-year history,"[47] partisans of R2P were relieved.

Two major developments at the summit are relevant for humanitarian intervention. The first is the creation of a Human Rights Council (HRC), which reflects an effort to bolster the human rights machinery of the United Nations, thereby enhancing the protection of individual rights. The second directly pertains to R2P, as the outcome document propelled forward, albeit gingerly, normative progress on the use of force in the face of conscience-shocking events by outright endorsing the responsibility to protect.

The performance of the UN's pre-existing Commission on Human Rights had been considered scandalous everywhere except in countries run by thugs. Creaking along since 1946, the commission's 53 members in 2005 included Sudan, while its government was pursuing genocide in Darfur, and Zimbabwe, while it was bulldozing the houses of 700,000 suspected opposition supporters and rounding up journalists and other critics. That China and Cuba played prominent roles, and that Libya was a former chair, added to the litany of embarrassments. The last session of the CHR took place in March, and it was abolished in June 2006 during the first session of the Human Rights Council.

The secretary-general's High-level Panel on Threats, Challenges and Change – assembled to evaluate threats to international peace and security, and offer recommendations for increasing UN effectiveness – produced its ideas as part of preparations for the World Summit. It recognized the "eroding credibility and professionalism" of the UN Commission on Human Rights, and that "States have sought membership of the Commission not to strengthen human rights but to protect themselves against criticism or to criticize others."[48] However, its recommendation was truly counterintuitive: universal membership instead of "only" one-quarter of the members.

In his only serious dissent from the panel's recommendations, the secretary-general proposed that member states "replace the Commission on Human Rights with a smaller standing Human Rights Council."[49] In September, leaders argued about whether the new council might one day become a principal organ, like the Security Council and the Economic and Social Council, one that could review the human rights of all members, not just those selected for special scrutiny.

World leaders found it easier to agree that the Commission on Human Rights was dysfunctional than to agree on an alternative. However, they "resolve[d] to create a Human Rights Council" as a subsidiary of the General Assembly, which would not only create it, under the provisions of Charter Article 22, but also decide its "mandate, modalities, functions, size, composition, membership, working methods, and procedures."[50]

Given the bitter disputes over the shape of the new council, it surprised some that the resumed General Assembly made any decision at all. Sweden's Jan Eliasson, the assembly's president at the time and now UN deputy secretary-general, managed to secure an agreement in March 2006 on a 47-member Human Rights Council with terms of three years with the assent of a simple majority of the General Assembly.

The new body has flaws. A majority vote in May 2006 by the General Assembly (rather than by two-thirds, as Annan originally proposed) facilitated the election of such abusers as China, Cuba, Russia, Pakistan, Saudi Arabia, and Azerbaijan. Nonetheless, elections replaced selection by regional powerbrokers, and candidates put forward platforms, which spurred open discussion of records. Some came close to acknowledging international concerns. For example, Pakistan emphasized its commitment to punishing all forms of violence against women, especially "the infamous honor killing." China drew attention to its invitations to UN investigators on freedom of religion, as well as on torture and arbitrary detention.

Two vocal critics of human rights measures, Venezuela and Iran, were defeated. Whereas, in the past, despotic regimes could evade scrutiny by joining the commission – indeed, that was often an incentive – inquiry into members' records is the first order of business for the new council. Hence, Zimbabwe, Sudan, Libya, Vietnam, Nepal, Syria, and Egypt did not even run.

Neither did the United States, which registered its negative views by not being a candidate for a seat in the council's first election. Rather than explain the tactic as pouting, some judged the decision as a calculation to avoid the potential embarrassment of possibly losing an election because of the American record at Abu Ghraib and Guantánamo. Indeed, Washington had earlier indicated its discontent with the modest level of change by voting against the council – one of only four countries (the others being Israel, the Marshall Islands, and Palau) to do so. Ambassador John Bolton told a public radio audience that the United States "wants a butterfly, not a caterpillar with lipstick on."[51] Many pundits and NGOs screamed that the firebrand conservative was doing the Bush administration's bidding and scuttling legitimate international initiatives. US opposition to the council was reversed under the Obama administration, which ran and won a seat in 2009. While conservative pundits continue to rail against the council, UN ambassador Susan Rice explained that the United States would work from within to bolster the flawed body.[52] Indeed, the Obama administration halted the pouting and boycott, and the United States has played a leading role since 2009.

By the time of a review in 2011 after five years of work, the fledgling council had conducted its first "universal periodic review" (UPR), a human rights report card for each UN member state. Preliminary assessments suggest that some gains have been made but that overall it remains closer to "business as usual" – the process is deeply politicized and state sovereignty continues to trump human rights. Robust follow-up mechanisms to the UPR, moreover, have yet to be established. As Bertrand Ramcharan explains:

> [T]he HRC has been heavily criticized on three main grounds: it fails to take principled action on many situations of gross human rights violations for political reasons; some in its membership seek to weaken the special procedures – the mandate-holders examining issues or situations of gross human rights violations; and it is biased in its treatment of countries as reflected in its narrow concentration on alleged violations committed by Israeli occupation forces in Palestine and refusal to take similar action on other equally or even more serious situations.[53]

We will have to wait and see if the actual behavior of the HRC over the longer run will distinguish it from its undistinguished predecessor. If past is prelude, this is unlikely. At the same time, if the promising sprouts of the council are to take root and not to shrivel, they must be actively nurtured by those committed to human rights – the Europeans, democracies of the global South such as India and South Africa, and especially the United States. An encouraging development was that the Human Rights Council referred to the responsibility to protect in its resolution S-15/1, which in turn led to the General Assembly's resolution 65/60 that suspended Libyan membership in the council. Some asked why Libya was a member in the first place, but the dramatic suspension was a precedent, as never before had a member state been bounced from an elected UN body.

The summit also agreed to strengthen the Office of the High Commissioner for Human Rights (OHCHR), a relatively recent addition to the UN's machinery (established after

the 1993 Vienna World Conference on Human Rights) that
is staffed by professionals (rather than run by governments)
who have, among other tasks, been establishing human rights
centers in troubled countries such as Cambodia, Guatemala,
and Nepal, and have assisted a series of special rapporteurs
working on such thematic issues as torture. The summit
document called for a doubling of the budget of the high commissioner's office, allowing recruitment of "highly competent
staff."[54] The OHCHR's budget, however, remains woefully
inadequate for the magnitude of the tasks confronting the
office.

   In addition to the creation of the Human Rights Council,
and most significant for the discussion here, was the World
Summit's blessing of R2P, an idea that has broken speed
records in the international normative arena. As Kofi Annan
told a 1998 audience, "state frontiers . . . should no longer be
seen as a watertight protection for war criminals or mass mur-
derers."[55] The High-level Panel reaffirmed the importance of
changing the terminology from the divisive "humanitarian
intervention" to "the responsibility to protect." It explicitly
endorsed the ICISS argument that "the issue is not the 'right
to intervene' of any State, but the 'responsibility to protect' of
every State." It proposed the same five criteria as ICISS: seriousness of threat, proper purpose, last resort, proportional
means, and balance of consequences.[56] In a significant break-
through for the growing acceptance of the new norm, China's
official paper on UN reforms and the Gingrich–Mitchell
taskforce commissioned by the US Congress both endorsed
the responsibility to protect.[57] In his own document for the
summit, In Larger Freedom, Annan made explicit reference to
ICISS and R2P, endorsed the legitimacy criteria, and urged
the Security Council to adopt a resolution "setting out these
principles and expressing its intention to be guided by them."
This would "add transparency to its deliberations and make its

decisions more likely to be respected, by both Governments and world public opinion."[58]

R2P was one of the few substantive items to survive relatively intact the negotiations at the World Summit – indeed, the concept was given its own subsection.[59] The final outcome document contained an unambiguous acceptance of individual state responsibility to protect populations from genocide, war crimes, ethnic cleansing, and crimes against humanity. Member states further declared that they "are prepared to take collective action, in a timely and decisive manner, through the Security Council, in accordance with the UN Charter, including Chapter VII . . . should peaceful means be inadequate and national authorities manifestly failing to protect their populations from genocide, war crimes, ethnic cleansing and crimes against humanity."

While ICISS was not enthusiastic about unilateral humanitarian intervention, it had left open the possibility that humanitarian intervention not be totally dependent on the procedural rules of the Charter governing the use of force. As such, the summit's language could be seen as a step backward, as "R2P lite" – because humanitarian intervention must be approved by the Security Council. Essentially, the effort to halt mass atrocities was back to where it had been in Kosovo's wake, subject to the lowest common denominator of the council's permanent members. And as we saw earlier, the double veto by Moscow and Beijing has prevented meaningful responses to Syria's bloodshed.

Moreover, the World Summit also kicked the issue of criteria back to the General Assembly, where a discussion is bound to stall. At the same time, the overall treatment of R2P suggests that consensus building can sometimes take place around even the most controversial issues and with opposition from the strangest of bedfellows – in this case, the United States and the Non-Aligned Movement (NAM). The summit's final text reaffirms the primary roles of states in protecting their own citizens and encourages international assistance to weak states to exercise this responsibility. At the same time, it also makes clear the requirement for international intervention when countries fail to shield their citizens from, or, more likely, to actively sponsor, mass atrocities.

NAM will undoubtedly continue to reiterate its rejection of the so-called right of humanitarian intervention, and the United States will continue to refuse to be committed to military action by others. But the proverbial bottom line is clear: when a state is incapable or unwilling to safeguard its own citizens and peaceful means fail, the resort to outside intervention, including military force (preferably with Security Council approval), remains a policy option. In short, there is an unambiguous acceptance by governments of the collective international responsibility to protect.

Significantly, the Security Council made use of the term "R2P" at the end of April 2006 in thematic resolution 1674 pertaining to the protection of civilians in armed conflict. And at the end of 2007, UN secretary-general Ban Ki-moon sought to institutionalize the norm with the creation of a new office at the under-secretary-general level. Following the Security Council's approval, Ban Ki-moon then appointed Edward C. Luck as his special adviser on the R2P. Luck collaborated closely with Francis Deng, the special adviser for the prevention of genocide and mass atrocities. Both left the UN in 2012 and were replaced by Jennifer Welsh and Adama Dieng, respectively.

In 2009, Ban Ki-moon sought to further advance the R2P agenda with his report *Implementing the Responsibility to Protect*, which he submitted to the General Assembly in 2009.[60] The 2010 and 2011 General Assembly interactive dialogues on R2P's implementation revealed growing consensus around the R2P norm. Indeed, only four states outright rejected R2P and sought to roll back normative progress – Cuba, Nicaragua, Sudan, and Venezuela – with many former skeptics adopting a more positive tone.[61] Subsequent interactive dialogues have continued the consolidation; and the largest one to date in September 2015 may have been the last informal "dialogue," as the suggestion was made to make R2P regular, formal agenda item of the General Assembly.

Although the first dialogue certainly was not what the secretary-general called "a watershed,"[62] the state members of the "Group of Friends" of the responsibility to protect in New York, the UN special adviser, and civil society successfully advanced the cause. The mobilization resembled successful earlier campaigns to forge wider constituencies for such issues as banning land mines and establishing the International Criminal Court.[63]

Initially, many observers feared that the debate would lead to a resolution diluting the September 2005 commitment. Fears about normative back-pedaling seemed concrete enough; for instance, on the eve of the debate, *The Economist* described opponents who were "busily sharpening their knives."[64] The Nicaraguan president of the General Assembly, Father Miguel d'Escoto Brockmann, unsheathed his Marxist dagger and suggested "a more accurate name for R2P would be ... redecorated colonialism."[65] He also invited Noam Chomsky to harangue delegates on the dangers of western imperialism and humanitarian intervention.

However, R2P-naysayers were deeply disappointed by the discernible shift from antipathy to wider public acceptance of the norm.[66] Countries that had suffered terrible atrocities continued to make rousing pleas to strengthen and implement R2P – for example, Rwanda, Bosnia, Guatemala, Sierra Leone, and East Timor. A wide variety of other countries, such as Chile, South Korea, and the entire West, continued their outspoken support. More surprising was the widening consensus with support from major regional powers that had previously been reticent or even hostile – including Brazil, Nigeria, India, South Africa, and Japan. Concerns remained about implementation, thresholds, and inconsistency. In September 2009, General Assembly resolution 63/208 registered tepid support for R2P across regions, but it was more widespread than previously.

In August 2010, the conversation continued around the secretary-general's report on early warning, and 42 states and four observers spoke at the informal interactive dialogue; the vast majority once again reaffirmed support for the norm, welcomed the report, and supported continued discussions.[67] Not surprisingly, the usual detractors continued to question the definition of R2P and previous agreements by the General Assembly; but, in December 2010, the assembly approved resolution 64/245, which funded the joint office and regularized the staff positions working on genocide prevention and R2P as part of the next UN biennium budget.

Successive UN interactive dialogues have witnessed a consolidation of consensus. In spite of the dispute over the intended results in Libya and with bombing still under way, the conversation in July 2011 was less heated than in previous summers with fewer of the usual suspects trying to torpedo consensus. The focus of the secretary-general's report on regional organizations was timely in that they had been so crucial in securing widespread political backing for the Libyan intervention. The fourth interactive dialogue in September 2012 focused on Ban Ki-moon's timid report about his "third pillar,"[68] R2P's coercive dimensions. The secretary-general earlier had repackaged ICISS recommendations to avoid this topic in favor of his other two pillars, the responsibility of states themselves to protect their citizens and international assistance to help them – a theme revisited in his sixth report in 2014.[69] The 2012 debate coincided with the impasse in

Syria, where coercion was required but blocked by multiple actual or threatened Russian and Chinese vetoes, which Bashar al-Assad correctly interpreted as a renewal for his license to continue atrocities. The fifth and sixth interactive dialogues in August 2013 and September 2014 continued the steady growth of state participation and the waning of dissent; the 2014 session included, for the first time, a joint statement read on behalf of the enlarged 45-state group, the "Friends of R2P." In 2015, almost 90 countries participated.

These annual dialogues have continued along with a number of state and nonstate initiatives. Most prominent were the informal group of like-minded countries in New York, the Group of Friends for R2P; the partnership to promote national R2P focal points; the International Coalition for the R2P; and the Global Centre for the R2P whose bi-monthly watchdog publication is *R2P Monitor*.[70] Likely the most visible efforts are governmental "focal points" meetings, where representatives from state capitals and UN officials gathered for the first time in May 2011 at the invitation of the foreign ministers from Denmark and Ghana (later joined by Australia and Costa Rica).[71] By the twentieth anniversary of the Rwandan genocide, almost 40 governments had established such focal points and 10 others only a year later in 2015, with still more considering them as Ban Ki-moon's 2013 report to the General Assembly had recommended.[72] Perhaps the most significant such structure resulted from US Presidential Study Directive-10, which, like action in Libya, emanated from the "dream team" of genocide prevention consisting then of Secretary of State Hillary Clinton, UN Ambassador Susan Rice, and Special Assistant to the President Samantha Power. In August 2011, President Barack Obama established the Atrocity Prevention Board – an interagency mechanism to facilitate rapid reaction across the government. It gathered for the first time at the White House in April 2012. Organizations are not the answers to all our prayers, but they provide a bureaucratic means to enhance the visibility of issues and ultimately accountability.

These gatherings afforded occasions to turn up the volume of lingering buyer's remorse, especially evident from Brazil's proposal at the 66th session of the UN General Assembly in fall 2011 that "the international community, as it exercises its responsibility to protect, must demonstrate a high level of responsibility while protecting (RwP)."[73] Reticence and even hostility are understandable for anyone familiar with the number of sins justified by colonial powers under a "humanitarian" rubric. The still raw memories of former colonies make them unlikely to welcome an interventionist doctrine merely because of a qualifying adjective. Moreover, naysayers have a special advantage in relationship to R2P in that the status quo of sovereignty is so deeply entrenched. They and others are uneasy about setting aside the principle of nonintervention in domestic affairs, the basis for international society and a restraint on major powers.

Wolfgang Seibel has described RwP as "hugging R2P to death."[74] While RwP reflects a mischievous ambivalence, it also reflects the norm's perceived power. Brazil's foreign policy must be unequivocally supportive of human rights; Brasilia could not be among R2P spoilers. At the same time, a prominent member of the global South also must communicate uneasiness about the use of military force for regime change, a sensitive topic for many developing countries. While critics emphasize state responsibility and prevention in the hopes of avoiding military force, James Pattison reminds readers that "humanitarian intervention is *only one part* of the doctrine of the responsibility to protect, but . . . it *is* part of the responsibility to protect."[75] Indeed.

The responsibility to protect has firmly taken root in today's international normative landscape – Chris Brown argues that

"it has driven out other vocabularies."[76] This normative reality leads us to trace its move from the prose and passion of
a blue-ribbon commission toward the international public
policy agenda. Perhaps most importantly in terms of decisions, as of July 2015 the Security Council had referred to R2P
in 37 resolutions – all except 5 were agreed after Libya – and
the Human Rights Council 13 resolutions.[77] David Rieff was
surely wrong to declare *resquiescat in pace.*[78] These numbers
alone suggest "that R2P is not about to die," as Alex Bellamy
notes. "Indeed, it is not even on life support."[79]

Mustering the cross-cultural political will to give concrete
and consistent protection to civilians is never going to be
easy, but Libya is pivotal for what Shannon Beebe and Mary
Kaldor call "human security intervention."[80] There will always
be acute dilemmas for humanitarians[81] and policymakers,
especially because of the lack of follow-up peacebuilding.
Combined with the Syrian disaster, future decision-making
about R2P's implementation could be even more problematic
than in the past. Historical perspective is in order. "Just as
any celebration about the triumph of the R2P principle would
have been premature after the Libyan resolutions in early
2011," cautions Gareth Evans, "so is it too early to despair now
about its future."[82]

However, the decibel level of claims will increase from
those naysayers who emphasize the potential of the responsibility to protect to backfire. Alan Kuperman, as we learned
in the previous chapter, argues that the mere expectation
of benefiting from possible outside "intervention" – and he
includes sanctions, embargoes, judicial pursuit, and military
force under this rubric – emboldens substate groups of rebels
either to launch or continue fighting, including the resort to
atrocities, so that a violent response from state authorities will
then spark international attention, perhaps even a military
intervention.[83] One of the more balanced critics, Roland Paris,

points to five "structural problems" that together constitute a seemingly unwinnable dilemma for R2P: mixed motives, counterfactual reasoning, conspicuous harm, end-state, and inconsistency.[84] However, they are hardly new; in fact, we have encountered all these problems previously and would encounter them in the use of military force in any context. As Ramesh Thakur points out in a lengthy criticism: "The choice therefore is not if intervention, but whether the intervention will be ad hoc or rules based, unilateral or multilateral, and divisive or consensual."[85]

International mumbling has possibly affected calculations by local militias and elites, even causing them to take action that perhaps has had the effect, intended and unintended, of prolonging the violence. But does this mean that robust humanitarianism is destined to constitute a genuine moral hazard? There might be a problem were there an insurance policy for humanitarians as there is for banks, which permits the latter to be reckless with other people's money. But there is no such global life insurance policy; surely all dissenters and rebels in Libya as well as Syria and Yemen understand that humanitarian talk is cheap. Is there a danger of too much military humanitarianism? Hardly. Political will remains problematic, and the threshold for military intervention high – not merely the existence of substantial human rights abuses, but crimes of a mass nature such as genocide, war crimes, crimes against humanity, and ethnic cleansing. That military force for human protection purposes remains a policy option at all, however, represents significant new middle ground in international relations.

Ramesh Thakur and this author were on target when we wrote that R2P's cumulative impact was "the most dramatic normative development of our time."[86] And new thinking was an essential contribution to this reality.

CHAPTER FIVE

So What? Moving from Rhetoric to Reality

The essential challenges of humanitarian intervention are not normative but, rather, operational. What political realities stand in the way of making R2P a reality – of turning "here we go again" into a genuine "never again," the fervent battle cry that resulted from the Holocaust of World War II? Constraints are certainly not in short supply, and five crucial ones are discussed here that act as a drag on humanitarian intervention. The first is that many developing countries are still concerned that R2P can be used to conceal the imperial designs of western powers under the guise of "humanitarian" motives. This worldview was made more plausible, second, by the blowback from the war on terrorism and the *ex post facto* morphing of the justification for the war in Iraq as somehow a humanitarian undertaking.

The third constraint is crucial in explaining why the robust humanitarian intervention of the 1990s has not become fashionable in the second decade of the twenty-first century. The notion that human beings matter more than sovereignty radiated, albeit briefly, across the international political horizon until the United States tied down its military in Afghanistan and Iraq.[1] The political will, as well as operational capacity for humanitarian intervention, diminished afterward because the United States as the preponderant power is disinclined to commit significant political and military resources to human protection. Meanwhile, other states complain but do little.[2]

The fourth and fifth constraints complicate matters further

and reside on the ground in war zones where civilians come to the rescue. The nature of local war economies is a major threat to the humanitarian enterprise, which is deep in the throes of questioning its *raison d'être*.

R2P, a Trojan horse for the Non-Aligned Movement?

Students of history who recall the so-called humanitarian interventions of the nineteenth century will find understandable the substantial residue of visceral anticolonialism in the Third World. Commercial and geopolitical calculations were cloaked in the language of humanitarian and religious motives, with an overlay of paternalism. As a result, the doctrine was discredited among countries gaining independence from colonial rule, and something akin to this condemnation can also be seen as applying to the responsibility to protect.

Conditional sovereignty uncomfortably resurrects "standards of civilization" and "the white man's burden."[3] From this perspective, R2P has the potential to divide the world into "civilized" and "uncivilized" arenas and to promote a return to semicolonial practices in the latter. Powerful states can determine whose human rights justify ignoring the principle of nonintervention. Most importantly, the responsibility to protect can seem a euphemism for western hegemony.

We earlier encountered the moral plea from Kofi Annan that human rights transcended claims of sovereignty, along with its outright rejection by many UN member states. Some have argued that the erosion of the principle of nonintervention could lead to chaos: "The use of force as a sanction for a breach of an international obligation may do more harm than the breach of the international obligation; the cure is often worse than the disease."[4]

Readers should recall Kosovo, which highlighted the need

for guidelines when nonintervention is morally repugnant but the Security Council is paralyzed. What nature and gravity of threats justify external military intervention?[5] ICISS proffered its response, but controversy continues over conflicting principles that produce normative incoherence, inconsistency, and contestation.[6] The result has been political and military paralysis in the face of Syria's bloodbath.

Algerian president Abdelaziz Bouteflika's remarks, after Annan's justification of two sovereignties at the General Assembly in 1999, capture the Non-Aligned Movement's position:

> We do not deny that the United Nations has the right and the duty to help suffering humanity, but we remain extremely sensitive to any undermining of our sovereignty, not only because sovereignty is our last defence against the rules of an unequal world, but because we are not taking part in the decision-making process of the Security Council.[7]

Venezuela's president Hugo Chavez played the same broken record at the September 2005 World Summit when he argued that the R2P would serve the interests of the powerful by making it easier to intervene inside weak countries without necessarily increasing cooperation for humanitarian crises.[8] This position remained a constant four years later during the General Assembly dialogues on R2P.

The NAM – with more than 130 members, and arguably the most representative group of countries outside the UN itself – has publicly rejected "the right of humanitarian intervention," even if Africans on their own are usually seeking more outside intervention to halt humanitarian disasters and the African Union's Constitutive Act contains a bullish Article 4(h).[9] Developing countries are not alone in their recalcitrance. For example, American "sovereigntists" launched three lines of counterattack: the emerging international legal order is vague and illegitimately intrusive on domestic affairs;

the international lawmaking process is unaccountable, and the resulting law unenforceable; and Washington can opt out of international regimes as a matter of power, legal right, and constitutional duty.[10]

In the last chapter, we saw that, amidst modest achievements, the World Summit's endorsement of R2P, as well as the statements made during the General Assembly's annual interactive dialogues, suggest that consensus continues to grow. However, it is difficult to disagree with Alex Bellamy, whose characterization was cited earlier, that the September 2005 consensus was possible only by "watering down" ICISS's original version by emphasizing that the Security Council alone must act and that the host state had the primary responsibility to act, and also by implying a higher threshold of "manifest failure" than had been present in several actual interventions in the preceding 15 years.[11] In effect, advances in norms have not changed the obvious reality that it is political will and military capacity, not considerations of state sovereignty, that determine whether or not humanitarian intervention takes place. This was most clearly demonstrated in the asymmetrical actions taken by the Security Council in confronting crises in Libya and Côte d'Ivoire in early 2011 and by the subsequent and continuing inability to stand up to the Syrian government's attacks on unarmed protestors.

We also encountered Brazil's effort to bridge the chasm between R2P's opponents and proponents. "Responsibility while protecting" enjoyed a short moment in the UN's limelight, but it disappeared with the change of the foreign minister (Antonio Patriota) who had been its champion.

Where does that leave us? David Rieff wonders whether the revolution of moral concern "has actually kept a single jackboot out of a single human face."[12] My own somber lament is that there still is appallingly sparse responsibility to protect those suffering from atrocities – unhumanitarian nonintervention. Or, as the moral philosopher Michael Walzer echoed, "It is more often the case that powerful states don't do enough, or don't do anything at all, in response to desperate need than that they respond in imperialist ways."[13]

The reticence, and in some cases hostility, of some developing countries toward humanitarian intervention is an important explanation. But this is unlikely to disappear as long as inconsistency and disingenuousness continue to characterize western responses to humanitarian catastrophes. This reality represents as great a threat to international society and global justice as preemptive or preventive war.

Recent research undertaken by scholars and activists of the global South, and more specifically from countries that have experienced violence and mass atrocities, suggests that there is a firm grounding of R2P norms in the diverse cultures in the global South. The research embodied in *The Responsibility to Protect: Cultural Perspectives in the Global South* is a small first step toward probing the normative underpinnings of R2P in the spiritual, philosophical, and aesthetic dimensions of southern cultures.[14] Further steps and dialogues among scholars, practitioners, and decision-makers within the global South and between North and South are needed to continue to advance the R2P doctrine in practice and in theory.

9/11 and the war on terror

Conventional wisdom now holds that terrorism and the attacks on US territory of September 2001 brought a paradigm change in international relations. It has become equally commonplace to hear that the UN is at a crossroads. Speaking before the General Assembly in September 2003, the secretary-general stated that the world organization was at a "fork in the road ... no less decisive than 1945 itself, when the United Nations was founded."[15]

The UN's credibility and legitimacy were the subjects of considerable debate well before 9/11. Selectivity and double standards in Security Council decisions about which conflicts warranted a response, for example, contributed to a sense that this UN organ was simply a conduit for western security interests. Why persist in Bosnia and withdraw from Rwanda? Why commit so fully to Kosovo and not to Sudan or the DRC? While few would make the ideal the enemy of the good – by insisting that humanitarian intervention must occur whenever and wherever a crisis exists, or not take place at all – nonetheless too much and too blatant inconsistency tarnishes the UN's reputation as an honest broker.

The trumpeting of self-defense by the United States as a response to 9/11 was understandable, and even approved by the Security Council for the military response against Afghanistan. However, that blanket authorization can now be seen as a prelude to the Bush administration's determination to take on Iraq with or without Security Council approval. Indeed, consensus building around R2P must be seen in this context. In 2003, the UN was sidelined in the war against Iraq. Everyone was unhappy – the UN could not impede US hegemony, and the UN could not approve requisite action against Saddam Hussein.

Many countries, in Europe and in the Third World, are unwilling to accept any use of military force that is not approved by the Security Council – not even for humanitarian or human rights purposes, let alone preemptive or preventive war. The logic is straightforward: the authority of the international political process, however flawed, is at least regulated internationally by the principles of the UN Charter. Setting aside agreed procedures, as NATO did in Kosovo and especially as Washington and London did in Iraq, could weaken or even destroy a tenuous but nonetheless essential rule governing international society.[16]

The wars in Iraq and on terror had three stifling effects on necessary normative conversations about actionable triggers (or criteria) in the General Assembly.[17] First, the selective use of the Security Council was compounded by Washington's and London's decisions to go to war against Iraq in March 2003 without Security Council approval after having assiduously sought it. Indeed, this was a conversation stopper for many when considering any loosening of criteria for intervention or setting aside the principle of nonintervention in the face of mass atrocity crimes.

Second, the legitimate idea of humanitarian intervention was contaminated by association with George W. Bush's and Tony Blair's spurious and largely *ex post facto* "humanitarian" justifications for invading Iraq. These disingenuous rationalizations were "difficult to reconcile with international law."[18] In a widely cited speech to his Sedgefield constituency in March 2004, Prime Minister Blair provided the clearest and most worrisome example of the potential for unilaterally abusing R2P when he applied it retroactively to Iraq: "But we surely have a duty and a right to prevent the threat materializing; and we surely have a responsibility to act when a nation's people are subjected to a regime such as Saddam's."[19] Fernando Tesón's judgments about the use of force for humanitarian purposes are usually apt, but his efforts to rationalize the end of Saddam Hussein's tyranny in such terms were implausible and erroneous.[20] Terry Nardin correctly commented that such "rationales strain the traditional understanding."[21]

It was thus harder in the second decade of the twenty-first century than at the beginning to gainsay those who are reluctant to codify norms about using military force for human protection purposes. The Bush and Blair doctrine was considered such a powerful threat as to require *renewing* the principle of nonintervention rather than any downgrading of sovereign prerogatives, even for a humanitarian rationale.

The *National Security Strategy of the United States of America*,[22] unveiled in September 2002, circumscribed discussions about using force. The Bush doctrine "had the effect of reinforcing fears both of US dominance and of the chaos that could ensue if what is sauce for the US goose were to become sauce for many other would-be interventionist ganders," wrote Adam Roberts.

> One probable result of the enunciation of interventionist doctrines by the USA will be to make states even more circumspect than before about accepting any doctrine, including on humanitarian intervention or on the responsibility to protect, that could be seen as opening the door to a general pattern of interventionism.[23]

The election of Barack Obama in 2008, however, attenuated momentarily some fears. His administration's renewed rhetorical commitment to multilateralism and re-engagement with the UN Human Rights Council, for example, helped undo the damage caused by the Bush administration. Security Council decisions under Chapter VII and action for human protection purposes in Libya and Côte d'Ivoire in early 2011 are additional illustrations. The premature award of the Nobel Peace Prize in 2009 was a high point of hope. Thereafter, domestic problems, Congressional gridlock, and the Democratic Party's drubbing in the 2012 elections made multilateralism a very second-order priority.

Third, the process of moving the General Assembly toward clarifying and agreeing on the criteria for intervention stalled. The atmosphere was simply too poisonous after the US and UK's blatant disregard for diplomacy in cavalierly using humanitarian vocabulary to justify their actions when other justifications evaporated.

The war in Iraq was without council approval and definitely has not improved the overall humanitarian situation on the ground, which remains tenuous. Indeed, over a decade after the ousting of Hussein's regime, the country remains unstable and turmoil-ridden. In the aftermath, Iraq's civilian populations continued to endure daily violence on a scale unknown under the Hussein regime prior to the invasion. Although civilian fatalities are highly disputed, actual reported deaths number about 150,000,[24] with many more not officially recorded. Indeed, one organization estimated Iraqi civilian fatalities at 865,000 in August 2010,[25] and countless have been injured since the March 2003 invasion.[26]

If R2P's "just cause thresholds" (and here the notion of criteria are pertinent) could have justified humanitarian intervention in 1999 in Kosovo, would not the same logic apply to Saddam Hussein's regime, whose history was certainly as ugly as Slobodan Milošević's? The just cause threshold could arguably have been invoked for Iraq, but it was not before the resort to force, and certainly was a minor factor in the decision to attack. Indeed, that human rights and human dignity were under assault during the Hussein period cannot be disputed. As such, the mass atrocity crime threshold might well have been invoked in March 1988 – when Saddam used chemical weapons against the Kurdish city of Halabja in northern Iraq, instantly killing 5,000 civilians – or on other occasions in the 1990s. And in the run-up to the March 2003 war, only the most perfunctory of references were made. Thus, the use of "humanitarian" has the hollow ring of rationalization after the fact, and after the earlier justifications – mainly weapons of mass destruction and links to Al Qaeda – proved vacuous.

It is more doubtful still that the other criteria could have been satisfied: right intention, last resort, proportional means, reasonable prospects, and right authority. Moreover, the primary purpose of the war in Iraq was the pursuit of geopolitical interests, while halting human suffering was at most an afterthought. There remains a question about whether reasonable nonmilitary options had been exhausted and whether the means were proportional (some 12,950 Iraqis were killed during the initial invasion, including 3,750 noncombatants[27]). Determining whether the consequences of the war are worse than inaction will require waiting to see how long the postwar misery lasts and on the future shape of Iraq. The disintegration of the country and the division between Shi'as and Sunnis does not augur well. And the control by ISIS of areas gives real pause especially because of the media-savvy use of atrocities against Yazidis, Shi'as, and even moderate Sunnis.

But most important, even if the five previous criteria had been met, which clearly they were not, ICISS emphasized just authority, which preferably means an overwhelming show of support from the Security Council or at least from a regional organization. Dissent within the council about the war in Iraq, and indeed across the planet, was far more visible than was the case for Kosovo or Libya. In withdrawing the resolution to authorize military force against Iraq in March 2003, Washington and London were not even assured a simple majority, and were also confronting three vetoes. In Kosovo, there were three negative votes and two vetoes in the offing. Moreover, there was not unanimous approval for the Iraq campaign from a 19-member regional body as there had been for Kosovo – in fact, both NATO and the European Union were split on the Iraq war between the "old" and "new" Europe. And all the regional organizations in the geographic area covered by the crisis were categorically against the war. In short, the "coalition" in Iraq was not legitimately constituted in any meaningful way, nor was the decision to wage war genuinely multilateral. Widespread international backing, let alone right authority, was conspicuously absent. Military intervention for human protection purposes using the framework spelled out in *The Responsibility to Protect* is one thing; military intervention for preventive war is quite another. The world requires capabilities to come to the rescue of vulnerable peoples, not fuzzy applications of legitimate concepts to obfuscate more sinister motivations.

Countries that earlier would have supported the R2P concept have on occasion subsequently been reluctant or hostile toward unilateral humanitarian intervention (that is, outside Security Council decision-making). As a result, "the Iraq war has undermined the standing of the United States and the UK as norm carriers . . . [and] the process of normative change is likely to be slowed or reversed."[28] One specific illustration took place immediately after the so-called victory in the Iraq war. At the July 13–14, 2003 Progressive Governance Summit of left-of-center government leaders, Canadian prime minister Jean Chrétien and British prime minister Tony Blair at first sought to quote ICISS's basic principles in the draft communiqué and to seek support for a continued discussion at the United Nations. When Argentina, Chile, and Germany strongly objected, a supportive passage was removed.

This reluctance even among countries that were previously counted among R2P's friends has not disappeared in UN corridors. The world's worst apprehensions regarding US military activism were rekindled by the Iraq crisis and confirmed by Blair's and Bush's attempts to twist the concept of the responsibility to protect. Is humanitarian intervention a convenient sleight of hand to conceal hidden – and in the case of Iraq, not so hidden – Western agendas? Would even enthusiasts now push for a doctrine that hinted at unauthorized humanitarian intervention, which could then provide a justification after the fact for the use of force in Iraq?

Such apprehensions were hardly assuaged as mainstream American academics pointed to the ethical underpinnings of preemptive and even preventive war. Extending R2P to prevention, Lee Feinstein and Anne-Marie Slaughter argued for a new "duty to prevent," while Allan Buchanan and Robert Keohane called for the "cosmopolitan" use of preventive military force.[29] The inevitable overextension of R2P was made by the Naval War College's Thomas Nichols:

> The Westphalian notion of sovereignty has already been breached by the necessity for humanitarian intervention, and now the international community must take the next step and legitimize action not only to prevent terrible regimes from annihilating their own people but also to coordinate preventive action against such regimes when they seek to undermine international order.[30]

According to Ivo Daalder and James Steinberg, the conditional terms of sovereignty include preventing not only genocide but also terrorism, the spread of weapons of mass destruction, and diseases. "It would be unfortunate," they concluded, "if President Bush's doctrine of preemption were a casualty of the Iraq war."[31]

The fallout from Iraq was immediately obvious and continues: humanitarian intervention and even R2P were no longer, Stephen Pinker notwithstanding,[32] on the side of the angels for fear that such notions could be manipulated to conceal imperialist agendas. The debate within the United Nations over the war in Iraq was at least as much about American power and its role in the world as about the risks posed by Iraq's disdain for UN resolutions and the search for weapons of mass destruction. UN diplomats almost unanimously described the debate surrounding the resolution withdrawn on the eve of the war in Iraq as "a referendum not on the means of disarming Iraq but on the American use of power."[33] It is to this challenge that we now turn.

The preoccupied and overstretched remaining superpower

Terrorism, and UN responses to it, reveal and accentuate the implications of the post-Cold War reality of an international

system based on a sole military superpower. The preponder-
ance of the United States represents a serious threat to the
health of the United Nations, particularly when the incumbent
regime goes into "unilateralist overdrive,"[34] as it was during
the George W. Bush administration. Throughout these pages,
a frequent refrain with both positive and negative implications for international society has been the role of the United
States. When the members of ICISS met in 2001 with French
foreign minister Hubert Védrine, they failed to appreciate his
apt depiction of American preeminence, *hyper-puissance*. On
the one hand, major power politics have always dominated the
United Nations and other international organizations. The
bitter East–West divide of the Cold War and the North–South
clashes of the 1960s and the 1970s provide extensive evidence
for this reality. On the other hand, there is no modern precedent for the current dimensions of the US goliath.

What exactly is the meaning of a collective security organization in a world so dominated by US power? Political scientists
who examine the United States are aware of the implications
for international institutions.[35] A dictionary, however, does
not define "hegemony" only in pejorative terms. Another
connotation is that the strongest member exerts natural leadership within a confederation – for example, it is an analytical
focus of political scientists who see "hegemonic stability"
as a necessary and desirable element in international political economy. First put forward by Charles Kindleberger in
the 1970s and developed by such analysts as Robert Gilpin
afterward, the theory points to the benefits of an open and
stable world economy of having one country dominate so that
others can feel secure enough to open their markets and avoid
beggar-thy-neighbor policies.[36] Indeed, many Americans and
non-Americans have often regretted the lack of US leadership and wished for more initiatives like those during World
War II and in the lead-up to the signing of the Charter in San

Francisco. The defeat of fascism was one result and the construction of multilateral institutions as the basis for peace and
prosperity was another.[37]

Washington's multilateral record in the twentieth century
conveys "mixed messages," as Edward Luck reminds us. The
United States has sometimes been the prime mover for new
international institutions and norms, but just as often has
kept a distance or stood in the way.[38] This historical pattern is
not about to change. In the past, Washington was careful and
somewhat reluctant to thumb its nose openly. The argument
was that American "exceptionalism" was, well, exceptional
– that is, to be saved for an unusual set of events when international cooperation was simply out of the question. The Bush
administration, by contrast, was committed to exceptionalism
as a routine, the normal bill of fare whether the context was
terrorism or the Kyoto Protocol, the ban on anti-personnel
land mines or the International Criminal Court.[39]

At the same time, the Bush administration provides an
anomalous contrast to the image and the actions of the previous administration's "assertive multilateralism." The Clinton
administration's missile strikes against Afghanistan and
Sudan in 1998 were launched without recourse to the United
Nations. In contrast, the Bush administration went immediately to the world organization after September 11. It also
persisted with protracted and difficult negotiations in the
Security Council on resolution 1411 in November 2002. While
it proceeded to war in the following March without the council's approval, it returned at several junctures to seek help with
the internationalization of the much contested occupation
that was an increasing political liability – in May for resolution 1483, in November for resolution 1511, and early in 2004
for help in finding a formula to identify an acceptable Iraqi
sovereign before June 30.

Scholars speculate about the nuances of economic and

cultural leverage resulting from US soft power, but the hardest currency in the international system remains military might. Before the war in Iraq, the "hyper-power" was already spending more on its military than the next 15–25 countries combined (depending on who was counting). With additional appropriations for Afghanistan and Iraq, Washington was spending more than the rest of the world's militaries combined.[40] Despite recent adjustments downwards the situation remains skewed in the western alliance – during the Cold War, the United States contributed about 50 percent of total military expenditures, whereas, since then, Washington's tab has been closer to 75 percent, which is also its contribution to total NATO expenditures. And even in the domain of soft power, the United States remains without challenge on the world stage for the foreseeable future, although some analysts see hegemony as more western than American.[41]

Even so, downsizing the armed forces in the post-Cold War era means an insufficient supply of equipment and manpower to meet the demands for humanitarian intervention. There are bottlenecks in the US logistics chain – especially in airlift capacity – that make improbable a rapid international response to a fast-moving, Rwanda-like genocide. With the US army still mired down in the aftermath of Iraq and Afghanistan and numerous reserves overseas, questions are being raised about the capacity to respond adequately to a serious national security threat or a natural disaster like Hurricane Katrina, let alone "distractions" like Liberia or Haiti. The Obama administration's outright decision of only "days not weeks" of air strikes and no boots on the ground in Libya illustrates the evident effects of such overstretch on humanitarian intervention. And the planning capacity of 1.5 instead of 2 wars promises to degrade US readiness still further.

Mass starvation, rape, and suffering continue in a post-9/11 world. For at least some conscience-shocking cases of mass suffering, there will simply be no viable alternative to military coercion for human protection purposes. The prediction that major powers other than the United States would not respond with military force to a new humanitarian emergency after September 11 proved somewhat too pessimistic. France led a European Union force into Ituri in summer 2003 and halted an upsurge of ethnic violence, which suggested to Washington that the EU could act outside the continent independently of NATO. This proposition was perhaps strengthened by Europe's takeover from NATO of the Bosnia operation in December 2004, the deployment of troops to the DRC for elections in July 2006, NATO's command of the air strikes in Libya in early 2011, and the assistance of French troops in ending the crisis in Côte d'Ivoire and taking the lead in Mali and the CAR.[42] These efforts provide a faint hope that an EU security identity could underpin a more operational responsibility to protect in circumscribed humanitarian crises of limited duration.

Europeans should share more of the burden of humanitarian boots-on-the-ground even if US air-lift capacity, military muscle, and technology are required for larger and longer-duration deployments. The imposition of the no-fly zone in Libya demonstrated once again that, for better or worse, the United States in the Security Council, as elsewhere, is what former secretary of state Dean Rusk once described as the fat boy in the canoe: "When we roll, everyone rolls with us."[43] Even after Washington began playing what was billed as a secondary role, NATO allies had to rely on American Airborne Early Warning and Control and refueling airplanes, as well as intelligence gathering and suppression of air defenses. With Washington's focus and equipment elsewhere, the danger is not too much but, rather, too little military humanitarianism.

Upgrading African capacities is a very long-term undertaking. The bullish Article 4(h) of the AU's Constitutive Act
provides for intervention in grave circumstances, but is as yet
unused.[44] In the near term, unless European and other populations support higher expenditures on their armed forces,
there is little alternative to the overworked global policeman.
Hence, we will have the kind of deployments for human protection purposes that we have seen since 1999, namely few
and far between.

US military power makes for an unusual multilateral
moment with implications for humanitarian intervention
as for other international decisions. There are two "world
organizations." The United Nations is global in membership, but the United States is global in reach and power.
American unilateralism in the early twenty-first century is
hardly new, and this reality creates acute difficulties for prin-
cipled multilateralists. For example, UN-led or UN-approved
operations with substantial military requirements take place
only when Washington approves, or at least acquiesces. For
other issues, moving ahead without the United States is problematic, although experiments are under way – for example,
the 1998 Rome Statute establishing the ICC and the 1997
Convention on the Prohibition of the Use, Stockpiling,
Production and Transfer of Anti-Personnel Mines and their
Destruction.

Departing US secretary of defense Robert Gates seized the
occasion of his mid-2011 *au revoir* in Brussels to lambaste
Washington's closest allies. He stated that the United States
had a "dwindling appetite"[45] to finance three-quarters of
the Western defense budget—an accurate metaphor for the
approach that had nourished American diplomacy toward
European freeriding since the end of World War II. In an
unusually undiplomatic speech, his valedictory visit to Europe
provided Gates with the opportunity to bluntly condemn

ongoing European defense cuts. Rather than a dividend for
the United Nations, Washington was seeking more European
participation in combat missions and peace operations –
non-UN as well as UN – from those who, in another sound
bite from Gates, "don't want to share the risks and the costs."
The mobilization in the corridors of the NATO summit in
Wales of a "core coalition" against ISIS was encouraging,
whereas the failure to agree on binding commitments by
individual countries to reach the defense spending target –
rather just to stop cutting and spend more in real terms – was
discouraging.

Whether the US presence and military power are overrated
and will wane in the coming decades remains to be seen.
Even if, as Joseph Nye claims, "the world's only superpower
can't go it alone,"[46] US power is likely to dominate future
UN affairs.[47] There is no danger that any US administration
would permit the UN or any other international institutions
to stand in the way of pursuing vital national interests for very
long. If "unilateralism and multilateralism are best understood as two ends of a continuum,"[48] would it not be more
profitable to identify the types of strategic considerations and
substantive issues that might optimize prospects for "tactical
multilateralism"?[49]

Conservative American pundits often overlook how the
UN system serves American interests and gives Washington
cause to proceed with international acquiescence, if not jubi-
lant support. The late Ted Sorensen, a former speechwriter
for President John F. Kennedy, asked: "What is more unrealistic than to believe that this country can unilaterally decide
the fate of others, without a decent respect for the opinions of
mankind, or for the judgment of world institutions and our
traditional allies?"[50] Princeton University's John Ikenberry
pointed to a striking irony: "The worst unilateral impulses
coming out of the Bush administration [were] so harshly

criticized around the world because so many countries have accepted the multilateral vision of international order that the United States has articulated over most of the twentieth century."[51]

The sobering experiences in occupied Afghanistan and Iraq have highlighted the limits of sheer military power. Postwar (if that is the term) Iraq has demonstrated that recovery, reconstruction, and rebuilding are not US strong suits. Meanwhile, the UN has accumulated substantial experience over several decades, and this comparative advantage makes its new Peacebuilding Commission sensible. Former US assistant secretary of state James Dobbins and a Rand Corporation evaluation team have argued that the world organization's performance in post-conflict situations is remarkably good by comparison with Washington's – they attribute success to seven out of eight UN operations versus only four out of eight for the United States.[52]

Moreover, most Americans would acknowledge that when it comes to spotting, warning, and managing international health hazards – Ebola, the severe acute respiratory syndrome (SARS), avian flu, and AIDS perennially – the World Health Organization is indispensable. Monitoring international crime statistics and narcotics, policing nuclear proliferation, and numerous other global oversight functions are properly based within the UN system.

The reality of US power means that, if the UN and multilateral cooperation are to have a chance of working, let alone flourishing, the globe's remaining superpower must be on board. The United States raced to be the first country to ratify the UN Charter, winning Senate approval on July 28, 1945, barely a month after the ink dried on the signatures on the Charter of the 50 countries present in San Francisco. The United States was as preponderant on the world stage then as it is now.

Looking back on that "remarkable generation of leaders and public servants," Brian Urquhart remembers: "They were pragmatic idealists more concerned about the future of humanity than the outcome of the next election; and they understood that finding solutions to postwar problems was much more important than being popular with one or another part of the American electorate."[53] Could that same far-sighted political commitment not dawn again?

War economies, spoilers, and privatization

Another crucial drag on the current international system's capacity to engage in humanitarian intervention is the nature of local war economies accompanied by spoilers and privatization.[54] Earlier, in the discussion of new wars and new humanitarianisms, a dominant theme was the prevalence of nonstate actors of various shapes, sizes, and sensibilities. Here, it is essential to unpack further the distinctive challenges for aid agencies and outside military forces that result when prevailing economic interests are better served by continuing violence than by ending war. "Spoilers"[55] – so-called because they seek to prevent turning a page on armed conflict and thus foster war – are perhaps better described as "war entrepreneurs," and have been present in previous armed conflicts. But the current generation is more numerous and better equipped to wreak havoc. The synergy of local and global economic conditions coupled with relatively inexpensive arms allows NSAs to assemble military capacity without much difficulty or investment.

Laurent Kabila was reported to have quipped that all that was required in (then) Zaire to have an "army" was $10,000 and a cell phone. Aid agencies and foreign militaries face a steep learning curve in negotiating access in such contexts. Reflection is more valuable than visceral reactions.

Humanitarian impulses and goodwill simply are no longer adequate, if indeed they ever were.

It would be useful here to revisit the two general types of economies that influence war and humanitarian action. First are "war economies," or those interests that directly profit from armed conflict. In his farewell speech in 1961, US president Dwight D. Eisenhower warned, "We need to guard against the acquisition of unwarranted influence ... by the 'military-industrial complex.'"[56] The new wars do not operate with the sophistication or technology of the US military-industrial complex, but a network of economically calculating actors profit from the production of violence. The second type that circumscribes humanitarian action is that of "aid economies" or interests that benefit from the provision of external assistance.

International efforts to thwart war economies follow two tracks, controlling means and ends. The former seeks to prevent or limit economically based actors from developing their ability to wage war. Examples are international efforts to restrict the spread of small arms and regulations to ban mercenaries. Several studies have spotlighted the former,[57] and numerous groups work to limit the production and distribution of these weapons by targeting arms sales.

Impeding or stopping the use of mercenaries is also crucial but less prevalent in analyses of intervening in new wars, where commercially inspired military actors have become standard players. Bad memories in the Third World have shaped perceptions of guns for hire, and international bodies have taken action: Article 47 of Additional Protocol I to the Geneva Conventions of 1977, the 1977 Convention for the Elimination of Mercenarism in Africa, and the 1989 UN Convention against the Recruitment, Use, Financing and Training of Mercenaries. The UN has also created the position of a special rapporteur to monitor developments. Despite bans, mercenaries have appeared throughout the world, mostly in Africa but also in the Balkans, Latin America, and Southeast Asia.

A different type of hired gun, contemporary private military companies (PMCs), is also crucial to the dynamics of the new wars. The war zones with PMCs are usually those in which international humanitarian law has been ignored by belligerents – for example, PMCs have had sizeable operations in such diverse sites as Sierra Leone, Bougainville, and Borneo.[58] The distinctions between "guns for hire" by aid agencies and by political-military actors are important,[59] but the larger issue is the presence of mercenaries in Afghanistan and Iraq on a scale not previously seen. The 20,000–25,000 private soldiers in Iraq in 2006 outnumbered the second largest national contingent, the United Kingdom's, by at least three to one. The 2015 conviction of several Blackwater employees for atrocities committed in Iraq was a reminder that such hires are not a guarantee of professionalism.

The second track seeks to regulate the resources over which new wars are waged. The UN has emphasized the role of plundered natural resources, particularly in Africa.[60] Natural resources used to be considered a blessing. But this truism has been called into question because a large variety of lootable resources – gold, silver, coltan, timber, copper, titanium, and diamonds – often sustain contemporary wars. As diamonds were the first resources to garner attention, it is worth noting progress since the early 1990s to regulate "blood diamonds."[61] Codes of conduct are becoming important in the industry. NGOs, such as Global Witness, have put pressure on it to accept regulation and clamp down on illicit trade responsible for fueling wars.[62] These efforts have led to broader efforts to regulate "conflict resources" pertaining to agricultural commodities and mineral deposits that often finance civil wars. Experts have long been aware of the links

between predation of natural resources and financing violence, but efforts to control such economies are becoming
more widespread.

Powerful external commercial interests that are vital to
national economic development – such as oil, mining, and
timber companies – can sometimes constitute additional
obstacles to relief efforts or even spark conflicts that trigger
humanitarian crises. Foreign oil companies in Africa alone
– their hands in the "scorched earth" of southern Sudan,
the charged ethnic environment of the delta in Nigeria, and
deposits that funded guerrillas and governments in Angola –
demonstrate their significance. Mining interests in the DRC,
Sierra Leone, and Indonesia typify how large multinational
corporations become powerbrokers in resource-rich countries. While oil represents the most substantial loot, other
natural resources provide substantial funds – illicit diamonds
in Angola are believed to generate some $700 million per
year, and in Sierra Leone probably $350 million.[63]

The focus of predators in aid economies is on benefiting not
so much from violence as from the generosity to relieve suffering. Aid can facilitate exploitation by greedy middlemen,
speculation, and hoarding, as well as generate conditions conducive to breeding future resentments and exacerbating local
tensions. Furthermore, outside aid can also be a disincentive
to indigenous capacity building.

Among humanitarians, the response to the new landscape
has been a modified Hippocratic Oath. Ignoring or eroding
local capacities, long a theme in the work of Mary Anderson,[64]
has led to the adoption of "do-no-harm" criteria. The idea is
to carry out emergency efforts to improve the ability of communities and public authorities to take control of their own
destinies, begin development, and react better to future
disasters – all of which is easier said than done.

Local commercial interests are pivotal in shaping the

operating environment for aid agencies. Merchants and traders are stakeholders in the price of basic commodities, which
can be undermined by the availability of relief goods in local
markets. Private sector providers of veterinary medicine, vac-
cinations and health care, agricultural supplies, and even
potable water see profits dwindle when aid agencies provide
goods for free. An astute measure in Somalia in 1993 was to
make foodstuffs available commercially rather than as grants,
which forced hoarders to dump their commodities and enticed
legitimate traders back into business,[65] thereby helping to
build the basis for development rather than dependency.
Well-intentioned relief can make enemies of legitimate local
businesspeople, prompting them to sabotage wells, drive food
convoys away, or even incite violence against aid agencies.

A related group of potentially problematic actors consists
of employment seekers. In many crises, external aid agencies constitute virtually the entire monetized sector. Drivers
working for external agencies can earn many multiples of
the salaries of senior government officials, highlighting the
skewed incentives in aid economies. When hiring procedures
are perceived as unfair, spurned applicants can confront aid
agencies. Local staff who are fired or whose contracts are
not renewed can themselves become a security problem.
These individuals tend to be the greatest threat when scarce
resources or other frustrations lead them to join a militarized
faction, but they can also present a challenge on purely economic grounds. Other negative factors for the local economy
include skyrocketing rents and inflation, prostitution, and
parallel markets.

To add to the list of possible woes, aid agencies have also
been criticized as the primary beneficiaries of aid. Alex de
Waal and Michael Maren stridently criticize outside humanitarian agencies as enriching themselves from the needs of
local populations on the dole.[66] MSF's Jean-Hervé Bradol

notes that "aid agencies [are] ever sensitive to the preservation and growth of their budgets."[67] Mark Duffield goes a step further and points to the needs of western aid agencies to continue to have wars as part of a new international political economy, which Naomi Klein labels "disaster capitalism."[68]

Although an in-depth analysis suggests that the economic impact of peacekeeping has been largely positive, nonetheless aid operations "are regularly criticized for a wide array of damage they are thought to do to the war-torn economies into which they deploy."[69] And whatever the quantitative data show, symbolically, when salaries, transportation, equipment, housing, insurance, and security rival the aid delivered, or international aid workers live lives of luxury next door to feeble shanties and squalid refugee camps, the humanitarian enterprise tarnishes its reputation.

The economies of war and of aid suggest the uncertain terrain on which aid workers tread while trying to help, and the complications are often especially acute after a military intervention. These elements were not unknown in earlier armed conflicts, but the magnitude of outside aid and a globalizing world economy create an unusual witches' brew in contemporary wars.

A humanitarian identity crisis

The expansion of the international humanitarian system – not only in terms of resources and actors, but also in the scope of tasks – was central to the earlier discussion of new humanitarianisms. The transformation of the sector has entailed substantial costs as well as benefits. Indeed, many practitioners are worried that humanitarianism as they have known it is under threat. There have been many more questions than answers about the nature of new wars and the actual results from new strategies and tactics guiding humanitarians. For example, if they are less effective than commercial alternatives, Stephen Hopgood asks, should we be saying "no" to Wal-Mart's encroachment on humanitarian jurisdiction?[70] If the industry were not a century and a half old, we might describe the present situation as a "mid-life crisis."

For the last two decades, humanitarian agencies have careened from one emergency to another. After barely recovering from Operation Lifeline Sudan in the late 1980s, the post-Cold War world promised a kinder, gentler 1990s, with more space for their action. But instead, humanitarians have confronted nearly unimaginable challenges, which means – as Michael Barnett and I have argued – that humanitarians are called upon to go "where angels fear to tread."[71] Some of these spectacles made front-page news and profiled heroic and not so heroic activities. In Somalia, humanitarians attempted to save hundreds of thousands from warlords who created a widening famine in order to attract food aid and feed ambitions. In Bosnia, they attempted to provide relief to those trapped in so-called safe havens – zones, resembling prisons, which were supposed to protect inhabitants from Serbian attacks but which were among the least safe places on the planet. In Rwanda, humanitarians were largely absent during the genocide itself, but began attempting to save millions of displaced people in camps militarized and controlled by the perpetrators of the mass murder. In Kosovo, Afghanistan, and Iraq, aid agency personnel were funded by and operated alongside invading and occupying soldiers, which meant that civilian helpers found themselves being treated as enemy combatants by insurgents. In addition to these high-profile disasters, there were so-called silent orphans in Pakistan, the DRC, northern Uganda, Chad, and Niger, which had their own brands of peculiar but thorny problems.

Twenty years of daunting challenges have compelled the members of the international humanitarian system to re-examine who they are, what they do, and how they do it. Questions that once essentially had ready-made replies, are now open for honest debate – indeed, must be interrogated. Perhaps the most gut-wrenching one is whether outside assistance actually helps or hinders conflict management. Good intentions clearly are no longer enough – if they ever were. The recognition that well-intentioned humanitarian action can lead to negative consequences has forced humanitarian organizations to measure their effectiveness. Such exercises require contemplating not only the values that motivate actions but also the consequences. "Accountability" has become a buzz-word, and Janice Stein reminds us that we need much better data and thinking, because it is not easy to answer "why, to whom, for what, and how?"[72]

These debates reflect a humanitarian enterprise in considerable flux – some would say in a full-blown identity crisis. Driving the debate are differences over the value of military intervention. There is substantial disagreement about how humanitarian organizations should respond, with some insisting that they have to adapt, and others arguing that adaptations might change humanitarianism beyond recognition. Indeed, while some suggest that the sector has improved its ability to deliver relief and protect rights, others contend that humanitarianism is in crisis because it has lost its soul by compromising with and conforming to the new world order.[73]

The off-the-rack humanitarian suit (independence, neutrality, impartiality) may fit some, but certainly not all, contemporary armed conflicts. What, if any, are the binding principles of humanitarianism? Can the humanitarian system adapt to new wars and new terrains?

The objective is not to question the honorable motivations of those who have worked heroically over a century and a half, but rather to indicate how new wars can distort traditionally cast humanitarian efforts. New wars have not only led to multiple humanitarian crises of a magnitude and simultaneity that dwarf those of previous generations; they have also led to debates among humanitarians about their purposes and practices. Earlier humanitarian agencies faced some of the elements found in contemporary wars. For example, confusion over responsibility and access in internal as opposed to international wars was present in the US Civil War (1861–5). The 1949 extensions of the Geneva Conventions included non-international armed conflict and considered those in unrecognized governments or in resistance movements as subject to restrictions and protections.

The plethora of wars in the 1990s hastened a realization: that the expiry date had passed for the previous orientations of the international humanitarian system. The performance of agencies created anxiety and doubts. David Rieff correctly characterized the responses of the 1990s as "humanitarianism in crisis."[74]

A philosophical chasm is widening about the political implications of humanitarian action.[75] On one side are the "classicists," who continue to uphold the traditional guiding principles. On the other are the "solidarists," who side with selected victims, publicly confront hostile governments, advocate partisan public policies in donor states, attempt to skew the distribution of aid resources, and refuse to respect the sovereignty of states. Moreover, many no longer view humanitarianism as being limited to short-term emergency relief to war victims, because job descriptions now include such broader objectives as protecting human rights, promoting democracy, fostering development, and hastening peacebuilding.

For many at the latter end of the spectrum, humanitarianism is no longer viewed as "pure," and acceptance of neutrality, a cornerstone of humanitarianism, is seen as naive. Proponents believe that aid should not be merely palliative and given without regard to political context. Rather, it should be ameliorative and address structural problems that foment humanitarian crises in the first place. And, when possible, it should be conceived in such a way as to help cement peace processes.

Among the earliest and most dramatic instances of the division among humanitarians arose from the so-called French Doctors' Movement that emerged in the late 1960s war between Nigeria and its Igbo inhabitants in the oil-rich eastern province of Biafra.[76] A group of dissidents, led by Bernard Kouchner – later humanitarian minister in several socialist governments in France and also foreign minister as well as the UN's first special representative in Kosovo – refused to keep quiet about systematic slaughter. Rather than pretending that working on both sides was essential and that keeping quiet was an operational advantage, the dissidents publicized the plight of the Igbos and worked to help them and to isolate the federal government. They took issue with the ICRC's orthodoxy and formed Médecins Sans Frontières (MSF) in 1971. The rebellious organization was awarded the Nobel Peace Prize in 1999 – the ICRC, its disapproving parent, was so acknowledged in 1944 and 1963.

An even more controversial cleavage appeared between classicists and solidarists with the advent of the most obviously politicized strain of humanitarianism, involving the use of military force. The spread of new wars and massive crises in Africa and the Balkans spawned a hot topic: whether or not the use of force could legitimately be advocated on humanitarian grounds; and if so, whether its use did more harm than good for war victims.

Since the 1990s, the goalposts have moved on several occasions. The explosion of new wars spurred rethinking about independence, neutrality, and impartiality as well as the use of force. Some humanitarians espoused a more muscular stance and pushed for soldiers as "humanitarian warriors." At a minimum, most aid agencies took advantage of military action to secure humanitarian goals – but usually with a somewhat defensive and begrudging posture – as a last resort and for a limited time. However, as armed aid convoys and security for refugee camps became more common, and insecurity remained, some humanitarians supported the use of force to defeat militarily those who cause or worsen crises. Indeed, some "human rights hawks" called for outside soldiers to overthrow governments that violate the rights of their citizens and to transform afflicted states and societies. One Canadian study group went so far as to propose an NGO-supported intervention force because governments moved too slowly.[77] As we have seen, the use of private military companies by aid agencies reflects a similar realization and need for effective protection.

At the other end of the spectrum, classicists still often view military forces as the antithesis of true humanitarianism, or at least as wishful thinking without the presence of substantial national interests to stay the course – which are rarely in evidence. These dichotomous categories are designed to shed light on the nature of differences and do not necessarily describe the specific behavior of any agency at all times. What unites the classicists, however, is their worry about the "risk of being associated with a potentially unwelcome military force, and thereby losing the protective patina of neutrality."[78]

The value of a humanitarian veneer for the military – aptly labeled WHAM (winning hearts and minds) – was obvious when US secretary of state Colin Powell described NGOs in Iraq as a "force multiplier." He was even clearer later in the same speech when he noted that they were part of his "combat team."[79] As one military analyst notes, "In the wake of 9/11, some Western countries, especially the United States, have stressed the strategic and force-protection benefits of assistance and reconstruction as part of broader military strategies."[80]

Laura Hammond reminds us that the United States and its allies are quite aware of humanitarianism's potential to win "hearts and minds" in countries where their militaries are deployed, as well as to help persuade constituencies at home of the righteousness of the cause.[81] A distinction thus should be made, as above, between the legitimate use of military force to foster humanitarian values – with specific triggers, just war precautions, and right authority along the lines of R2P – and the illegitimate manipulation of humanitarian values to facilitate militarism and the pursuit of geopolitical interests.

The crises stemming from the new wars frame the peculiar international collective action problems facing the new humanitarianisms, but they encounter a very old problem – the fragmentation of the international humanitarian system. With no central power of the purse and no wherewithal to ensure compliance, it should come as no surprise that cohesive action in an atomized system is the exception rather than the rule. Cohesion is more necessary than ever, but remains unlikely.

The use of outside military forces for humanitarian intervention and peace enforcement felled barriers to entry for aid agencies. As a result, in the 1990s, a growing number of organizations became involved in active war zones – evidenced by the fact that in the immediate aftermath of the Rwandan genocide there were some 200 relief agencies, and even more in Kosovo, in what Ian Smillie and Larry Minear called "the humanitarian free-for-all."[82] There were fewer moving parts during the Cold War; "[t]he ICRC's and UN's monopoly on humanitarian action was broken by the mid-1990s," according to Joanna Macrae.[83] Global longitudinal data are lacking,[84] but a detailed survey of US-based private voluntary agencies suggests considerable growth over the last 75 years. Shortly after the start of World War II, the number of US-based organizations rose from 240 to 387, but the numbers dropped to 103 in 1946 and 60 in 1948. They rose steadily thereafter and reached 543 in 2005. The growth was especially dramatic from 1986 to 1994, when the number increased from 178 to 506.[85] There are currently at least 2,500 NGOs in the business, with about 260 being serious players.[86]

Not only has the total number increased but so too have the funds and market share of the largest. Specific emergencies account for spikes, and the numbers of people working in the NGO sector grew by 91 percent between 1997 and 2005. Already by 2001 the half dozen or so largest NGOs controlled between $2.5 billion and $3 billion, about half of global humanitarian assistance.[87] A little over a decade later, the total sum for international NGOs approached $3.5 billion, with probably an additional half-billion coming from national NGOs.[88] Overall, the international humanitarian system (including the UN system and the ICRC) experienced a 77 percent surge in personnel.[89]

Alongside the explosion of new NGOs, increased availability of humanitarian funding, and greater personnel presence, individual agencies are expanding the scope of their projects. The Office of the UN High Commissioner for Refugees was created to help displaced persons, but the bulk of UN agencies were founded to foster development.[90] However, they too are increasingly involved in relief, including the United Nations Development Programme (UNDP) and the World Bank, both of which have steadily expanded programming for disasters. Until recently, most UN specialized agencies had virtually nonexistent disaster programs, but have also decided to pursue available funding. Organizations that were once focused on a narrower range of activities are now active in many other domains, moving "upstream" (helping in the midst of war) and "downstream" (post-conflict peacebuilding and ultimately development). As a result, virtually no UN organizations or NGOs can be indifferent about creating more humanitarian space or the "scramble" for funds and turf because their business plans are built on continuing expansion.[91]

Another indicator of growth is the number of international and regional organizations whose primary responsibility is coordination, including the UN's Inter-Agency Standing Committee (IASC) and the Office for the Coordination of Humanitarian Affairs (OCHA). The same phenomenon exists for NGOs in the United States and Europe, including InterAction in Washington, DC, the International Council for Voluntary Action and Emergency Committee for Humanitarian Response in Geneva, and both the European Commission's Humanitarian Aid and Civil Protection department and the Voluntary Organizations in Cooperation in Emergencies in Brussels.

States, for-profit disaster firms, businesses, and foundations are also increasingly prominent contributors to humanitarian action. More and more governments are responding to disasters of all sorts. Whereas 16 states pledged their support to Bosnia in the mid-1990s, most from the West, a more diverse group of 73 attended the 2003 pledging conference in Madrid for Iraq, and 92 responded to the December 2004 tsunami. One overview summarized, "From as few as a dozen government financiers just over a decade ago, it is now commonplace to see 50 or 60 donor governments supporting a humanitarian response."[92]

Such non-western donors as China, Saudi Arabia, and India have accounted for up to 12 percent of official humanitarian assistance in a given year; and their influence in certain crises – for example, Afghanistan or Palestine – is significant. Most countries that are not members of the Organisation for Economic Co-operation and Development's Development

Assistance Committee concentrate on immediate neighbors; and the bulk of such assistance has traditionally emanated from the Gulf states. For many years, Saudi Arabia accounted for three-quarters of the non-OECD/DAC sum and was the third largest humanitarian donor,[93] and Turkey now is. Along with the United Arab Emirates and Kuwait, these states now contribute larger humanitarian resources than some of the smaller western countries.

We know little about whether nontraditional donors follow the major western states in their rationales for aid disbursements, their priorities and policy options, or their choices for response channels,[94] but they resemble their OECD counterparts in preferring bilateral aid to increase influence. Geopolitics trumps humanitarian values for nontraditional donors as well. For instance, non-DAC humanitarian funds increased dramatically from 2011 to 2012 as Turkey almost doubled its allocation and then doubled it again in 2013. Driven by neighboring Syria's refugees and disruption of its economy and domestic politics, Turkey's $1.6 billion made it the third largest country donor (after the United States and the United Kingdom) and the "most generous" in terms of a percentage of gross national income – Norway is the most generous in per capita terms.[95]

Moreover, NGOs are now major players. For instance, expenditures by MSF in 2007 were larger than Saudi Arabia's, while those by World Vision and Caritas outstripped all except four DAC donor countries.[96]

Nonetheless, the international humanitarian system remains essentially a North American and Western European enterprise, accounting for about $11 billion of the total of just over $12 billion of official humanitarian assistance in 2008.[97] In short, "It works wherever it can in international society but is not really owned by all of international society."[98]

Private contributions have increased, but the growth in

official (i.e., governmental) assistance has been most impressive. Between 1990 and 2000, aid levels rose nearly threefold, from $2.1 billion to $5.9 billion – and in 2005–6 amounted to over $10 billion.[99] In the last year for which data are available, 2014, the best "guesstimate" was a total of some $18.7 billion, up about $3.5 billion from the previous year.[100]

Earlier we learned that the best guesstimate for aid workers was around 30,000. But whatever the number in 2014, 329 of them in 27 countries suffered a major attack – 120 killed, 88 seriously wounded, and 121 kidnapped. And this was a 30 percent decrease from the record-setting previous year.[101]

It is difficult for newcomers to understand the bevy of governmental, intergovernmental, and nongovernmental aid agencies that flock to emergencies along with other external actors. Hence, the label "IGO" fails to capture the complexity of the European Union or the dizzying acronyms within the UN system – the main abbreviations being UNHCR, UNICEF, WFP, UNDP, and OCHA. And behind the label of "NGO" reside literally thousands of international nongovernmental bodies – some with budgets of hundreds of millions of dollars, others mom-and-pop operations.

Readers may also have to stretch to understand the extent to which calls for enhanced "coordination" are usually sung by a passionate chorus of bureaucrats, while actual behavior is accompanied by lower decibel levels that reflect administrative inertia and dominant economic incentives pushing in the opposite direction. The widespread shorthand is usually the international humanitarian "system." This word disguises the fact that overall performance reflects the sum of individual actions rather than a planned, singular, and coherent whole. The use of another image, the international humanitarian "family," might be more apt in that it allows for several eventualities, including being extremely dysfunctional.

The need to make better use of the many moving parts of international humanitarian machinery seems obvious on the face of it. But the need to have less waste and more impact, at least within the humanitarian part of the international delivery system, seems especially compelling when huge numbers of lives are at stake in humanitarian disasters.

Everyone is for coordination as long as it implies no loss of autonomy. One retired UN practitioner, Antonio Donini, draws distinctions among three broad categories of coordination within the United Nations, which apply equally to NGOs:

- *coordination by command* – in other words, coordination where strong leadership is accompanied by some sort of leverage and authority, whether carrot or stick;
- *coordination by consensus* – where leadership is essentially a function of the capacity of the "coordinator" to orchestrate a coherent response and to mobilize the key actors around common objectives and priorities;
- *coordination by default* – where, in the absence of a formal coordination entity, only the most rudimentary exchange of information and division of labor takes place among the actors.[102]

Given the feudal nature of the UN system and the ferocious independence of NGOs, coordination by command is clearly unrealistic, however desirable in the context of coercive military operations. While exceptions occur – for instance, some have argued that UNHCR exercised "benign coercive coordination" as lead agency in the Balkans[103] – nonetheless, the experience under the best of circumstances could undoubtedly be most readily described as coordination by consensus. The experience under the worst of circumstances – for instance, in the uncharted waters of Liberia or Afghanistan or Iraq – demonstrated the absence of meaningful coordination, and what little existed could accurately be labeled as coordination by default.

The clearest central theme emerging from earlier descriptions of the new wars and the new humanitarianisms is the urgent requirement for fewer outsiders and better orchestration among those coming to the rescue – the military, IGOs and especially the members of the UN system, international NGOs, private contractors, and the ICRC. Nonetheless, no expression in the public policy lexicon is more used, or less understood, than "coordination." Autonomy, not meaningful coordination, is the key goal of proprietary UN agencies and market share-oriented NGOs. Officials who lament waste and the lack of effectiveness should make genuine efforts to forgo financial and operational independence in the interests of common humanitarian efforts and address its collective action problems.

At the same time, it would be unfair to imply a total absence of adaptation. Largely as a result of having to respond to the challenges of new wars, the organization of humanitarian action has begun to evolve into a better defined field of professional activity, with improved and appropriate career development. Previously, a relatively limited number of agencies had few sustained interactions and rarely focused on principles of action, codes of conduct, or standards. Those who presented themselves as humanitarian usually limited themselves to emergency relief – except for the ICRC and the UNHCR whose mandates include protection. Their operations were sometimes staffed by individuals with little experience, who jumped into the fray believing that a can-do attitude and good intentions were sufficient.

Since the mid-1990s, what Larry Minear aptly calls the "humanitarian enterprise"[104] has become a recognized field, with more donors, deliverers, and regulators. Not only have the numbers grown, but the field is now characterized by regular interactions among the members, a greater reliance on specialized knowledge, and a collective awareness of a common undertaking. Since 1997, the Active Learning Network for Accountability and Performance in Humanitarian Action – better known by its acronym, ALNAP – has produced some 5,000 evaluations and an annual *Review of Humanitarian Action*. Practitioners have begun to rationalize conduct by developing codes of conduct, methodologies for calculating results, abstract rules to guide standardized responses, training programs, exchanges of personnel among various types of agencies, and procedures to improve efficiency and identify best practices and lessons learned.

Although some old-timers protest the fading of volunteerism and the onset of bureaucratization, the dominant reality is that agencies and managers are both familiar with and value specialized knowledge, spheres of competence, rules for standardized responses, and means–ends calculations.[105] Nothing could be more obvious than the need for professionalism among aid workers who act side by side with soldiers during humanitarian interventions.

In short, military force has opened up not only "humanitarian space" but also the marketplace for more resources and institutions. However, all is not well. In spite of some rethinking, the international humanitarian system is struggling to determine the extent to which the crises in Afghanistan and Iraq, or in the DRC and Darfur, in Libya and Syria, are aberrations or the new "normal." Moreover, there is little coherence and no centralization – either in the UN system or in the NGO arena. As demonstrated earlier, "coordination" rolls easily from bureaucratic lips, but is absent from the incentive structures of the system.

Furthermore, collective action problems are exacerbated by the lack of an agreement concerning the scope and nature of humanitarian activity. Some humanitarians pursue a broad range of tasks with military protection. Others, such as the ICRC, remain more closely committed to traditional principles, preferring not to be tainted by politicized activity that may endanger not only the fulfillment of goals, but also the lives of aid providers. Thus, in addition to the multiplicity of actors on the scene, an incentive structure that encourages resource grabbing, and donor preferences that may have geopolitical underpinnings, the humanitarian identity crisis is yet another centrifugal force pulling actors in multiple directions.

In February 2006, for example, the UN secretary-general set up a 15-member High-level Panel on UN System-wide Coherence in the areas of development, humanitarian aid, and the environment. Thus far, this effort – co-chaired by the prime ministers of Mozambique, Norway, and Pakistan – has resulted in tinkering rather than a substantial rationalization of the system. Certainly there will be no consolidation into a central humanitarian pillar. The numerous moving parts of the international humanitarian system will continue to function far less effectively than they should to aid and protect war victims into the foreseeable future.

Conclusion

ICISS was originally established because of the Security Council's failure to address dire and conscience-shocking humanitarian crises in Rwanda and Kosovo. The view of Yale historian Paul Kennedy is quite accurate: namely, that the absence of meaningful military might in Rwanda was "the single worst decision the United Nations ever made"[106] – much like the do-nothing approach in the Darfur region of Sudan, Uganda, Zimbabwe, and the DRC – and represents a more serious threat to international order and justice than the council's paralysis in Kosovo. Not all claims to justice are equally valid, and NATO's was superior to China's and

Russia's (the "no" double vetoes). At least in the Balkans, a regional organization took a unanimous decision to deploy military force to halt bloodshed by coercing a political solution to conflict, and ultimately for human protection. Justified criticism arose about timidity: Washington's domestic politics meant that military action remained at an altitude of 15,000 feet when ground troops would have prevented the initial mass exodus. Nonetheless, past or potential victims would undoubtedly support NATO's decision. A 1999 survey of affected populations in several war zones reports, not surprisingly, that fully two-thirds of civilians under siege who were interviewed by the ICRC wanted more intervention, and only 10 percent wanted none.[107]

The disarray of humanitarian agencies has polarized perspectives on the ground. While the majority of victims who benefit from relief and protection undoubtedly hold positive views about the overall enterprise and most operations, instances of hostile reactions to the presence of agencies, as well as profound differences among humanitarians, highlight the seriousness of its "identity crisis." A 2005 mapping exercise of operational contexts for humanitarian agencies finds that recipients rightly "are more concerned about *what* is provided than about *who* provides it."[108]

It is soothing for those of us who are preoccupied with normative developments to point proudly to paragraphs 138–9 about R2P as the success story of the World Summit. On the one hand, that clearly is true. Cosmopolitanism is compelling normatively, and R2P is an important step "to promote a society-of-states morality, given the fact that sovereignty is one of the few principles that has universal appeal among national elites and mass publics."[109]

On the other hand, the summit could do nothing to change the geopolitical reality that "never again" is an inaccurate description of the actual impact of the 1948 Genocide

Convention – "here we go again" is closer to the truth in Darfur and Syria, just as it was in Rwanda. There are limits to analysis and advocacy with neither the political will nor the operational capacity among major powers to act on new norms. Simon Chesterman notes that political desires and means, not sovereignty considerations, determine whether states intervene to save strangers in the improved international society that Nicholas Wheeler urges.[110] Stephen Lewis's lament is blunter: "Alas, man and woman cannot live by rhetoric alone."[111]

Today, the main challenge facing the responsibility to protect is how to act, not how to build additional normative consensus. The shibboleth of western imperialism is a distraction with foundations across the global South on which to build a case for robust humanitarian action;[112] in this regard, the Arab League's and the African Union's support for outside intervention in Libya is noteworthy, as was military participation by Qatar and the United Arab Emirates. "Though some critics fret that R2P could prove to be a humanitarian veneer by which powerful states could justify military intervention in the development world, more often the problem has been the opposite," Edward Luck tells us. "The capable have stood by as the slaughter of civilians unfolded before the world's – and sometimes even UN peacekeepers' – eyes. They have looked for excuses not to act, rather than for reasons to intervene."[113]

Perhaps Libya will make policy- and decision-makers realize that between 1999 and 2011 we hardly witnessed too much military intervention to protect human beings but, rather, nothing significant. The international action against Libya was not about bombing for democracy, sending messages to Iran, implementing regime change, keeping oil prices low, or pursuing narrow interests. These may result, but the dominant motivation for using military force was to protect civilians, and Qaddafi's "model" for repression can no longer automatically be interpreted as an acceptable policy option by other autocratic regimes, although the lack of peacebuilding was an unfortunate follow on. Mustering cross-cultural political will to protect civilians or build the foundations for stability will always reflect the art of the possible, as the lack of reaction to Bahrain in 2011 and Syria since 2011 underlined.

Speaking in Brazil shortly after imposing the no-fly zone for Libya, US president Barack Obama saw no contradiction with his Nobel Prize – one can be in favor of peace but still authorize force to halt the "butchering" of civilians. Later, when addressing the US public, Obama defended this decision, which provided no political advantage but prevented massacres that would have "stained the conscience of the world." Libya suggests that we can say no more Holocausts, Cambodias, and Rwandas – and occasionally mean it even if the blow-back from the post-intervention lawlessness reduced the value of that humanitarian intervention.

To this end, in August 2011, President Obama issued the Presidential Study Directive on Mass Atrocities (PSD-10), which stated clearly that mass atrocity and genocide prevention is not only a core national security interest but also a moral responsibility of the United States. In addition to asking individual agencies to assess how to accomplish this task, PSD-10 also created an interagency Atrocity Prevention Board, an important step in embedding the norm in a bureaucracy.

We are living in a new world for which the International Commission on Intervention and State Sovereignty has reiterated the central role of the Security Council – reformed and enlarged or not – and urged it to act when mass atrocities threaten, once again, to stain the collective conscience. But if it does not, humanitarians and victims are left where Kofi Annan was in September 1999 when he questioned his dignified diplomatic audience in the General Assembly about their potential reactions had there actually been a state or a group of states willing to act early in April 1994 without a

Security Council imprimatur: "Should such a coalition have stood aside," he asked rhetorically, "and allowed the horror to unfold?"[114]

While the answers in UN diplomatic circles remain equivocal, those from any of the 800,000 dead Rwandans – or millions of murdered Syrians, Sudanese, Ugandans, and Congolese – would have been a resounding "no."

What is yours?

Selected Readings

Readers may already have been exposed to more endnotes than they would have liked. The brief selection below highlights a few key books that cover essential reading for the main topics covered in each chapter.

In terms of the conceptual building blocks for chapter 1, readers may wish to consult Stephen Krasner, *Sovereignty: Organized Hypocrisy* (Princeton: Princeton University Press, 1999), to learn more about the "normal" reasons why Westphalian sovereignty is routinely violated and non-intervention may or may not be respected in international relations. Kalevi J. Holsti, *Taming the Sovereigns: Institutional Change in International Politics* (Cambridge: Cambridge University Press, 2004), provides an overview of how to conceptualize continuity and change. Robert Jackson, *The Global Covenant: Human Conduct in a World of States* (Oxford: Oxford University Press, 2000), revisits the classical international society approach (or "English school") and brings it into the new era, including war and intervention, human rights, and humanitarian disasters. Up-to-date annual overviews of international military efforts in Center for International Cooperation, *Annual Review of Global Peace Operations 2010* (Boulder, CO: Lynne Rienner, 2010).

For historical overviews of humanitarian action, see Gary Bass, *Freedom's Battle: The Origins of Humanitarian Intervention* (New York: Knopf, 2008), Michael J. Barnett, *Empire of Humanity: A History of Humanitarianism* (Ithaca,

NY: Cornell University Press, 2011), and Michael J. Barnett and Janice Stein (eds.), *Sacred Aid: Faith and Humanitarianism* (Oxford: Oxford University Press, 2012). More detailed political analyses of the more recent humanitarian interventions in chapter 2 can be found in Nicholas J. Wheeler, *Saving Strangers: Humanitarian Intervention in International Society* (Oxford: Oxford University Press, 2000), and more legal insights in Simon Chesterman, *Just War or Just Peace? Humanitarian Intervention and International Law* (Oxford: Oxford University Press, 2001), and Anne Orford, *International Authority and the Responsibility to Protect* (Cambridge: Cambridge University Press, 2011). For the coming together of military forces and humanitarians in the post-Cold War era, see Thomas G. Weiss, *Military–Civilian Interactions: Humanitarian Crises and the Responsibility to Protect*, 2nd edn (Lanham, MD: Rowman & Littlefield, 2005), and James Pattison, *Humanitarian Intervention and the Responsibility to Protect* (Oxford: Oxford University Press, 2010). For attitudes about the use of force, see Martha Finnemore, *The Purpose of Intervention: Changing Beliefs about the Use of Military Force* (Ithaca, NY: Cornell University Press, 2003). For case studies of various types of humanitarian military action (logistics, protection of operations and populations, and defeat of perpetrators of violence), see Taylor Seybolt, *Humanitarian Military Operations: Conditions for Success and Failure* (Oxford: Oxford University Press, 2007). Two collections of essays on a wide range of related topics are Jennifer Welsh (ed.), *Humanitarian Intervention and International Relations* (Oxford: Oxford University Press, 2004), and J. L. Holzgrefe and Robert O. Keohane (eds.), *Humanitarian Intervention: Ethical, Legal, and Political Dilemmas* (Cambridge: Cambridge University Press, 2003).

For chapter 3, good places to start reading about the nature of contemporary wars are Mary Kaldor, *New and Old Wars:*

Organized Violence in a Global Era (Stanford, CA: Stanford University Press, 1999), Mark Duffield, *Global Governance and the New Wars* (London: Zed Books, 2001), Mohammed Ayoob, *The Third World Security Predicament: State Making, Regional Conflict, and the International System* (Boulder, CO: Lynne Rienner, 1995), and Mats Berdal and David M. Malone (eds.), *Greed and Grievance: Economic Agendas in Civil Wars* (Boulder, CO: Lynne Rienner, 2000). For the nature of humanitarian challenges resulting from them and new approaches, intriguing examinations are available, including Fiona Terry, *Condemned to Repeat? The Paradox of Humanitarian Action* (Ithaca, NY: Cornell University Press, 2002), David Rieff, *A Bed for the Night: Humanitarianism in Crisis* (New York: Simon & Schuster, 2002), Alex de Waal, *Famine Crimes: Politics & the Disaster Relief Industry in Africa* (Oxford: James Currey, 1997), and Fabrice Weissman (ed.), *In the Shadow of "Just Wars": Violence, Politics and Humanitarian Action* (Ithaca, NY: Cornell University Press, 2004). Peter J. Hoffman and Thomas G. Weiss, *Sword and Salve: Confronting New Wars and Humanitarian Crises* (Lanham, MD: Rowman & Littlefield, 2006), provide an overview of the historical, philosophical, legal, and political foundations of war (interstate and intrastate) and traditional and newer varieties of humanitarian action. Michael Byers's *War Law: Understanding International Law and Armed Conflict* (New York: Grove Press, 2005) is a readable primer that examines under what conditions it is appropriate to use military force when diplomacy has failed.

For international efforts to help and protect internally displaced persons, discussed in chapter 4, readers may consult Roberta Cohen and Francis M. Deng, *Masses in Flight: The Global Crisis of Internal Displacement* (Washington, DC: Brookings Institution, 1998), and their edited volume of case studies, *The Forsaken People: Case Studies of the Internally Displaced* (Washington, DC: Brookings Institution, 1998).

For the history of efforts to improve the knowledge base, law, norms, and operational responses, see Thomas G. Weiss and David A. Korn, *Internal Displacement: Conceptualization and its Consequences* (London: Routledge, 2006). Those wishing to examine the use of the bully pulpit should consult Kofi A. Annan, *The Question of Intervention – Statements by the Secretary-General* (New York: UN, 1999). There is a veritable cottage analytical industry for the responsibility to protect (R2P) – a key-worded bibliography at http://web.gc.cuny. edu/RalphBuncheInstitute/ICISS/index.htm contains some 5,000 sources in English. Readers should consult the actual report of the International Commission on Intervention, *The Responsibility to Protect* (Ottawa: International Development Research Centre, 2001), and an accompanying research volume by Thomas G. Weiss and Don Hubert, *The Responsibility to Protect: Research, Bibliography, Background* (Ottawa: International Development Research Centre, 2001). Useful interpretations of R2P from two commissioners are Ramesh Thakur, *The United Nations, Peace and Security: From Collective Security to the Responsibility to Protect* (Cambridge: Cambridge University Press, 2006), and Gareth Evans, *The Responsibility to Protect: Ending Mass Atrocities Once and For All* (Washington, DC: Brookings Institution, 2008). In addition to works cited above, readers could consult Alex Bellamy, *Responsibility to Protect: The Global Effort to End Mass Atrocities* (Cambridge: Polity, 2009), and Aidan Hehir, *The Responsibility to Protect: Rhetoric, Reality and the Future of Humanitarian Intervention* (Basingstoke, UK: Palgrave Macmillan, 2012).

In looking to the future, the topic of chapter 5, readers may wish to begin with a collection of essays about the UN's limitations and strengths after 9/11 by Jane Boulden and Thomas G. Weiss (eds.), *Terrorism and the UN: Before and After September 11* (Bloomington: Indiana University Press, 2004). The role of the United States in the multilateral era is discussed in several edited volumes: Rosemary Foot, S. Neil MacFarlane, and Michael Mastanduno (eds.), *The United States and Multilateral Organizations* (Oxford: Oxford University Press, 2003), Michael Byers and Georg Nolte (eds.), *United States Hegemony and the Foundations of International Law* (Cambridge: Cambridge University Press, 2003), Stewart Patrick and Shepard Forman (eds.), *Multilateralism and US Foreign Policy: Ambivalent Engagement* (Boulder, CO: Lynne Rienner, 2002), and David M. Malone and Yuen Foong Khong (eds.), *Unilateralism and US Foreign Policy: International Perspectives* (Boulder, CO: Lynne Rienner, 2003). Overviews of the ongoing philosophical and operational problems, respectively, of humanitarian action can be found in Hugo Slim, *Humanitarian Ethics: A Guide to the Morality of Aid in War and Disaster* (Oxford: Oxford University Press, 2015), Stephen Hopgood, *The Endtimes of Human Rights* (Ithaca, NY: Cornell University Press, 2013), David Kennedy, *The Dark Sides of Virtue: Reassessing International Humanitarianism* (Princeton: Princeton University Press, 2004), Larry Minear, *The Humanitarian Enterprise: Dilemmas and Discoveries* (Bloomfield, CN: Kumarian, 2002), and Michael Barnett and Thomas G. Weiss (eds.), *Humanitarianism in Question: Politics, Power, Ethics* (Ithaca, NY: Cornell University Press, 2007) as well as their *Humanitarianism Contested: Where Angels Fear to Tread* (London: Routledge, 2011).

Notes

PREFACE AND ACKNOWLEDGMENTS

1 Larry Minear et al., *Humanitarianism under Siege: A Critical Review of Operation Lifeline Sudan* (Trenton, NJ: Red Sea Press, 1991).

2 Thomas G. Weiss and Don Hubert, *The Responsibility to Protect: Research, Bibliography, Background* (Ottawa: International Development Research Centre, 2001).

3 Peter J. Hoffman and Thomas G. Weiss, *Sword & Salve: Confronting New Wars and Humanitarian Crises* (Lanham, MD: Rowman & Littlefield, 2006).

4 Thomas G. Weiss and David A. Korn, *Internal Displacement: Conceptualization and its Consequences* (London: Routledge, 2006).

5 Michael Barnett and Thomas G. Weiss (eds.), *Humanitarianism in Question: Politics, Power, Ethics* (Ithaca, NY: Cornell University Press, 2008); Michael Barnett and Thomas G. Weiss, *Humanitarianism Contested: Where Angels Fear to Tread* (London: Routledge, 2011).

6 See Louis Emmerij, Richard Jolly, and Thomas G. Weiss, *Ahead of the Curve? UN Ideas and Global Challenges* (Bloomington: Indiana University Press, 2001); Thomas G. Weiss, Tatiana Carayannis, Louis Emmerij, and Richard Jolly, *UN Voices: The Struggle for Development and Social Justice* (Bloomington: Indiana University Press, 2005); Richard Jolly, Louis Emmerij, and Thomas G. Weiss, *UN Ideas That Changed the World* (Bloomington: Indiana University Press, 2009). Further information on the project can be found at www.unhistory.org.

7 Thomas G. Weiss and Sam Daws (eds.), *The Oxford Handbook on the United Nations* (Oxford: Oxford University Press, 2007).

8 Gareth Evans, *The Responsibility to Protect: Ending Mass Atrocity Crimes Once and for All* (Washington, DC: Brookings Institution, 2008).

INTRODUCTION

1 Global Centre for the Responsibility to Protect, "Implementing the Responsibility to Protect. The 2009 General Assembly Debate: An Assessment," GCR2P Report, August 2009; available at: http://www.globalr2p.org/media/files/gcr2p_-general-assembly-debate-assessment.pdf. "'Early Warning, Assessment and the Responsibility to Protect': Informal Interactive Dialogue of the General Assembly held on 9 August 2010," GCR2P Report, September 2010; available at: http://www.globalr2p.org/media/files/gcr2p-report-_informal-interactive-dailogue-2010.pdf.

CHAPTER 1 CONCEPTUAL BUILDING BLOCKS

1 Adam Roberts, "The So-Called 'Right' of Humanitarian Intervention," in *Yearbook of International Humanitarian Law 2000*, vol. 3 (The Hague: T. M. C. Asser, 2002), pp. 3–51; emphasis added.
2 Louise Doswald-Beck, "The Legal Validity of Military Intervention by Invitation of the Government," in *1985 British Yearbook of International Law* (Oxford: Clarendon Press, 1985), p. 194.
3 Michael Walzer, *Just and Unjust Wars: A Moral Argument with Historical Illustrations*, 3rd edn (New York: Basic Books, 2000); *Arguing about War* (New Haven: Yale University Press, 2004).
4 This discussion draws on Thomas G. Weiss, "Peace Operations and the Responsibility to Protect," in *Armed Conflict Survey 2015* (London: International Institute for Strategic Studies, 2015), pp. 55–68.
5 Thomas G. Weiss and Kurt M. Campbell, "Military Humanitarianism," *Survival* 33(5) (1991): 451–65.
6 Robert Pape, "When Duty Calls: A Pragmatic Standard of Humanitarian Intervention," *International Security* 37(1) (2012): 41–80.

7 International Commission on Intervention and State Sovereignty, *The Responsibility to Protect* (Ottawa: International Development Research Centre, 2001).

8 Boutros Boutros-Ghali, *An Agenda for Peace: Preventive Diplomacy, Peacemaking and Peace-keeping* (New York: United Nations, 1992).

9 Boutros Boutros-Ghali, *Supplement to "An Agenda for Peace"* (New York: United Nations, 1995).

10 United Nations, *Report of the Panel on United Nations Peace Operations*, UN document A/55/305, August 21, 2000.

11 Samantha Power, "On Peacekeeping." Remarks at the American Enterprise Institute on UN Peacekeeping Reform, November 7, 2014; available at: http://www.huffingtonpost.com/samantha-power/on-peacekeeping_b_6124822.html.

12 For a discussion, see Thomas G. Weiss, David P. Forsythe, Roger A. Coate, and Kelly-Kate Pease, *The United Nations and Changing World Politics*, 8th edn (Boulder, CO: Westview, 2016), chs 2–3.

13 Marrack Goulding, "The Evolution of United Nations Peacekeeping," *Journal of International Affairs* 69(3) (1993): 457.

14 See Victoria Holt and Tobias Berkman, *The Impossible Mandate? Military Preparedness, the Responsibility to Protect, and Modern Peace Operations* (Washington, DC: Stimson Center, 2006).

15 Kofi Annan, "Opening Remarks," Humanitarian Action: A Symposium, November 20, 2000, in *International Peace Academy Conference Report* (New York: International Peace Academy, 2001), p. 11.

16 David Rieff, *At the Point of a Gun: Democratic Dreams and Armed Intervention* (New York: Simon & Schuster, 2005).

17 Taylor Seybolt, *Humanitarian Military Intervention: The Conditions for Success and Failure* (Oxford: Oxford University Press, 2007), p. 259.

18 Ban Ki-moon, *Implementing the Responsibility to Protect*. Report of the Secretary-General, UN document A/63/677, January 12, 2009.

19 Ban Ki-moon, *The Role of Regional and Sub-regional Arrangements in Implementing the Responsibility to Protect*. Report of the Secretary-General, UN document A/65/877, June 27, 2011, para. 11.

20 Ban Ki-moon, *Early Warning, Assessment and the Responsibility to Protect*. Report of the Secretary-General, UN document A/64/864, July 14, 2010.

21 Alex J. Bellamy, "The Responsibility to Protect – Five Years On," *Ethics & International Affairs* 24(2) (2010): 166.
22 I. William Zartman, *Preventing Identity Conflicts Leading to Genocide and Mass Killings* (New York: International Peace Institute, 2010), p. 4.
23 Kwame Akonor, "Assessing the African Union's Right of Humanitarian Intervention," *Criminal Justice Ethics* 29(2) (2010): 157–73.
24 James Pattison, *Humanitarian Intervention and the Responsibility to Protect: Who Should Intervene?* (Oxford: Oxford University Press, 2010), p. 250; emphasis in original.
25 The International Commission on Intervention and State Sovereignty, "The Responsibility to Protect," December 2001; available at: http://responsibilitytoprotect.org/ICISS%20Report. pdf.
26 Gareth Evans, "Commission Diplomacy," in *The Oxford Handbook of Modern Diplomacy*, ed. Andrew F. Cooper, Jorge Heine, and Ramesh Thakur (Oxford: Oxford University Press, 2013), p. 289.
27 United Nations, *A Vital and Enduring Commitment: Implementing the Responsibility to Protect: Report of the Secretary-General*, UN document A/69/981-S/2015/500, 13 July 2015, para. 7.
28 Anne-Marie Slaughter, "A Day to Celebrate, but Hard Work Ahead," *Foreign Policy*, March 18, 2011.
29 Ramesh Thakur, "R2P's 'Structural' Problems: A Response to Roland Paris," *International Peacekeeping* 22(1) (2015); available at: http://www.tandfonline.com/loi/finp20.
30 Simon Chesterman, "Hard Casers Make Bad Law: Law, Ethics, and Politics in Humanitarian Intervention," in *Just Intervention*, ed. Anthony F. Lang, Jr (Washington, DC: Georgetown University Press, 2003), p. 54.
31 Jennifer Welsh, "Implementing the Responsibility to Protect: Where Expectations Meet Reality," *Ethics & International Affairs* 24(4) (2010): 428.
32 Jarat Chopra and Thomas G. Weiss, "Sovereignty Is No Longer Sacrosanct: Codifying Humanitarian Intervention," *Ethics & International Affairs* 6 (1992): 95–117.
33 Ramesh Thakur and William Maley, eds., *Theorising the Responsibility to Protect* (Cambridge: Cambridge University Press, 2015).

34 For the history of the concept and its development, see Craig
    Calhoun, "The Imperative to Reduce Suffering: Charity, Progress,
    and Emergencies in the Field of Humanitarian Action," in
    Humanitarianism in Question: Power, Politics, Ethics, ed. Michael
    Barnett and Thomas G. Weiss (Ithaca, NY: Cornell University
    Press, 2007).
35 *Oxford English Dictionary* (Oxford: Oxford University Press, 1933).
36 Boutros Boutros-Ghali, *An Agenda for Peace,* para. 17.
37 Stephen D. Krasner, *Sovereignty: Organized Hypocrisy* (Princeton:
    Princeton University Press, 1999), p. 9.
38 See, e.g., Anthony Giddens, *Runaway World* (New York:
    Routledge, 2000); David Held, Anthony McGrew, David
    Goldblatt, and Jonathan Perraton, *Global Transformations: Politics,
    Economics and Culture* (Stanford, CA: Stanford University Press,
    1999).
39 Mohammed Ayoob, "The New-Old Disorder in the Third World,"
    Global Governance 1(1) (1995): 59–78.
40 Nico Schrijver, "The Changing Nature of State Sovereignty,"
    in *The British Year Book of International Law 1999* (Oxford:
    Clarendon Press, 2000), pp. 69–70.
41 Francis Hinsley, *Sovereignty* (London: Basic Books, 1966);
    Louis Henkin, *International Law: Politics and Values* (London:
    M. Nijhoff, 1995).
42 Robert Jackson and Carl Rosberg, "Why Africa's Weak States
    Persist: The Empirical and Juridical in Statehood," *World Politics*
    35(1) (1982): 1–24.
43 Max Weber, *Politics as Vocation* (Philadelphia: Fortress Press,
    1965; first published in 1919).
44 *ICJ Reports,* 1949, p. 35.
45 *ICJ Reports,* 1986, para. 263.
46 Quoted by Shashi Tharoor and Sam Daws, "Humanitarian
    Intervention: Getting Past the Reefs," *World Policy Journal* 18(2)
    (2001): 25.
47 Emphasis added. This is an interpretation similar to that made
    by the Permanent Court of International Justice in its Advisory
    Opinion concerning the *Tunis and Morocco Nationality Decrees*
    (1923), Series B, No. 4(4).
48 *Aegean Sea Case, ICJ Reports,* 1978, p. 22.
49 Kofi A. Annan, "Secretary-General's Speech to the 54th Session
    of the General Assembly," September 20, 1999.

50 See Brian D. Lepard, *Rethinking Humanitarian Intervention* (University Park: Pennsylvania State University Press, 2002), pp. 7–23.

51 Boutros-Ghali, *An Agenda for Peace*, para. 17.

52 Ramesh Thakur, "Humanitarian Intervention," in *The Oxford Handbook on the United Nations*, ed. Thomas G. Weiss and Sam Daws (Oxford: Oxford University Press, 2007), p. 390.

53 Donald C. F. Daniel and Bradd C. Hayes with Chantal de Jonge Oudraat, *Coercive Inducement and the Containment of International Crises* (Washington, DC: US Institute of Peace, 1999).

54 Robert Jennings and Arthur Watts (eds.), *Oppenheim's International Law* (London: Longmans, 1996), pp. 428–34; Ian Brownlie, *International Law and the Use of Force by States* (Oxford: Clarendon Press, 1963), pp. 44–5.

55 See Julie A. Mertus, *The United Nations and Human Rights: A Guide for a New Era*, 2nd edn (London: Routledge, 2009); Sarah Zaidi and Roger Normand, *Human Rights Ideas at the United Nations: The Political History of Universal Justice* (Bloomington: Indiana University Press, 2007).

56 Kofi Annan, "Two Concepts of Sovereignty," *The Economist* 352 (September 18, 1999): 49–50.

57 Roberta Cohen and Francis M. Deng, *Masses in Flight: The Global Crisis of Internal Displacement* (Washington, DC: Brookings Institution, 1998); Roberta Cohen and Francis M. Deng (eds.), *The Forsaken People: Case Studies of the Internally Displaced* (Washington, DC: Brookings Institution, 1998).

58 See S. Neil MacFarlane and Yuen Foong-Khong, *The UN and Human Security: A Critical History* (Bloomington: Indiana University Press, 2006).

59 Commission on Human Security, *Human Security Now* (New York: Commission on Human Security, 2003).

60 Lloyd Axworthy, "Human Security and Global Governance: Putting People First," *Global Governance* 7(1) (2001): 23.

61 Louis Henkin, "Kosovo and the Law of Humanitarian Intervention," *American Journal of International Law* 93 (1999): 824.

62 See Robert Jackson, *The Global Covenant: Human Conduct in a World of States* (Oxford: Oxford University Press, 2000), chs 10 and 11. See also Mohammed Ayoob, "Humanitarian Intervention and International Society," *Global Governance* 7(3) (2001): 225–30.

63 Charles E. Merriam, *History of the Theory of Sovereignty since Rousseau* (New York: Columbia University Press, 1958), p. 11.
64 Ramesh Thakur, "Global Norms and International Humanitarian Law: An Asian Perspective," *International Review of the Red Cross* 83(841) (2001): 35.
65 Statement by the President of the Security Council, October 30, 1992; UN document S/24744.
66 Theodore Meron, "International Criminalization of Internal Atrocities," *American Journal of International Law* 89 (July 1995): 554.
67 Robert H. Jackson, *Quasi-States: Sovereignty, International Relations, and the Third World* (Cambridge: Cambridge University Press, 1990). See also Christopher Clapham, *Africa and the International System: The Politics of State Survival* (Cambridge: Cambridge University Press, 1996); I. William Zartman (ed.), *Collapsed States* (Boulder, CO: Lynne Rienner, 1995).
68 Statement by President Robert Mugabe of Zimbabwe, quoted by Lori F. Damrosch (ed.), *Reinforcing Restraint: Collective Intervention in Internal Conflicts* (New York: Council on Foreign Relations, 1993), p. 364.
69 Thomas G. Weiss and Sam Daws, "World Politics: Continuity and Change since 1945," in *The Oxford Handbook on the United Nations*; Michael Barnett and Thomas G. Weiss, "Contemporary Humanitarianism in Global, Historical, and Theoretical Perspective," in *Humanitarianism in Question*.
70 Adam Roberts and Benedict Kingsbury, "Introduction: The UN's Roles in International Society since 1945," in *United Nations: Divided World*, 2nd edn, ed. Adam Roberts and Benedict Kingsbury (Oxford: Oxford University Press, 1993), p. 1.
71 Hedley Bull, *The Anarchical Society: A Study of Order in World Politics* (New York: Columbia University Press, 1977).
72 Craig Murphy, *International Organization and Industrial Change: Global Governance since 1850* (Cambridge: Polity, 1994).

CHAPTER 2 "HUMANITARIAN" INTERVENTIONS: THUMBNAIL SKETCHES

1 Augustus Stapleton, *Intervention and Non-Intervention* (London: Murray, 1866); *The Foreign Policy of Great Britain from 1790 to*

1865 (London: Murray, 1866); Ellery Stowell, *Intervention in International Law* (Washington, DC: J. Bryne, 1921); Ian Brownlie, *International Law and the Use of Force by States* (Oxford: Clarendon Press, 1963).

2 Danish Institute of International Affairs, *Humanitarian Intervention: Legal and Political Aspects* (Copenhagen: Danish Institute for International Affairs, 1999), p. 79.

3 Stowell, *Intervention in International Law*, p. 53.

4 Dino Kritsiotis, "Reappraising Policy Objections to Humanitarian Intervention," *Michigan Journal of International Law* 19 (1998): 1005.

5 Ramesh Thakur, "Global Norms and International Humanitarian Law: An Asian Perspective," *International Review of the Red Cross* 83(841) (2001): 31.

6 Brownlie, *International Law*, p. 340.

7 Hersch Lauterpacht, "The Grotian Tradition in International Law," *British Year Book of International Law* 23 (1946): 1.

8 Richard Lillich, *Humanitarian Intervention and the United Nations* (Charlottesville: University Press of Virginia, 1973).

9 International Court of Justice, *Military and Paramilitary Activities In and Against Nicaragua (Nicaragua v. United States)*, June 27, 1986, paras 267–8 and 243.

10 Bruno Simma (ed.), *The Charter of the United Nations: A Commentary* (Oxford: Oxford University Press, 1995), p. 7.

11 United Nations, Dag Hammarskjöld Library, "Security Council – Veto List"; available at http://research.un.org/en/docs/sc/quick/veto.

12 Sebastian von Einsiedel, David M. Malone, and Bruno Stagno (eds.), *The UN Security Council: From the Cold War to the 21st Century* (Boulder, CO: Lynne Rienner, 2016).

13 See Global Policy Forum, "Number of Security Council Resolutions and Presidential Statements, 1988–2011"; available at: http://www.globalpolicy.org/images/pdfs/Number_of_Security_Council_Resolutions.pdf. In 1987, 13 resolutions were passed, bringing the total to 1,373.

14 United Nations, Security Council, "Security Council Resolutions"; available at http://www.un.org/en/sc/documents/resolutions/.

15 United Nations Peacekeeping, "List of Peacekeeping Operations 1948–2013"; available at http://www.un.org/en/peacekeeping/

documents/operationslist.pdf. Despite its title, this list includes missions through MINUSCA (UN Multidimensional Integrated Stabilization Mission in the Central African Republic), which was authorized in April 2014.

16 United Nations Peacekeeping, "United Nations Peacekeeping Operations Fact Sheet: 31 March 2015." Updated fact sheets available at http://www.un.org/en/peacekeeping/resources/ statistics/factsheet.shtml. For these and other updated statistics, see *Annual Review of Global Peace Operations 2015*, published annually by the Centre for International Cooperation of New York University.

17 Stephen J. Stedman, "The New Interventionists," *Foreign Affairs* 72(1) (1993): 1–16; Thomas G. Weiss, "Whither the United Nations," *Washington Quarterly* 17(1) (1993): 109–28.

18 Thomas G. Weiss, "Military–Civilian Humanitarians: The Age of Innocence is Over," *International Peacekeeping* 2(2) (1995): 157–74.

19 Mario Bettati and Bernard Kouchner (eds.), *Le Devoir d'ingérence: peut-on les laisser mourir?* (Paris: Denoël, 1987); Mario Bettati, *Le Droit d'ingérence: mutation de l'ordre international* (Paris: Odile Jacob, 1987).

20 The criteria were absent in outside military operations in several countries in the 1990s that are not included in Table 2.1. Meaningful consent, e.g., was expressed and justified the Russian military efforts in Georgia and Tajikistan and the Commonwealth of Independent States in Tajikistan; and they were not based on explicitly humanitarian justifications. Similarly, three interventions in Africa had the consent of democratically elected governments, but again humanitarian concerns were not paramount: in 1998 in Guinea-Bissau, the Senegalese and Guinean and ECOWAS efforts; in 1997 in the Central African Republic, Inter-African Force to Monitor the Implementation of the Bangui Agreements (MISAB); and in 1998 in Lesotho, the efforts by South Africa and Botswana in accordance with agreements of the South African Development Community (SADC). Italy intervened in Albania in 1996 for humanitarian reasons, but with Tirana's consent.

21 William J. Durch (ed.), *UN Peacekeeping, American Politics, and the Uncivil Wars of the 1990s* (New York: St. Martin's, 1996) and *The Evolution of UN Peacekeeping: Case Studies and Comparative*

Analysis (New York: St. Martin's, 1993); Thomas G. Weiss,
*Military–Civilian Interactions: Humanitarian Crises and the
Responsibility to Protect*, 2nd edn (Lanham, MD: Rowman &
Littlefield, 2005); Simon Chesterman, *Just War or Just Peace?
Humanitarian Intervention and International Law* (Oxford: Oxford
University Press, 2001); Nicholas J. Wheeler, *Saving Strangers:
Humanitarian Intervention in International Society* (Oxford: Oxford
University Press, 2000); Francis Kofi Abiew, *The Evolution
of the Doctrine and Practice of Humanitarian Intervention* (The
Hague: Kluwer Law International, 1999); Fernando Tesón,
Humanitarian Intervention: An Inquiry into Law and Morality,
2nd edn (Irvington-on-Hudson, NY: Transnational Publishers,
1997); Sean D. Murphy, *Humanitarian Intervention: The United
Nations in an Evolving World Order* (Philadelphia: University of
Pennsylvania Press, 1996).

22 David Cortright and George A. Lopez, *Sanctions Decade: Assessing
UN Strategies in the 1990s* (Boulder, CO: Lynne Rienner, 2000).

23 In the case of Cambodia, the sanctions were not imposed under
Chapter VII. On Angola, see United Nations, *Report of the Panel of
Experts on Violations of Security Council Sanctions against UNITA*,
UN document S/2000/203, March 10, 2000.

24 Thomas G. Weiss, David Cortright, George A. Lopez, and Larry
Minear, *Political Gain and Civilian Pain: Humanitarian Impacts of
Economic Sanctions* (Boulder, CO: Lynne Rienner, 1997).

25 Cortright and Lopez, *Sanctions Decade*, p. 46. See, e.g., Manuel
Bessler, Richard Garfield, and Gerard McHugh, *Sanctions
Assessment Handbook: Assessing the Humanitarian Implications of
Sanctions* (New York: OCHA, 2004), p. 7.

26 Fourth Freedom Forum, *Towards Smarter, More Effective United
Nations Sanctions* (Goshen, IN: Fourth Freedom Forum, 1999);
David Cortright, Alistair Millar, and George A. Lopez, *Smart
Sanctions: Restructuring UN Policy in Iraq*, Policy Brief Series
(Goshen, IN: Fourth Freedom Forum, 2001); *Expert Seminar
on Targeting United Nations Financial Sanctions* (Interlaken:
Swiss Federal Office for Foreign Economic Affairs, Department
of Economy), March 17–19, 1998; UN document S/1999/92,
January 29, 1999; and UN document S/2000/319, April 17,
2000.

27 The International Law Commission between 1977 and 1986
produced a "Draft Convention on the Jurisdictional Immunities

of States and Their Property," which sought to change the then existing rules, including by allowing legal actions against officials who committed crimes.

28 See Richard Goldstone, "International Criminal Court and Ad Hoc Tribunals," in *The Oxford Handbook on the United Nations*, ed. Thomas G. Weiss and Sam Daws (Oxford: Oxford University Press, 2007), pp. 463–78.

29 *Report of the International Inquiry on Darfur to the United Nations Secretary-General*, Geneva, January 25, 2005, p. 4; available at www.un.org/News/dh/sudan/com_inq_darfur.pdf.

30 *Prosecutor v. Tadic*, IT-94–1-AR72 (October 1995), para. 30.

31 International Committee of the Red Cross, "Report on the Protection of War Victims," *International Review of the Red Cross*, 296 (September–October 1993): 391–445.

32 The Commission on Global Governance, *Our Global Neighbourhood* (Oxford: Oxford University Press, 1995), p. 90.

33 Simon Chesterman, *Just War or Just Peace?* (New York: Oxford University Press, 2003), p. 98.

34 See Tom Farer, "Collectively Defending Democracy in a World of Sovereign States: The Western Hemisphere's Prospect," *Human Rights Quarterly* 15 (November 1993): 716–50; Michael E. Brown, Sean M. Lynn Jones, and Steven E. Miller (eds.), *Debating the Democratic Peace* (Cambridge, MA: MIT Press, 1996).

35 Jeremy Levitt, "African Interventionist States and International Law," in *African Interventionist States: The New Conflict Resolution Brokers*, ed. Oliver Furley and Roy May (Aldershot: Ashgate, 2001), p. 35; emphasis in original.

36 James Cockayne and David M. Malone, "Creeping Unilateralism: How Operation Provide Comfort and the No-fly Zones in 1991 and 1992 Paved the Way for the Iraq Crisis of 2003," *Security Dialogue* 37(1) (2006): 123–41.

37 *Supplement to An Agenda for Peace: Position Paper of the Secretary-General on the Occasion of the Fiftieth Anniversary of the United Nations*, UN document A/50/60-S/1995/1 (1995), paras 77–80.

38 *Report of the Panel on United Nations Peace Operations*, UN document A/55/305-S/2000/809, August 21, 2000.

39 United Nations, Report of the High-Level Independent Panel on United Nations Peace Operations, "Uniting Our Strengths for Peace – Politics, Partnership and People," June 16, 2015; available at http://www.un.org/sg/pdf/HIPPO_Report_1_June_2015.pdf.

40 Victoria Holt, "The Military and Civilian Protection: Developing Roles and Capacities," in *Resetting the Rules of Engagement: Trends and Issues in Military–Humanitarian Relations*, ed. Victoria Wheeler and Adele Hammer (London: Overseas Development Institute, 2006), p. 65.

41 Martha Finnemore, *The Purpose of Intervention: Changing Beliefs about the Use of Force* (Ithaca, NY: Cornell University Press, 2003), p. 3. See especially her discussion of humanitarian cases in ch. 3.

42 International Rescue Committee, "Conflict in Congo Deadliest since World War II, Says the IRC," April 8, 2003; available at http://www.theirc.org/news/conflict_in_congo_deadliest_since _world_war_ii_says_the_irc.html.

43 Herbert Weiss and Tatiana Carayannis, "The Enduring Idea of the Congo," in *Borders, Nationalism, and the African State*, ed. Ricardo René Larémont (Boulder, CO: Lynne Rienner, 2005), pp. 135–77.

44 Refugees International, DR Congo; available at: www. refugeesinternational.org/where-we-work/africa/dr-congo.

45 International Rescue Committee, "Mortality in the Democratic Republic of Congo: An Ongoing Crisis," 2007; available at www.rescue.org/sites/default/files/resource-file/2006-7_congo MortalitySurvey.pdf.

46 MONUSCO Facts and Figures; available at http://www.un.org/ en/peacekeeping/missions/monusco/facts.shtml.

47 Human Rights Watch, *World Report 2011* (New York: HRW, 2011); available at http://www.hrw.org/sites/default/files/related_ material/wr2011_book_complete.pdf.

48 International Rescue Committee, "Congo Crisis"; available at www.http://www.rescue.org/special-reports/congo-forgotten-crisis.

49 Olara A. Otunnu, "The Secret Genocide," *Foreign Policy* (July/ August 2006): 45–6.

50 International Criminal Court, "Case Information Sheet. Situation in Uganda, *The Prosecutor v. Joseph Kony, Vincent Otti, and Okot Odhiambo*"; available at http://www.icc-cpi.int/iccdocs/PIDS/ publications/KonyEtAlEng.pdf.

51 Pew Research Center, "The Viral KONY 2012 Video," March 15, 2012; available at http://www.pewinternet.org/files/old-media/ Files/Reports/2012/The_Viral_Kony_2012_Video.pdf.

52 Caitlin Dewey, "#Bringbackourgirls, #Kony2012, and the complete, divisive history of 'hashtag activism,'" *Washington Post*; available at http://www.washingtonpost.com/news/the-intersect/wp/2014/05/08/bringbackourgirls-kony2012-and-the-complete-divisive-history-of-hashtag-activism/.

53 International Criminal Court, "Case Information Sheet, Situation in Uganda, *The Prosecutor v. Joseph Kony, Vincent Otti, and Okot Odhiambo.*"

54 Internal Displacement Monitoring Centre, *The Many Faces of Displacement: IDPs in Zimbabwe* (Geneva: IDMC, 2008); available at http://www.internal-displacement.org/sub-saharan-africa/zimbabwe/2008/the-many-faces-of-displacement-idps-in-zimbabwe

55 Internal Displacement Monitoring Centre, "Zimbabwe," updated December 2014; available at http://www.internal-displacement.org/sub-saharan-africa/zimbabwe/.

56 United Nations Mission in Sudan, Public Information Office, Media Monitoring Report, April 23, 2008; available at http://unmis.unmissions.org/Portals/UNMIS/2008Docs/patch1/mmr-apr23.pdf.

57 Samantha Power, *"A Problem from Hell": America and the Age of Genocide* (New York: Basic Books, 2001).

58 Nicholas D. Kristof, "Genocide in Slow Motion," *New York Review of Books* 53(2) (February 9, 2006): 14. See also Julie Flint and Alex de Waal, *A Short History of a Long War* (London: Zed Books, 2005); Gérard Prunier, *Darfur: The Ambiguous Genocide* (Ithaca, NY: Cornell University Press, 2005); and a special issue on "Genocide in Darfur," *Genocide Studies and Prevention* 1(1) (2006).

59 UN OCHA, "Sudan: US Congress Unanimously Defines Darfur Violence as 'Genocide'," July 23, 2004; available at http://reliefweb.int/report/sudan/sudan-us-congress-unanimously-defines-darfur-violence-genocide.

60 "The Crisis in Darfur," written remarks before the Senate Foreign Relations Committee, Washington, DC, September 9, 2004.

61 Physicians for Human Rights, "Call for Intervention to Save Lives in the Sudan: Field Team Compiles Indicators of Genocide," June 23, 2004; available at http://reliefweb.int/sites/reliefweb.int/files/resources/81DA5DF0B5E4A50F85256EBD0008EB73-phr-sud-23jun.pdf.

62 *Agence France Presse*, "EU Lawmakers Call Darfur 'Crisis Genocide'," September 16, 2004.

63 William G. O'Neill and Violette Cassis, *Protecting Two Million Internally Displaced: The Successes and Shortcomings of the African Union in Darfur* (Washington, DC: Brookings Institution – University of Bern Project on Internal Displacement, 2005).

64 Lydia Polgreen, "As Darfur War Rages On: Hunger and Disease Kill," *New York Times*, May 30, 2006.

65 "Strongly Condemning Escalation of Violence in Sudan, Secretary-General Tells Security Council 'It Is Time to Act,'" Press Release SG/SM/10628, September 11, 2006.

66 Human Rights Watch, *Darfur in the Shadows: The Sudanese Government's Ongoing Attacks on Civilians and Human Rights* (New York: HRW, 2011), p. 1.

67 Human Rights Watch, *Men with No Mercy*, September 2015; available at https://www.hrw.org/report/2015/09/09/men-no-mercy/rapid-support-forces-attacks-against-civilians-darfur-sudan.

68 Human Rights Watch, "World Report 2015: South Sudan, Events of 2014"; available at https://www.hrw.org/world-report/2015/country-chapters/south-sudan.

69 United Nations Mission in the Republic of South Sudan, "Flash Human Rights Report on the Escalation of Fighting in Greater Upper Nile, April/May 2015," June 29, 2015; available at http://reliefweb.int/report/south-sudan/flash-human-rights-report-escalation-fighting-greater-upper-nile-aprilmay-2015.

70 Iain Levine, "Dispatches: Unhappy Birthday, South Sudan," Human Rights Watch, July 8, 2015; available at https://www.hrw.org/news/2015/07/09/dispatches-unhappy-birthday-south-sudan.

71 Alex J. Bellamy, "What Will Become of the 'Responsibility to Protect?,'" *Ethics & International Affairs* 20(2) (2006): 143–69.

72 David Rieff, "A Nation of Pre-emptors?" *New York Times Magazine*, January 15, 2006, p. 12.

73 Quoted in Mimi Hall, "Obama cites US 'Responsibility' in Libya Intervention," *USA Today*, March 28, 2011; available at www.usatoday.com/news/washington/2011-03-29-RWIAObama29_ST_N.htm.

74 Helene Cooper and Steven Lee Myles, "Obama Takes Hardline with Libya after Shift by Clinton," *New York Times*, March 18, 2011; available at www.nytimes.com/2011/03/19/world/africa/19policy.html.

75 This section draws on Thomas G. Weiss, "Military Humanitarianism: Syria Hasn't Killed It," *Washington Quarterly* 37(1) (2014): 7–20.

76 Aidan Hehir, "The Permanence of Inconsistency: Libya, the Security Council, and the Responsibility to Protect," *International Security* 38(1) (2013): 137–59. The author's views are Thomas G. Weiss, "RtoP Alive and Well after Libya," *Ethics & International Affairs* 25(3) (2011): 287–92.

77 Thomas G. Weiss, "The Responsibility to Protect (R2P) and Modern Diplomacy," in *The Oxford Handbook of Modern Diplomacy*, ed Andrew Cooper, Jorge Heine, and Ramesh Thakur (Oxford: Oxford University Press, 2013), pp. 763–78.

78 For interpretations by commissioners, see Gareth Evans, *The Responsibility to Protect: Ending Mass Atrocity Crimes Once and For All* (Washington, DC: Brookings, 2008); Ramesh Thakur, *The United Nations, Peace and Security: From Collective Security to the Responsibility to Protect* (Cambridge: Cambridge University Press, 2006). See also Alex J. Bellamy, *Responsibility to Protect: The Global Effort to End Mass Atrocities* (Cambridge: Polity, 2009); Anne Orford, *International Authority and the Responsibility to Protect* (Cambridge: Cambridge University Press, 2011); Aidan Hehir, *The Responsibility to Protect: Rhetoric, Reality and the Future of Humanitarian Intervention* (Houndmills, Basingstoke, UK: Palgrave Macmillan, 2012).

79 Derek Chollet and Ben Fishman, "Who Lost Libya?" *Foreign Affairs* 94(3) (2015): 154–7.

80 Ramesh Thakur, "R2P after Libya and Syria: Engaging Emerging Powers," *Washington Quarterly* 36(2) (2013): 61.

81 International Criminal Court, Resumed thirteenth session at the Ministry of Foreign Affairs of the Netherlands – The Hague, June 24–25, 2015, "Assembly of States Parties. To the Rome Statute of the International Criminal Court. Handbook for Participants, June 15, 2015"; available at http://www.icc-cpi.int/iccdocs/asp_docs/ASP13R/ASP13R-Handbook-ENG.pdf.

82 General Salah Abdallah Gosh, quoted in Alex de Waal and Gregory H. Stanton, "Should President Omar al-Bashir of Sudan be Charged and Arrested by the International Criminal Court? An Exchange of Views," *Genocide Studies and Prevention* 4(3) (December 2009): 347.

83 De Waal and Stanton, "Should President Omar al-Bashir of

Sudan Be Charged and Arrested by the International Criminal
Court?"
84 International Criminal Court, "Case Information Sheet: *The
Prosecutor v. Omar Hasan Ahmed al Bashir*"; available at http://
www.icc-cpi.int/iccdocs/PIDS/publications/AlBashirEng.pdf.
85 Open Society Foundations, Open Society Justice Initiative,
Briefing Paper, "Kenya: Trial of William Samoei Ruto and Joshua
arap Sang at the International Criminal Court," September
2013; available at http://www.opensocietyfoundations.org/sites/
default/files/briefing-paper-kenya-ruto-sang-%2020130909.pdf.
86 International Criminal Court, "Case Information Sheet: *The
Prosecutor v. Uhuru Muigai Kenyatta*"; available at http://www.icc-
cpi.int/iccdocs/PIDS/publications/KenyattaEng.pdf.
87 Uhuru Kenyatta, quoted in International Federation for Human
Rights, "Kenya: One Year in Office for Uhuru Kenyatta and
William Ruto," April 2014: 16. Available at https://www.fidh.org/
IMG/pdf/kenya631a2014bassdef.pdf.
88 International Criminal Court, "Case Information Sheet: *The
Prosecutor v. Uhuru Muigai Kenyatta*."
89 International Federation for Human Rights, "Kenya: One Year
in Office for Uhuru Kenyatta and William Ruto." The Rome
Statute can be found at http://www.icc-cpi.int/iccdocs/asp_docs/
Publications/Compendium/Compendium.3rd.01.ENG.pdf.
90 International Criminal Court, Assembly of States Parties, Twelfth
session, The Hague, November 20–28, 2013, "Special Segment
as Requested by the African Union: 'Indictment of Sitting Heads
of State and Government and its Consequences on Peace and
Stability and Reconciliation'"; available at http://www.icc-cpi.int/
iccdocs/asp_docs/ASP12/ICC-ASP-12-61-ENG.pdf.
91 De Waal and Stanton, "Should President Omar al-Bashir of
Sudan Be Charged and Arrested by the International Criminal
Court," pp. 332–3.

CHAPTER 3 NEW WARS AND NEW
HUMANITARIANISMS

1 United Nations Office on Drugs and Crime (UNODC), "Research
Report: Estimating Illicit Financial Flows Resulting from Drug
Trafficking and Other Transnational Organized Crimes," October

2011; available at https://www.unodc.org/documents/data-and-analysis/Studies/Illicit_financial_flows_2011_web.pdf.

2 United Nations Development Programme, *Human Development Report 1999* (New York: UN, 1999).

3 Luis Martinez, "Opium Production Booming in Free Afghanistan: State Department Says Country Produces 90 Percent of the World's Opium," *ABC News*, March 1, 2006; available at http://abcnews.go.com/Health/story?id=1675283& page1.

4 United Nations Office on Drugs and Crime (UNODC), *World Drug Report 2009* (New York: UN, 2009).

5 For essays on this topic, see Mats R. Berdal and David Malone (eds.), *Greed and Grievance: Economic Agendas in Civil Wars* (Boulder, CO: Lynne Rienner, 2000).

6 Mark Duffield, "Globalization, Transborder Trade, and War Economies," in *Greed and Grievance*, ed. Berdal and Malone, pp. 70–4.

7 Peter Wallensteen and Margareta Sollenberg, "Armed Conflict, 1989–2000," *Journal of Peace Research* 38(5) (2001): 632.

8 Adam Roberts, "Lives and Statistics: Are 90% of War Victims Civilians?" *Survival* 52(3) (2010): 115–36.

9 James Rosenau, *Along the Domestic–Foreign Frontier: Exploring Governance in a Turbulent World* (Cambridge: Cambridge University Press, 1997). See also Joseph A. Camilleri and Jim Falk, *Worlds in Transition: Evolving Governance across a Stressed Planet* (Cheltenham, UK: Edward Elgar, 2009).

10 This count is now considered the reliable number of deaths in Bosnia during the war. See the UN ICTY's website at www.icty.org/sid/10591.

11 Mary Kaldor, *New and Old Wars: Organized Violence in a Global Era* (Stanford, CA: Stanford University Press, 1999) and *New and Old Wars: Organized Violence in a Global Era*, 3rd edn. (Cambridge: Polity, 2012); Mark Duffield, *Global Governance and the New Wars: The Merging of Development and Security* (London: Zed Books, 2001); Robert Kaplan, "The Coming Anarchy," *Atlantic Monthly* (February 1994): 44–76, and *The Coming Anarchy: Shattering the Dreams of the Post-Cold War* (New York: Random House, 2000).

12 See Bertrand Badie, *The Imported State: The Westernization of the Political Order* (Stanford, CA: Stanford University Press, 2000).

13 John Gerard Ruggie, "Territoriality and Beyond: Problematizing Modernity in International Relations," *International Organization* 47 (Winter 1993): 165.

14 Janice E. Thomson, "State Sovereignty in International Relations: Bridging the Gap Between Theory and Empirical Research," *International Studies Quarterly* 39 (June 1995): 213–33; Kalevi J. Holsti, *The State, War, and the State of War* (Cambridge: Cambridge University Press, 1996), pp. 82–98.

15 Samuel Huntington, *Political Order in Changing Societies* (New Haven: Yale University Press, 1968); Joel Migdal, *Strong States, Weak Societies: State–Society Relations and State Capabilities in the Third World* (Princeton: Princeton University Press, 1988).

16 Gerald B. Helman and Steven R. Ratner, "Saving Failed States," *Foreign Policy* 89 (Winter 1992–3): 3–20.

17 Robert I. Rotberg, "Failed States in a World of Terror," *Foreign Affairs* 81(4) (2002): 127–40.

18 Hedley Bull, *The Anarchical Society: A Study of Order in World Politics* (New York: Columbia University Press, 1977).

19 Jessica Matthews, "Power Shift," *Foreign Affairs* 76 (January/February 1997): 61.

20 Mohammed Ayoob, *The Third World Security Predicament: State Making, Regional Conflict, and the International System* (Boulder, CO: Lynne Rienner, 1995).

21 Kalevi J. Holsti, *Taming the Sovereigns: Institutional Change in International Politics* (Cambridge: Cambridge University Press, 2004), p. 318.

22 James N. Rosenau, *Turbulence in World Politics* (Princeton: Princeton University Press, 1990).

23 Stephen J. Stedman and Fred Tanner (eds.), *Refugee Manipulation: War, Politics, and the Abuse of Human Suffering* (Washington, DC: Brookings Institution, 2003), p. 14.

24 Beatrice Hibou, "The 'Social Capital' of the State as an Agent of Deception," in *The Criminalization of the State in Africa*, ed. Jean-François Bayart, Stephen Ellis, and Beatrice Hibou (Bloomington: Indiana University Press, 1999), p. 102.

25 Bernard Frahi, "Organized Crime and Conflict – Interaction and Policy Implications," in *Organized Crime as an Obstacle to Successful Peacebuilding: Lessons Learned from the Balkans, Afghanistan, and West Africa – 7th International Berlin Workshop*, ed. Alexander Austin, Tobias von Gienanth, and Wibke Hansen

(Berlin: Zentrum für Internationale Friedenseinsätze, 2003), pp. 35–6.

26 Peter W. Singer, *Corporate Warriors: The Rise of the Privatized Military Industry* (Ithaca, NY: Cornell University Press, 2003), pp. 45–7; Robert Mandel, *Armies without States: The Privatization of Security* (Boulder, CO: Lynne Rienner, 2002), pp. 9–10.

27 David Keen, "Incentives and Disincentives for Violence," in *Greed and Grievance*, ed. Berdal and Malone, p. 27; emphasis in original.

28 For the author's extended views, see Thomas G. Weiss, *Humanitarian Business* (Cambridge: Polity, 2013). See also Berdal and Malone (eds.), *Greed and Grievance*, in particular chapters by Keen, "Incentives and Disincentives for Violence," pp. 24–7, 29–31, and Reno, "Shadow States and the Political Economy of Civil War," pp. 44–5. See also Halvor Mehlum, Karl Ove Moene, and Ragnar Torvik, "Plunder & Protection, Inc," *Journal of Peace Research* 39(4) (2002): 447–59.

29 Alexander B. Downes, "Desperate Times, Desperate Measures: The Causes of Civilian Victimization in War," *International Security* 30(4) (2006): 152.

30 See "Special Feature: The Great War in Numbers"; available at www.worldwar1.com/sfnum.htm.

31 Carnegie Commission on Preventing Deadly Conflict, *Preventing Deadly Conflict: Final Report* (Washington, DC: Carnegie Commission on Preventing Deadly Conflict, 1998), p. 11.

32 Kaldor, *New and Old Wars*, pp. 8, 100.

33 Holsti, *Taming the Sovereigns*, pp. 284–5.

34 Virgil Hawkins, "The Price of Inaction: The Media and Humanitarian Intervention," *Journal of Humanitarian Assistance*, May 15, 2001; available at https://sites.tufts.edu/jha/archives/1504.

35 Roberts, "Lives and Statistics"; and Human Security Report Project, *Human Security Report 2009/2010: The Causes of Peace and the Shrinking Costs of War* (Oxford: Oxford University Press, 2011). See also Mary Kaldor, "In Defence of New Wars," *Stability* 2(1) (2013): 1–16.

36 Jean-Paul Azam and Anke Hoeffler, "Violence against Civilians in Civil Wars: Looting or Terror?," *Journal of Peace Research* 39(4) (July 2002): 461–85.

37 Committee to Protect Journalists, "Iraq: Journalists in Danger"; available at www.cpj.org/Briefings/Iraq/Iraq_danger.html.

38 Michael Astor, "Iraq's Heavy Journalist Death Toll Keeps Climbing," Huffpost Media, September 7, 2010; available at www.huffingtonpost.com/2010/09/07/iraqs-heavy-journalist-de_n_708299.html.

39 Cate Buchanan and Mireille Widmer, "Putting Guns in their Place: A Resource Pack for Two Years of Action by Humanitarian Agencies," Centre for Humanitarian Dialogue, October 2004, p. 35.

40 Afghanistan Watch, "Afghanistan by the Numbers," January 18, 2006.

41 Sune Engel Rasmussen, "Attacks on Aid Workers Reflects Rising Danger in Afghanistan," *Guardian*, June 4, 2015; available at http://www.theguardian.com/global-development/2015/jun/04/afghanistan-attack-aid-workers-danger-gunmen-humanitarian-staff.

42 Abby Stoddard, Adele Harmer, and Katherine Haver, *Providing Aid in Insecure Environments: Trends in Policy and Operations* (London: Overseas Development Institute, 2006), HPG Report 23, 1, 13. Also see National Intelligence Council, *Global Humanitarian Emergencies: Trends and Projections, 1999–2000* (Washington, DC: National Intelligence Council, August 1999), p. 14; UN Department of Public Information, *Basic Facts about the United Nations* (New York: United Nations, 2000), p. 251.

43 UN OCHA, *To Stay and Deliver: Good Practice for Humanitarians in Complex Security Environments* (New York: OCHA, 2011); available at http://ochanet.unocha.org/p/Documents/Stay_and_Deliver.pdf.

44 Humanitarian Outcomes, *The Aid Worker Database*, updated August 16, 2015; available at https://aidworkersecurity.org/incidents/report/summary.

45 UN Convention on the Safety of United Nations and Associated Personnel, adopted December 9, 1994, came into force January 15, 1999.

46 Jeffrey Goldberg, "Before the Beheadings," *The Atlantic* (December 2014).

47 Quoted by Rick Gladstone, "World Briefings/Worldwide; Growing Dangers for Journalists Cited," *New York Times*, April 28, 2015. See also Committee to Protect Journalists, *Attacks on*

the Press, 2015 Edition; available at https://www.cpj.org/2015/04/attacks-on-the-press.php.

48 Michael Barnett and Thomas G. Weiss (eds.), *Humanitarianism in Question: Politics, Power, Ethics* (Ithaca, NY: Cornell University Press, 2007), and *Humanitarianism Contested: Where Angels Fear to Tread* (London: Routledge, 2011).

49 For a parsing by a practitioner of contemporary humanitarianism as an ideology, a movement, a profession, and a business, see Antonio Donini, "The Far Side: The Meta-functions of Humanitarianism in a Globalised World," *Disasters* 34(2) (2010): 220–37.

50 Michael Barnett, *The Empire of Humanity: A History of Humanitarianism* (Ithaca, NY: Cornell University Press, 2011).

51 Thomas G. Weiss, "The Dialectics of Humanitarian Space," in *Negotiating Relief: The Politics of Humanitarian Space*, ed. Michael Acuto (London: Hurst, 2014), pp. xxi–xxix.,

52 Data drawn from Monty G. Marshall, "Major Episodes of Political Violence, 1946–1999"; available at http://www.systemicpeace.org/warlist.htm.

53 Since 1998, the number of deaths in the DRC has approached 5.5 million or is closer to 200,000 – depending on the source. See International Rescue Committee, "Mortality in the Democratic Republic of Congo: Results from a Nationwide Survey," conducted from April to July 2004; available at http://www.rescue.org/sites/default/files/migrated/resources/DRC_MortalitySurvey2004_RB_8Dec04.pdf. Human Security Report Project, *Human Security Report 2009–2010: The Causes of Peace and the Shrinking Costs of War*; available at http://www.hsrgroup.org/docs/Publications/HSR20092010/20092010HumanSecurityReport-CoverPage.pdf.

54 *Global Humanitarian Assistance Report 2014* (Somerset, UK Development Initiatives, 2014), pp. 4 and 21; available at http://www.globalhumanitarianassistance.org/wp-content/uploads/2014/09/GHA-Report-2014-interactive.pdf, pp. 4–5 (hereafter GHA)

55 Linda Polman, *The Crisis Caravan: What's Wrong with Humanitarian Aid?* (New York: Henry Holt, 2010). The estimate for current NGOs comes from Glyn Taylor et al., *The State of the Humanitarian System* (London: ALNAP and ODI, 2012), p. 9

56 *GHA 2013* (Somerset, UK Development Initiatives, 2013), p. 6; available at http://www.globalhumanitarianassistance.org/wp-content/uploads/2013/07/GHA-Report-20131.pdf, pp. 20, 30; and *GHA 2014*, pp. 4–5, 15.

57 *GHA 2014*, pp. 4–7, 34

58 A few years back the number was estimated to be 274,000: see Taylor et al., *The State of the Humanitarian System*, p. 9. Six years earlier, it was 200,000: see Abby Stoddard, Adele Harmer, and Katherine Haver, *Providing Aid in Insecure Environments: Trends in Policy and Operations*, HPG Report 23 (London: Overseas Development Institute, 2006).

59 Peter Walker and Catherine Ross, *Professionalizing the Humanitarian Sector: A Scoping Study*, Report Commissioned by the Enhancing Learning and Research for Humanitarian Assistance, April 2010, pp. 11–12.

60 Alexander Cooley and James Ron, "The NGO Scramble: Organizational Insecurity and the Political Economy of Transnational Action," *International Security* 27(1) (2002): 13.

61 Anna Jeffreys, "Giving Voice to Silent Emergencies," April 3, 2002; available at www.reliefweb.int/rw/rwb.nsf/AllDocsByUNID/dfa2cbec597f702c85256b920059b28f.

62 Toby Porter, "The Partiality of Humanitarian Assistance – Kosovo in Comparative Perspective," *The Journal of Humanitarian Assistance*, June 2000.

63 See Susan Woodward, *Balkan Tragedy: Chaos and Dissolution after the Cold War* (Washington, DC: Brookings Institution, 1995). As UNHCR special envoy to the former Yugoslavia Nicholas Morris explains, the distinction between civilians and combatants was extremely difficult in the Bosnian context because most families had members who fought in the war. See Nicholas Morris, "Humanitarian Aid and Neutrality," paper presented at the Conference on the Promotion and Protection of Human Rights in Acute Crisis, London, February 1998; available at www.essex.ac.uk/rightsinacutecrisis/report/morris.htm.

64 See Joanna Macrae (ed.), *New Humanitarianisms: A Review of Trends in Global Political Action* (London: ODI, 2002); available at: http://www.odi.org/sites/odi.org.uk/files/odi-assets/publications-opinion-files/293.pdf; and Thomas G. Weiss, "Principles, Politics, and Humanitarian Action," *Ethics & International Affairs* 13 (1999): 1–22.

65 Michael Barnett, "Humanitarianism Transformed," *Perspectives on Politics* 3(4) (2005): 723–41.
66 This was popularized by Roberta Cohen and Francis M. Deng, *Masses in Flight: The Global Crisis of Internal Displacement* (Washington, DC: Brookings Institution, 1998), p. 10; and "Exodus within Borders," *Foreign Affairs* 77(4) (1998): 15.
67 Antonio Donini, *The Future of Humanitarian Action: Implications of Iraq and Other Recent Crises* (Medford, MA: Tufts University, 2004); F. Fox, "New Humanitarianism: Does it Provide a Moral Banner for the 21st Century?," *Disasters* 25(4) (2001): 275–89.
68 Michael Bryans, Bruce D. Jones, and Janice Gross Stein, *"Mean Times": Humanitarian Action in Complex Political Emergencies – Stark Choices, Cruel Dilemmas* (Toronto: Programme on Conflict Management and Negotiation, Center for International Studies, University of Toronto, 1999), pp. 9–10.
69 Bruce M. Oswald, "The Creation and Control of Places of Protection during United Nations Peace Operations," *International Review of the Red Cross* 83(844) (December 2001): 1013.
70 See Michael Barnett and Martha Finnemore, *Rules for the World: International Organizations in Global Order* (Ithaca, NY: Cornell University Press, 2004), ch. 4, "Defining Refugees and Voluntary Repatriation at the United Nations High Commissioner for Refugees," pp. 73–120, esp. pp. 75 and 95. For UNHCR's views on repatriation, see its publication *State of the World's Refugees: Fifty Years of Humanitarian Action* (New York: Oxford University Press, 2000), pp. 155–83.
71 Bob Haywood and Roberta Spivak, *Maritime Piracy* (London: Routledge, 2011); Danielle A. Zach, D. Conor Seyle, and Jens Vestergaard Madsen, *Burden-Sharing Multilevel Governance: A Study of the Contact Group on Piracy off the Coast of Somalia* (Broomfield, CO: One Earth Future Foundation, 2013).
72 "Haiti earthquake Death Toll Exaggerated, US Report Finds," *Telegraph*, June 1, 2011; available at www.telegraph.co.uk/news/worldnews/centralamericaandthecaribbean/haiti/8549193/Haiti-earthquake-death-toll-exaggerated-US-report-finds.html. The article also notes that these figures conflict with the UN's International Organization for Migration (IOM) displacement figures, which estimated that the camp population reached about 1.5 million.

73 Barnett, "Humanitarianism Transformed."
74 Roland Paris, *At War's End: Building Peace after Civil Conflict* (New York: Cambridge University Press, 2004).
75 Myron Wiener, "The Clash of Norms: Dilemmas in Refugee Policies," in *Workshop on the Demography of Forced Migration* (Washington, DC: National Academy of Sciences, 1997), p. 5.
76 David Kennedy, *The Dark Sides of Virtue: Reassessing International Humanitarianism* (Princeton: Princeton University Press, 2004).
77 Mary B. Anderson, *Do No Harm: How Aid Can Support War – or Peace* (Boulder, CO: Lynne Rienner, 1999). See also Hugo Slim, "Doing the Right Thing: Relief Agencies, Moral Dilemmas, and Moral Responsibility in Political Emergencies and War," *Disasters* 21(3) (1997): 244–57; Duffield, *Global Governance and the New Wars*, pp. 90–5; and Des Gasper, "'Drawing a Line' – Ethical and Political Strategies in Complex Emergency Assistance," *European Journal of Development Research* 11(2) (1999): 87–114.
78 James Fearon, "The Rise of Emergency Relief Aid," in *Humanitarianism Contested: Power, Politics, and Ethics*, ed. Michael Barnett and Thomas G. Weiss (Ithaca, NY: Cornell University Press, 2008), pp. 49–72.
79 Ian Smillie and Larry Minear, *The Charity of Nations: Humanitarian Action in a Calculating World* (Bloomfield, CN: Kumarian, 2004), p. 1.
80 Marc Lindenberg and Coralie Bryant, *Going Global: Transforming Relief and Development NGOs* (Bloomfield, CN: Kumarian, 2001), p. 76.
81 Thomas G. Weiss, *Military–Civilian Interactions: Humanitarian Crises and the Responsibility to Protect*, 2nd edn (Lanham, MD: Rowman & Littlefield, 2005), pp. 192–7.
82 Thomas G. Weiss, "The Humanitarian Action, Impulse Not Imperative," in *The United Nations Security Council: From Cold War to the 21st Century*, ed. Sebastian von Einsedel, David Malone, and Bruno Stagno (Boulder, CO: Lynne Rienner, 2016), ch. 11.
83 Alan J. Kuperman, "Mitigating the Moral Hazard of Humanitarian Intervention: Lessons from Economics," *Global Governance* 14(2) (2008): 219–40. See also his "Obama's Libya Debacle," *Foreign Affairs* 94(2) (2015): 66–77; and a reply by Derek Chollet and Ben Fishman, "Who Lost Libya?" *Foreign Affairs* 94(3) (2015): 154–7.

84 See Simon Chesterman, *Just War or Just Peace? Humanitarian Intervention and International Law* (Oxford: Oxford University Press, 2001).
85 Thomas G. Weiss, "RtoP Alive and Well after Libya," *Ethics & International Affairs* 25(3) (2011): 1–6.
86 Fiona Terry, *Condemned to Repeat? The Paradox of Humanitarian Action* (Ithaca, NY: Cornell University Press, 2002).

CHAPTER 4 NEW THINKING: THE RESPONSIBILITY TO PROTECT

1 For interpretations of this normative advance, see Ramesh Thakur, *The United Nations, Peace and Security: From Collective Security to the Responsibility to Protect* (Cambridge: Cambridge University Press, 2006); Gareth Evans, *The Responsibility to Protect: Ending Mass Atrocities Once and For All* (Washington, DC: Brookings Institution, 2008); Alex Bellamy, *Responsibility to Protect: The Global Effort to End Mass Atrocities* (Cambridge: Polity, 2009); James Pattison, *Humanitarian Intervention and the Responsibility to Protect: Who Should Intervene?* (Oxford: Oxford University Press, 2010); Anne Orford, *International Authority and the Responsibility to Protect* (Cambridge: Cambridge University Press, 2011); Aidan Hehir, *The Responsibility to Protect: Rhetoric, Reality and the Future of Humanitarian Intervention* (Houndmills, UK: Palgrave Macmillan, 2012).
2 Anthony Lewis, "The Challenge of Global Justice Now," *Daedalus* 132(1) (2003): 8.
3 Edward Newman, "Humanitarian Intervention, Legality and Legitimacy," *International Journal of Human Rights* 6(4) (2002): 102–20; Danish Institute of International Affairs, *Humanitarian Intervention: Legal and Political Aspects* (Copenhagen: Danish Institute of International Affairs, 1999); Advisory Council on International Affairs and Advisory Committee on Issues of Public International Law, *Humanitarian Intervention* (The Hague: Advisory Council on International Affairs, 2000); Independent International Commission on Kosovo, *The Kosovo Report: Conflict, International Response, Lessons Learned* (Oxford: Oxford University Press, 2000).
4 Mohammed Ayoob, "Humanitarian Intervention and

International Society," *The International Journal of Human Rights* 6(1) (2002): 84.

5 The figures come from UNHCR estimates at http://www.unhcr.org.uk/about-us/key-facts-and-figures.html.

6 Anthony M. Messina and Gallya Lahav (eds.), *The Migration Reader: Explaining Politics and Policies* (Boulder, CO: Lynne Rienner, 2006).

7 David A. Korn, *Exodus within Borders* (Washington, DC: Brookings Institution, 1999).

8 Statistics are often uncontested because of disputes as to who counts and when displacement ends. See Erin D. Mooney, "The Concept of Internal Displacement and the Case for IDPs as a Category of Concern," *Refugee Survey Quarterly* 24(3) (2005): 9–26.

9 Donald Steinberg, *Orphans of Conflict: Caring for the Internally Displaced* (Washington, DC: US Institute of Peace, 2005), Special Report #148.

10 Centers for Disease Control, "Famine-Affected, Refugee, and Displaced Populations: Recommendations for Public Health Issues," *Morbidity and Mortality Weekly Report* 41, RR-13 (1992). Subsequent evaluations are essentially unchanged. See Peter Salama, Paul Spiegel, and Richard Brennan, "Refugees – No Less Vulnerable: The Internally Displaced in Humanitarian Emergencies," *The Lancet* 357(9266) (May 5, 2001): 1430–1.

11 See Francis M. Deng and I. William Zartman (eds.), *Conflict Resolution in Africa* (Washington, DC: Brookings Institution, 1991); Francis M. Deng and Terrence Lyons (eds.), *African Reckoning: A Quest for Good Governance* (Washington, DC: Brookings Institution, 1998); Francis M. Deng, "Reconciling Sovereignty with Responsibility: A Basis for International Humanitarian Action," in *Africa in World Politics: Post-Cold War Challenges*, ed. John W. Harbeson and Donald Rothschild (Boulder, CO: Westview, 1995), pp. 295–310.

12 Francis M. Deng, *Protecting the Dispossessed: A Challenge for the International Community* (Washington, DC: Brookings Institution, 1993). See also two earlier articles: "Dealing with the Displaced: A Challenge to the International Community," *Global Governance* 1(1) (1995): 45–57, and "Frontiers of Sovereignty," *Leiden Journal of International Law* 8(2) (1995): 249–86.

13 Roberta Cohen and Francis M. Deng, *Masses in Flight: The Global*

Crisis of Internal Displacement (Washington, DC: Brookings Institution, 1998); and Roberta Cohen and Francis M. Deng (eds.), *The Forsaken People: Case Studies of the Internally Displaced* (Washington, DC: Brookings Institution, 1998).

14 The first was Janie Hampton (ed.), *Internally Displaced People: A Global Survey* (London: Earthscan, 1998), which now appears annually as *Internal Displacement: Global Overview of Trends and Development* (Geneva: Norwegian Refugee Council). Updates are on the website at www.internal-displacement.org.

15 See Nicholas Van Hear and Christopher McDowell (eds.), *Catching Fire: Containing Complex Displacement in a Volatile World* (Lanham, MD: Lexington Books, 2006); Susan F. Martin et al., *The Uprooted: Improving Humanitarian Responses to Forced Migration* (Lanham, MD: Lexington Books, 2005); special issue on "Internally Displaced Persons: The Challenges of International Protection – Articles, Documents, Literature Survey," *Refugee Survey Quarterly* 24(3) (2005); Simon Bagshaw and Diane Paul, *Protect or Neglect? Toward a More Effective United Nations Approach to the Protection of Internally Displaced Persons* (Washington, DC: Brookings Institution and OCHA, 2004); Catherine Phuong, *The International Protection of Internally Displaced Persons* (Cambridge: Cambridge University Press, 2004); Kathleen Newland, with Erin Patrick and Monette Zard, *No Refuge: The Challenge of Internal Displacement* (New York and Geneva: OCHA, 2003); Cécile Dubernet, *The International Containment of Displaced Persons: Humanitarian Spaces without Exit* (Aldershot, UK: Ashgate, 2001).

16 "Guiding Principles on Internal Displacement," UN document E/CN.4/1998/53/Add.2, February 11, 1998, has subsequently been published by the OCHA and several other institutions.

17 Susan Martin, *The Handbook for Applying the Guiding Principles on Internal Displacement* (New York: OCHA, 1999); and Inter-Agency Standing Committee Working Group, *Manual on Field Practice in Internal Displacement* (Geneva: OCHA, 1999).

18 Stephen Castles et al., *Developing DfID's Policy Approach to Refugees and Internally Displaced Persons*, vol. 1 (Oxford: Queen Elizabeth House, University of Oxford, February 2005), p. 77.

19 John Borton, Margie Buchanan-Smith, and Ralf Otto, *Support to Internally Displaced Persons: Learning from Evaluations* (Stockholm: Swedish International Development Agency, 2005), p. 12.

20 Louis Emmerij, Richard Jolly, and Thomas G. Weiss, *Ahead of the Curve? UN Ideas and Global Challenges* (Bloomington: Indiana University Press, 2001), p. 214.

21 A detailed history of 1992–2004 is Thomas G. Weiss and David A. Korn, *Internal Displacement: Conceptualization and its Consequences* (London: Routledge, 2006).

22 Kersten Martens, *NGOs and the United Nations: Institutionalization, Professionalization and Adaptation* (Houndsmill, UK: Palgrave Macmillan, 2005).

23 Kofi Annan, "Two Concepts of Sovereignty," *The Economist* 352 (September 18, 1999): 49–50.

24 Five speeches from 1998 and 1999 are reproduced in Kofi A. Annan, *The Question of Intervention – Statements by the Secretary-General* (New York: UN, 1999). See also *"We the Peoples": The United Nations in the 21st Century* (New York: UN, 2000). For a discussion of the September 1999 speech, see Thomas G. Weiss, "The Politics of Humanitarian Ideas," *Security Dialogue* 31(1) (2000): 11–23.

25 Gareth Evans, "Foreword," in Ramesh Thakur, *The United Nations, Peace and Security*, p. xiv.

26 Michael Reisman, "Sovereignty and Human Rights in Contemporary International Law," *American Journal of International Law* 84(4) (1990): 866–76.

27 Louis Henkin, "Kosovo and the Law of 'Humanitarian Intervention,'" *American Journal of International Law* 93(4) (1999): 824–8.

28 The analysis draws on Thomas G. Weiss, "To Intervene or Not to Intervene?," *Canadian Journal of Foreign Policy* 9(2) (2002): 141–57.

29 World Commission on Environment and Development, *Our Common Future* (Oxford: Oxford University Press, 1987).

30 For interpretations by commissioners, see Evans, *The Responsibility to Protect*; Thakur, *The United Nations, Peace and Security*, esp. ch. 11.

31 International Commission on Intervention and State Sovereignty, *The Responsibility to Protect* (Ottawa: ICISS, 2001), p. xi. All quotes are from the "Synopsis," pp. xi–xiii.

32 Roland Paris, *At War's End: Building Peace after Civil Conflict* (Cambridge: Cambridge University Press, 2004), p. ix.

33 Stanley Hoffmann, *The Ethics and Politics of Humanitarian*

Intervention (South Bend, IN: University of Notre Dame Press, 1997), p. 39.

34 Ramesh Thakur, "Iraq and the Responsibility to Protect," *Behind the Headlines* 62(1) (2004): 1–16, and "A Shared Responsibility for a More Secure World," *Global Governance* 11(3) (2005): 281–9.

35 See Michael Walzer, *Just and Unjust Wars: A Moral Argument with Historical Illustrations*, 3rd edn (New York: Basic Books, 2000), including a revised discussion on humanitarian intervention, pp. 101–8; J. Bryan Hehir, "The Just-War Ethic Revisited," in *Ideas and Ideals: Essays on Politics in Honor of Stanley Hoffmann*, ed. Linda B. Miller and Michael Joseph Smith (Boulder, CO: Westview, 1993), pp. 144–61; and J. Bryan Hehir, "Intervention: From Theories to Cases," *Ethics & International Affairs* 9 (1995): 1–13.

36 Chantal de Jonge Oudraat, *Intervention in Internal Conflicts: Legal and Political Conundrums* (Washington, DC: Carnegie Endowment for International Peace, 2000).

37 International Law Association, *Report of the Fifty-Fourth Conference* (1971), pp. 633, 641; *Report of the Fifty-Fifth Conference* (1974), p. 608; *Report of the Fifty-Sixth Conference* (1976), p. 217; *Report of the Fifty-Seventh Conference* (1978), pp. 519, 521.

38 Lawyers' Committee for Human Rights, *In the National Interest 2001 – Human Rights Policies for the Bush Administration* (New York: Lawyers' Committee for Human Rights, 2001); International Council in Human Rights Policy, "NGO Responses to Military Interventions in Human Rights Crises," draft report, September 2001.

39 Michael Ignatieff, *The Warrior's Honor: Ethnic War and the Modern Conscience* (New York: Henry, 1997); Simon Chesterman, *Just War or Just Peace? Humanitarian Intervention and International Law* (New York: Oxford University Press, 2001); Nicholas J. Wheeler, *Saving Strangers: Humanitarian Intervention in International Society* (Oxford: Oxford University Press, 2000); Fernando Tesón, *Humanitarian Intervention: An Inquiry into Law and Morality*, 2nd edn (Irvington-on-Hudson, NY: Transnational Publishers, 1997).

40 Independent International Commission on Kosovo, *Kosovo Report: Conflict, International Response, Lessons Learned* (Oxford: Oxford University Press, 2000), p. 4.

41 The lowest estimate – *only* 125,000 lives would have been saved

from a plausible intervention – comes from Alan J. Kuperman, *The Limits of Humanitarian Intervention: Genocide in Rwanda* (Washington, DC: US Institute of Peace Press, 2001), p. 76.

42 Christine Bourloyannis, "The Security Council of the United Nations and the Implementation of International Humanitarian Law," *Denver Journal of International Law and Policy* 20(3) (1993): 43.

43 David P. Forsythe, *Humanitarian Politics* (Baltimore, MD: Johns Hopkins University Press, 1977), and *The Humanitarians: The International Committee of the Red Cross* (Cambridge: Cambridge University Press, 2005). For a compendium of relevant documents with commentary, see Adam Roberts and Richard Guelff (eds.), *Documents on the Laws of War*, 3rd edn (Oxford: Oxford University Press, 2000).

44 Th. A. van Baarda, "The Involvement of the Security Council in Maintaining International Law," *Netherlands Quarterly of Human Rights* 12(1) (1994): 140.

45 José E. Alvarez, *International Organizations as Law-makers* (Oxford: Oxford University Press, 2005), p. 591.

46 "The Lost UN Summit Meeting," *New York Times*, September 14, 2005.

47 Kofi A. Annan, "In Larger Freedom: Decision Time at the UN," *Foreign Affairs* 84(3) (2005): 66.

48 High-level Panel on Threats, Challenges and Change, *A More Secure World: Our Shared Responsibility* (New York: UN, 2004), paras 283 and 285.

49 Kofi Annan, *In Larger Freedom: Towards Development, Security and Human Rights for All*, UN document A/59/2005, March 21, 2005, para. 183.

50 *2005 World Summit Outcome*, adopted by General Assembly resolution A/RES/60/1, October 24, 2005, paras 157 and 160.

51 Interview on March 29, 2006; available at www.vibewire.net.

52 Jane Morse, "US Wins Seat on the UN Human Rights Council," May 12, 2009; available at http://iipdigital.usembassy.gov/st/english/article/2009/05/20090512171515ajesromo.7585108.html#axzz3m7c8s7XY.

53 Bertrand Ramcharan, *The UN Human Rights Council* (London: Routledge, 2011), p. 9.

54 *2005 World Summit Outcome*, para. 124.

55 Annan, *Question of Intervention*, p. 7.

56 High-level Panel, *A More Secure World*, para. 201, emphasis in original, and para. 207.
57 *Position Paper of the People's Republic of China on the United Nations Reforms* (Beijing, June 7, 2005), Part III.1, "Responsibility to Protect"; available at http://news.xinhuanet.com/english/2005-06/08/content_3056817_3.htm; *American Interests and UN Reform: Report of the Task Force on the United Nations* (Washington, DC: US Institute of Peace, 2005), p. 15.
58 Annan, "In Larger Freedom," paras 122–35.
59 *2005 World Summit Outcome*, paras 138–9.
60 Ban Ki-moon, *Implementing the Responsibility to Protect* (New York: UN, 2009).
61 Global Centre for the Responsibility to Protect (GCR2P), "Implementing the Responsibility to Protect: The 2009 General Assembly Debate: An Assessment," August 2009; available at: http://www.globalr2p.org/publications/42.
62 Ban Ki-moon, *Early Warning, Assessment and the Responsibility to Protect*. Report of the Secretary-General, UN document A/64/864, July 14, 2010, para. 14.
63 Martha Finnemore and Kathryn Sikkink, "International Norm Dynamics and Political Change," *International Organization* 52(4) (1998): 887–917; Thomas Risse, Stephen Ropp, and Kathryn Sikkink, *The Power of Human Rights: International Norms and Domestic Change* (Cambridge: Cambridge University Press, 1999); Margaret Keck and Kathryn Sikkink, *Activists beyond Borders: Advocacy Networks in International Politics* (Ithaca, NY: Cornell University Press, 1998).
64 "An Idea whose Time Has Come – and Gone?" *The Economist*, July 23, 2009.
65 "Statement by the President of the General Assembly, Miguel d'Escoto Brockmann, at the Opening of the 97th Session of the General Assembly," July 23, 2009.
66 GCR2P, "Implementing the Responsibility to Protect."
67 GCR2P, "'Early Warning, Assessment, and the Responsibility to Protect': Informal Interactive Dialogue of the General Assembly held on 9 August 2010," September 2010; available at http://www.globalr2p.org/publications/86.
68 Ban Ki-moon, *The Responsibility to Protect, Pillar III: Timely and Decisive Response*, Report of the Secretary-General, UN document S/2012/578, July 24, 2012.

69 Ban Ki-moon, *Fulfilling Our Collective Responsibility: International Assistance and the Responsibility to Protect*, UN document S/2014/449, July 11, 2014.

70 Alex J. Bellamy, "The Responsibility to Protect – Five Years On," *Ethics and International Affairs* 24(2) (2010): 143–69; Edward C. Luck, "The Responsibility to Protect: Growing Pains or Early Promise?" *Ethics & International Affairs* 24(2) (2010): 349–65.

71 Global Centre for the Responsibility to Protect, "Meeting of National Focal Points on R2P Convened by Costa Rica, Denmark and Ghana, New York, May 17 and 18, 2011," *GCR2P Report*, June 2011; available at http://www.globalr2p.org/our_work/r2p_focal_points.

72 Ban Ki-moon, *Report of the Secretary-General on the Responsibility to Protect: State Responsibility and Prevention*, UN document A/67/929-S/2013/399, July 9, 2013, paras. 33 and 72. For the most recent document, see Ban Ki-moon, *A Vital and Enduring Commitment: Implementing the Responsibility to Protect*, UN document A/69/981-S/2015/500.

73 "Letter Dated 9 November 2011 from the Permanent Representative of Brazil to the United Nations Addressed to the Secretary-General," UN document A/66/551-S/2011/701, 1.

74 Wolfgang Seibel, "R2P and German Foreign Policy 'after Libya,'" in *Norms and Practice of the Responsibility to Protect*, ed. C. Daase, J. Junk, and W. Seibel (London: Routledge, forthcoming).

75 Pattison, *Humanitarian Intervention and the Responsibility to Protect*, p. 250; emphasis in original.

76 Chris Brown, "The Antipolitical Theory of Responsibility to Protect," *Global Responsibility to Protect* 5(4) (2013): 440.

77 See Global Center for the Responsibility to Protect, "R2P References in United Nations Security Council Resolutions and Presidential Statements"; available at http://www.globalr2p.org/media/files/unsc-resolutions-and-statements-with-r2p-table-as-of-december-2014.pdf.

78 David Rieff, "R2P, R.I.P.," *New York Times*, November 7, 2011. The author's response is Thomas G. Weiss, "Military Humanitarianism: Syria Hasn't Killed It," *Washington Quarterly* 37(1) (2014): 7–20.

79 Alex Bellamy, "R2P – Dead or Alive?" in *The Responsibility to Protect – From Evasive to Reluctant Action? The Role of Global Middle Powers* (Johannesburg: United Litho, 2012), p. 12.

80 Shannon D. Beebe and Mary Kaldor, *The Ultimate Weapon Is No Weapon: Human Security and the New Rules of War and Peace* (New York: Public Affairs, 2010).
81 Michael Barnett and Thomas G. Weiss, *Humanitarianism Contested: Where Angels Fear to Tread* (London: Routledge, 2011).
82 Gareth Evans, "The Evolution of the Responsibility to Protect: From Concept and Principle to Actionable Norm," in *Theorising the Responsibility to Protect*, ed. Ramesh Thakur and William Maley (Cambridge: Cambridge University Press, 2015), p. 34.
83 See Alan J. Kuperman, "Mitigating the Moral Hazard of Humanitarian Intervention: Lessons from Economics," *Global Governance* 14(2) (2008): 219–40; "The Moral Hazard of Humanitarian Intervention: Lessons from the Balkans," *International Studies Quarterly* 52 (2008): 49–80; "Darfur: Strategic Victimhood Strikes Again?" *Genocide Studies and Prevention* 4(3) (2009): 281–303.
84 Roland Paris, "The 'Responsibility to Protect' and the Structural Problems of Preventive Humanitarian Intervention," *International Peacekeeping* 21(5) (2015): 569–603.
85 Ramesh Thakur, "R2P's 'Structural' Problems: A Response to Roland Paris," *International Peacekeeping* 22(1) (2015); available at: http://www.tandfonline.com/loi/finp20.
86 Ramesh Thakur and Thomas G. Weiss, "R2P: From Idea to Norm – and Action?" *Global Responsibility to Protect* 1(1) (2009): 22.

CHAPTER 5 SO WHAT? MOVING FROM RHETORIC TO REALITY

1 Jane Boulden and Thomas G. Weiss (eds.), *Terrorism and the UN: Before and After September 11* (Bloomington: Indiana University Press, 2004); Thomas G. Weiss, Margaret E. Crahan, and John Goering (eds.), *Wars on Terrorism and Iraq: Human Rights, Unilateralism, and U.S. Foreign Policy* (London: Routledge, 2004).
2 Thomas G. Weiss, "The Responsibility to Protect in a Unipolar Era," *Security Dialogue* 35(2) (2004): 135–53.
3 Mohammed Ayoob, "Humanitarian Intervention and International Society," *International Journal of Human Rights* 6(1)

(2002): 81–102; David Chandler, *From Kosovo to Kabul: Human Rights and International Intervention* (London: Pluto Press, 2002).

4 Michael Akehurst, "Humanitarian Intervention," in *Intervention in World Politics*, ed. Hedley Bull (Oxford: Clarendon Press, 1984), p. 111.

5 Albrecht Schnabel and Ramesh Thakur (eds.), *Kosovo and the Challenge of Humanitarian Intervention: Selective Indignation, Collective Action, and International Citizenship* (Tokyo: United Nations University Press, 2000).

6 Ramesh Thakur, *The United Nations, Peace and Security: From Collective Security to the Responsibility to Protect* (Cambridge: Cambridge University Press, 2006), ch. 12.

7 Quoted by Kathleen Newland with Erin Patrick and Monette Zard, *No Refuge: The Challenge of Internal Displacement* (New York and Geneva: UN, Office for the Coordination of Humanitarian Affairs, 2003), p. 37.

8 Statement by Hugo Chavez, President of Venezuela, at the General Debate of the 60th Session of the United Nations General Assembly, September 15, 2005; available at http://www.un.org/en/ga/65/meetings/generaldebate/Portals/1/statements/634213735343437500VE_en.pdf.

9 Philip Nel, "South Africa: The Demand for Legitimate Multilateralism," in Schnabel and Thakur (eds.), *Kosovo and the Challenge of Humanitarian Intervention*, pp. 245–59.

10 Peter J. Spiro, "The New Sovereigntists," *Foreign Affairs* 79(6) (2000): 9–15.

11 Alex J. Bellamy, "What Will Become of the 'Responsibility to Protect'?," *Ethics & International Affairs* 20(2) (2006): 143–69.

12 David Rieff, *A Bed for the Night: Humanitarianism in Crisis* (New York: Simon & Schuster, 2002), p. 11.

13 Michael Walzer, "On Humanitarianism," *Foreign Affairs* 90(4) (2011): 77.

14 Rami Mani and Thomas G. Weiss (eds.), *The Responsibility to Protect: Cultural Perspectives in the Global South* (London: Routledge, 2011).

15 The secretary-general's address to the General Assembly, New York, September 23, 2003; available at http://www.un.org/webcast/ga/58/statements/sg2eng030923.

16 For a readable account of the law for non-lawyers, see Michael

Byers, *War Law: Understanding International Law and Armed Conflict* (New York: Grove Press, 2005).

17 See Thomas G. Weiss, "R2P after 9/11 and after the World Summit," *Wisconsin International Law Journal* 24(3) (2006): 741–60.

18 Richard Falk, in special section "Humanitarian Intervention: A Forum," *The Nation*, July 2003, p. 12.

19 "Speech Given by the Prime Minister in Sedgefield, Justifying Military Action in Iraq and Warning of the Continued Threat of Global Terrorism," March 5, 2004; available at http://politics. guardian.co.uk/iraq/story/0,12956,1162991,00.html.

20 Fernando Tesón, "Ending Tyranny in Iraq," *Ethics & International Affairs* 19(2) (2005): 1–20.

21 Terry Nardin, "Humanitarian Imperialism," *Ethics & International Affairs* 19(2) (2005): 21.

22 *National Security Strategy of the United States of America*, September 2002; available at http://www.state.gov/documents/ organization/63562.pdf.

23 Adam Roberts, "The United Nations and Humanitarian Intervention," in *Humanitarian Intervention and International Relations*, ed. Jennifer Welsh (Oxford: Oxford University Press, 2004), p. 90.

24 Iraq Body Count; available at www.iraqbodycount.org/ (accessed August 27, 2015).

25 Unknown News; available at http://www.unknownnews.org/ casualties.html This is the latest figure as of August 2010. The website explains its methodology and the differences with the Iraq Body Count figure documented in the previous citation. This number still seems to be the best civilian-specific death toll, and the number has not been updated since 2010. Further, the newest data would be complicated by ISIS-related violence, which is arguably distinct from the consequences of the earlier intervention.

26 Unknown News estimated this figure to be about 1,560,000 in August 2010.

27 Carl Conetta, "The Wages of War: Iraqi Combatant and Noncombatant Fatalities in the 2003 Conflict," Project on Defense Alternatives Research Monograph #8, October 20, 2003; available at http://www.comw.org/pda/fulltext/0310rm8. pdf.

28 Alex J. Bellamy, "Responsibility to Protect or Trojan Horse? The Crisis in Darfur and Humanitarian Intervention after Iraq," *Ethics & International Affairs* 19(2) (2005): 32–3.
29 Lee Feinstein and Anne-Marie Slaughter, "A Duty to Prevent," *Foreign Affairs* 83(1) (2004): 136–50; Allan Buchanan and Robert O. Keohane, "The Preventive Use of Force: A Cosmopolitan Institutional Proposal," *Ethics & International Affairs* 18(1) (2004): 1–22.
30 Thomas M. Nichols, "Anarchy and Order in the New Age of Prevention," *World Policy Journal* 22(3) (2005): 20.
31 Ivo Daalder and James Steinberg, "Preventive War, A Useful Tool," *Los Angeles Times*, December 4, 2005; available at http://articles.latimes.com/2005/dec/04/opinion/op-preemptivewar4. See the full argument in "The Future of Preemption," *The American Interest* 1(2) (2005): 30–9.
32 Steven Pinker, *The Better Angels of Our Nature* (New York: Viking 2011).
33 James Traub, "The *Next* Resolution," *New York Times Magazine*, April 13, 2003, p. 51.
34 Chris Patten, "Jaw-Jaw, Not War-War," *Financial Times*, February 15, 2002.
35 Rosemary Foot, S. Neil MacFarlane, and Michael Mastanduno (eds.), *The United States and Multilateral Organizations* (Oxford: Oxford University Press, 2003); Michael Byers and Georg Nolte (eds.), *United States Hegemony and the Foundations of International Law* (Cambridge: Cambridge University Press, 2003).
36 Charles Kindleberger, *The World in Depression, 1929–39* (Berkeley: University of California Press, 1973); Robert Gilpin, *The Political Economy of International Relations* (Princeton: Princeton University Press, 1987).
37 See Stephen C. Schlesinger, *Act of Creation: The Founding of the United Nations* (Boulder, CO: Westview, 2003); Dan Plesch and Thomas G. Weiss (eds.), *Wartime Origins and the Future United Nations* (London: Routledge, 2015).
38 Edward C. Luck, *Mixed Messages: American Politics and International Organization, 1919–1999* (Washington, DC: Brookings Institution 1999).
39 Patrice C. McMahon and Andrew Wedeman, "Sustaining American Power in a Globalized World," and John Gerard

Ruggie, "Doctrinal Unilateralism and Its Limits: America and Global Governance in the New Century," both in *American Foreign Policy in a Globalized World*, ed. David P. Forsythe, Patrice C. McMahon, and Andrew Wedeman (New York: Routledge, 2006), pp. 1–45, 46–76.

40 "Last of the Big Time Spenders: US Military Budget Still the World's Largest, and Growing," Center for Defense Information, Table on "Fiscal Year 2004 Budget," based on data provided by the US Department of Defense and International Institute for Strategic Studies, Washington, DC.

41 Donald J. Puchala, "The United Nations and Hegemony," *International Studies Review* 7(4) (2005): 571–84.

42 See Thomas G. Weiss and Martin Welz, "The UN and the African Union in Mali and Beyond: A Shotgun Wedding?" *International Affairs* 90(4) (2014): 889–905; "Military Twists and Turns in World Politics: Downsides or Dividends for UN Peace Operations?" *Third World Quarterly* (2015): 1493–1509.

43 Quoted by Lincoln Palmer Bloomfield, *Accidental Encounters with History (and some lessons learned)* (Cohasset, MA: Hot House Press, 2005), p. 14.

44 Kwame Akonor, "Assessing the African Union's Right of Humanitarian Intervention," *Criminal Justice Ethics* 29(2) (2010): 157–73.

45 "The Security and Defense Agenda (as delivered by Secretary of Defense Robert Gates, Brussels, Belgium, January 10, 2011)"; available at http://www.washingtonpost.com/world/the-security-and-defense-agenda-as-delivered-by-secretary-of-defense-robert-gates-brussels-belgium-june-10-2011/2011/06/10/AGqlZhOH_story.html.

46 Joseph E. Nye, Jr, *The Paradox of American Power: Why the World's Only Superpower Can't Go It Alone* (Oxford and New York: Oxford University Press, 2002).

47 Stewart Patrick and Shepard Forman (eds.), *Multilateralism & US Foreign Policy: Ambivalent Engagement* (Boulder, CO: Lynne Rienner, 2002); David M. Malone and Yuen Foong Khong (eds.), *Unilateralism & US Foreign Policy: International Perspectives* (Boulder, CO: Lynne Rienner, 2003).

48 Stephen G. Brooks and William C. Wohlforth, "International Relations Theory and the Case against Unilateralism," *Perspectives on Politics* 3(3) (2005): 509.

49 Jane Boulden and Thomas G. Weiss, "Tactical Multilateralism: Coaxing America Back to the UN," *Survival* 46(3) (2004): 103–14.

50 Theodore C. Sorensen, "JFK's Strategy of Peace," *World Policy Journal* 20(3) (2003): 4.

51 G. John Ikenberry, "Is American Multilateralism in Decline?," *Perspectives on Politics* 1(3) (2003): 545.

52 James Dobbins et al., *The UN's Role in Nation-Building: From the Congo to Iraq* (New York: Rand Corporation, 2005), p. xxxvii.

53 Brian Urquhart, "The New American Century," *New York Review of Books*, August 11, 2005, p. 42.

54 Thomas G. Weiss, *Humanitarian Business* (Cambridge: Polity, 2013); Thomas G. Weiss and Peter J. Hoffman, "Making Humanitarianism Work," in *Making States Work: State Failure and the Crisis of Governance*, ed. Simon Chesterman, Michael Ignatieff, and Ramesh Thakur (Tokyo: UN University Press, 2005), pp. 296–317.

55 Stephen John Stedman, Donald S. Rothschild, and Elizabeth Cousens (eds.), *Ending Civil Wars: The Implementation of Peace Agreements* (Boulder, CO: Lynne Rienner, 2002).

56 Dwight D. Eisenhower, farewell address, 1961, in *A Documentary History of the United States*, ed. Richard D. Heffner (New York: Mentor Books, 1976), p. 314.

57 United Nations, *Programme of Action to Prevent, Combat and Eradicate the Illicit Trade in Small Arms and Light Weapons in All Its Aspects*, UN document A/CONF.192/1.5, July 20, 2001. For a discussion, see Keith Krause, "Multilateral Diplomacy, Norm Building, and UN Conferences: The Case of Small Arms and Light Weapons," *Global Governance* 8(2) (2002): 247–63.

58 Michael T. Klare, *Resource Wars: The New Landscape of Global Conflict* (New York: Henry Holt, 2002), pp. 190–212.

59 Peter W. Singer, "Humanitarian Principles, Private Military Agents: Some Implications of the Privatised Military Industry for the Humanitarian Community," in *Resetting the Rules of Engagement: Trends and Issues in Military–Humanitarian Relations*, ed. Victoria Wheeler and Adele Hammer (London: Overseas Development Institute, 2006), pp. 67–79.

60 United Nations, *The Causes of Conflict and the Promotion of Durable Peace and Sustainable Development in Africa*, Report of

the UN secretary-general to the Security Council, April 1998.
With direct reference to the DRC, see *Final Report of the Panel
of Experts on the Illegal Exploitation of Natural Resources and
Other Forms of Wealth of the Democratic Republic of Congo*, UN
Document S/2002/1146, October 16, 2002; available at http://
www.pcr.uu.se/digitalAssets/96/96819_congo_20021031.pdf.

61 Greg Campbell, *Blood Diamonds: Tracing the Deadly Path of the
World's Most Precious Stones* (Boulder, CO: Westview, 2002).
62 Global Witness website, www.globalwitness.org/campaigns/
diamonds/.
63 Klare, *Resource Wars*, p. 192.
64 Mary B. Anderson and Peter J. Woodrow, *Rising from the
Ashes: Development Strategies in Times of Disaster* (Boulder, CO:
Westview, 1987); Mary B. Anderson, *Do No Harm: How Aid Can
Support Peace – or War* (Boulder, CO: Lynne Rienner, 1999).
65 Andrew S. Natsios, "Humanitarian Relief Intervention in
Somalia: The Economics in Chaos," *International Peacekeeping*
3(1) (1996): 68–91.
66 Alex de Waal, *Famine Crimes: Politics & the Disaster Relief Industry
in Africa* (Oxford: James Currey, 1997); Michael Maren, *The
Road to Hell: The Ravaging Effects of Foreign Aid and International
Charity* (New York: Free Press, 1997).
67 Jean-Hervé Bradol, "Introduction: The Secretarial International
Order and the Humanitarian," in *In the Shadow of "Just Wars":
Violence, Politics and Humanitarian Action*, ed. Fabrice Weissman
(Ithaca, NY: Cornell University Press, 2004), p. 12.
68 Mark Duffield, *Global Governance and the New Wars: The Merging
of Development and Security* (London: Zed Books, 2001), and *Aid
Policy and Post-Modern Conflict: A Critical Review*, Occasional
Paper 19 (Birmingham: School of Public Policy, 1998); Naomi
Klein, *The Shock Doctrine: The Rise of Disaster Capitalism* (New
York: Metropolitan Books, 2007).
69 Michael Carnahan, William Durch, and Scott Gilmore,
Economic Impact of Peacekeeping: Final Report (New York: UN
Peacekeeping Best Practices Unit, 2006), p. iii.
70 Stephen Hopgood, "Saying 'No' to Wal-Mart? Money
and Morality in Professional Humanitarianism," in
Humanitarianism in Question: Politics, Power, Ethics, ed. Michael
Barnett and Thomas G. Weiss (Ithaca, NY: Cornell University
Press, 2007), pp. 98–123.

71 Michael Barnett and Thomas G. Weiss, *Humanitarianism Contested: Where Angels Fear to Tread* (London: Routledge, 2011).
72 Janice Stein, "Humanitarian Organizations: Accountable Why, to Whom, for What, and Why?," in *Humanitarianism in Question*, ed. Barnett and Weiss, pp. 124–42.
73 See Hugo Slim, *Humanitarian Ethics: A Guide to the Morality of Aid in War and Disaster* (Oxford: Oxford University Press, 2015).
74 David Rieff, "Humanitarianism in Crisis," *Foreign Affairs* 81(6) (2002): 111–21.
75 This discussion draws on Thomas G. Weiss, "Principles, Politics, and Humanitarian Action," *Ethics & International Affairs* 13 (1999): 1–22.
76 Anne Vallarys, *Médecins Sans Frontières: La Biographie* (Paris: Fayort, 2004).
77 Michael Bryans, Bruce D. Jones, and Janice Gross Stein, *"Mean Times": Humanitarian Action in Complex Political Emergencies – Stark Choices, Cruel Dilemmas: Report of the NGOs in Complex Emergencies Projects* (Toronto: Program on Conflict Management and Negotiation, Centre for International Studies, University of Toronto, 1999).
78 Victoria Wheeler and Adele Hammer, "Executive Summary," in *Resetting the Rules of Engagement*, p. 2.
79 Colin L. Powell, "Remarks to the National Foreign Policy Conference for Leaders of Non-Governmental Organizations," US Department of State, Oct. 26, 2001.
80 Stuart Gordon, "The Changing Role of the Military in Assistance Strategies," in *Resetting the Rules of Engagement*, ed. Wheeler and Hammer, p. 39.
81 Laura Hammond, "The Power of Holding Humanitarianism Hostage and the Myth of Protective Principles," in *Humanitarianism in Question*, ed. Barnett and Weiss, pp. 172–95.
82 Ian Smillie and Larry Minear, *The Charity of Nations: Humanitarian Action in a Calculating World* (Bloomfield, CN: Kumarian, 2004), ch. 8.
83 Joanna Macrae, "Defining the Boundaries: International Security and Humanitarian Engagement in the post-Cold War World," in OCHA, *Humanitarian Decade*, p. 117.
84 James Fearon, "The Rise of Emergency Relief Aid," and Janice Gross Stein, "Humanitarian Organizations: Accountable – Why,

to Whom, for What and How?" in *Humanitarianism in Question,* ed. Barnett and Weiss, pp. 49–72 and 124–42.

85 Rachel McCleary, *Global Compassion: Private Voluntary Organizations and US Foreign Policy since 1939* (Oxford: Oxford University Press, 2009), p. 16 and especially ch 1.

86 These figures are drawn from a 2003 OCHA roster (which no longer is updated).

87 Development Initiatives, *Global Humanitarian Assistance 2003* (London: Overseas Development Institute, 2003), p. 56.

88 *Global Humanitarian Assistance Report 2015* (Somerset, UK Development Initiatives, 2015): 75; available at http://www.globalhumanitarianassistance.org/wp-content/uploads/2015/06/GHA-Report-2015_-Interactive_Online.pdf.

89 Abby Stoddard, Adele Harmer, and Katherine Haver, *Providing Aid in Insecure Environments: Trends in Policy and Operations* (London: Overseas Development Institute, 2006), HPG Report 23, p. 16.

90 Gil Loescher, Alexander Betts, and James Milner, *UNHCR*, 2nd edn (London: Routledge, 2012); Peter Walker and Daniel G. Maxwell, *Shaping the Humanitarian Order* (London: Routledge, 2009).

91 Alexander Cooley and James Ron, "The NGO Scramble: Organizational Insecurity and the Political Economy of Transnational Action," *International Security* 27(1) (2002): 5–39.

92 Adele Harmer and Ellen Martin, *Diversity in Donorship: Field Lessons* (London: Overseas Development Institute, 2010), HPG Report 30, p. 1.

93 Relief Web, "International: Changes in Aid Pose Challenges," April 15, 2010; available at www.reliefweb.int/rw/rwb.nsf/db900osid/VDUX-84JSAS?OpenDocument.

94 Harmer and Martin, *Diversity in Donorship,* quotes from 3 and 6, statistics from 7 and 5.

95 *Global Humanitarian Assistance Report 2014* (Somerset, UK Development Initiatives, 2014), pp. 4–7 and 30; available at http://www.globalhumanitarianassistance.org/wp-content/uploads/2014/09/GHA-Report-2014-interactive.pdf.

96 Global Humanitarian Assistance, "03/Global Humanitarian Assistance," in *Global Humanitarian Assistance 2009* (Somerset, UK: Development Initiatives, 2009), p. 14; available at: www.

globalhumanitarianassistance.org/analyses-and-reports/gha-reports/gha-reports-2009.

97 Global Humanitarian Assistance, "01/Executive Summary," in *Global Humanitarian Assistance 2009* (Somerset, UK: Development Initiatives, 2009), p. 1.

98 Hugo Slim, "Global Welfare," *ALNAP Review of Humanitarian Action in 2005*, p. 21.

99 Smillie and Minear, *The Charity of Nations*, pp. 8–10, 195.

100 *Global Humanitarian Assistance Report 2015* (Somerset, UK Development Initiatives, 2015): 75; available at http://www.globalhumanitarianassistance.org/wp-content/uploads/2015/06/GHA-Report-2015_-Interactive_Online.pdf.

101 "Aid Worker Security Report 2015, Figures at a Glance"; available at https://aidworkersecurity.org/sites/default/files/HO_AidWorkerSectyPreview_V1.pdf.

102 Antonio Donini, "The Evolving Nature of Coordination," in *OCHA, Humanitarian Decade*, UN 131, which updates his work *The Policies of Mercy: UN Coordination in Afghanistan, Mozambique and Rwanda*, Occasional Paper #22 (Providence, RI: Watson Institute, 1996), p. 14.

103 Personal communication from Nicholas Morris, a retired UNHCR staff member.

104 Larry Minear, *The Humanitarian Enterprise: Dilemmas and Discoveries* (Bloomfield, CN: Kumarian, 2002).

105 Stephen Hopgood, *Keepers of the Flame: Understanding Amnesty International* (Ithaca, NY: Cornell University Press, 2006).

106 Paul Kennedy, *The Parliament of Man: The Past, Present, and Future of the United Nations* (New York: Random House, 2006), p 103.

107 Greenberg Research, *The People on War Report* (Geneva: ICRC, 1999), p. xvi.

108 Antonio Donini, Larry Minear, Ian Smillie, Ted van Baarda, and Anthony C. Welch, *Mapping the Security Environment: Understanding the Perceptions of Local Communities, Peace Support Operations, and Assistance Agencies* (Medford, MA: Feinstein International Famine Center, June 2005), p. 53.

109 J. Martin Rochester, *Between Peril and Promise: The Politics of International Law* (Washington, DC: CQ Press, 2006), p. 95.

110 Simon Chesterman, *Just War or Just Peace? Humanitarian Intervention and International Law* (Oxford: Oxford University

Press, 2001); Nicholas J. Wheeler, *Saving Strangers: Humanitarian Intervention in International Society* (Oxford: Oxford University Press, 2000).

111 Stephen Lewis, *Race against Time* (Toronto: Anansi Press, 2005), p. 145.

112 Rama Mani and Thomas G. Weiss (eds.), *The Responsibility to Protect: Cultural Perspectives in the Global South* (London: Routledge, 2011); Mónica Serrano and Thomas G. Weiss (eds.), *The International Politics of Human Rights: Rallying to the R2P Cause?* (London: Routledge, 2014).

113 Edward C. Luck, "The Responsibility to Protect: Growing Pains or Early Promise?" *Ethics & International Affairs* 24(4) (2010): 361.

114 Kofi A. Annan, *The Question of Intervention – Statements by the Secretary-General* (New York: UN, 1999), p. 39.

Index